# FOREWARNED IS FOREARMED

The centuries have borne witness to Nostradamus' often uncanny accuracy—over 400 years ago, he predicted the fall of communism in the former Soviet Union.

If his final prophecies are correct, then a huge disaster will occur here on Earth in a few short years. This disaster will be so far-reaching that it will touch the life of everyone on this planet.

Consider: scientists speculate that an Ice Age began when a meteor struck the Earth millions of years ago. Imagine the devastation such an event would cause today: tidal waves and volcanoes. . . nuclear winter. . . famine. . . and almost inevitably, World War III.

In this believable and highly readable book, Stephen Paulus pieces together the jigsaw puzzle of Nostradamus' final prophecies. Using the prophet's last dated quatrain as the starting point, Paulus arranges a total of 181 quatrains in their original sequence to give you an alarming picture of what the new millennium may bring.

Forewarned is forearmed. You have a unique opportunity to prepare for a possible disaster that is fast approaching, a disaster that will change the lives of everyone on this planet. Find out what's coming and increase your chances of surviving it.

## ABOUT THE AUTHOR

Stefan Paulus was always familiar with Nostradamus but it wasn't until 1991 that he began interpreting Nostradamus' predictions as a hobby. While watching an old quasi-documentary on the French prophet, Paulus realized that the analysis of Nostradamus' quatrains (four-line poems of prediction) seemed faulty and inadequate. That prompted Paulus' intense research and study of Nostradamus and his prophecies, which he has now turned into this book.

A committed Christian actively involved in his church as a member, council member, and organizer in major fund-raising campaigns, Paulus enjoys organic gardening, aerobic exercising, and construction handy work. He studied yoga, eastern and western meditation techniques, and is a former martial arts instructor.

Stefan Paulus is married and the proud parent or three children. He lives in Chicago but hopes to retire to a more rustic setting where he can further experiment with organic farming techniques and live a calmer, more sustainable lifestyle.

## TO WRITE TO THE AUTHOR

If you wish to contact the author or would like more information about this book, please write to Stefan Paulus in care of Llewellyn Worldwide, and we will forward your request. Both the author and publisher appreciate hearing from you and learning of your enjoyment of this book and how it has helped you. Llewellyn Worldwide cannot guarantee that every letter written to the author can be answered, but all will be forwarded. Please write to:

Stefan Paulus
c/o Llewellyn Worldwide
P.O. Box 64383, Dept. K515–0,
St. Paul, MN 55164-0383, U.S.A.

Please enclose a self-addressed, stamped envelope for reply or $1.00 to cover costs.
If outside the U.S.A., enclose international postal reply coupon.

## FREE CATALOG
## FROM LLEWELLYN WORLDWIDE

For more than ninety-five years Llewellyn has brought its readers knowledge in the fields of metaphysics and human potential. Learn about the newest books in spiritual guidance, natural healing, astrology, occult philosophy, and more. Enjoy book reviews, New Age articles, a calendar of events, plus current advertised products and services. To get your free copy of the *Llewellyn's New Worlds of Mind and Spirit* magazine, send your name and address to:

*Llewellyn's New Worlds of Mind and Spirit*
P.O. Box 64383, Dept. K515–0,
St. Paul, MN 55164-0383, U.S.A.

# NOSTRADAMUS 1999

# 1999

# NOSTRADAMUS

## WHO WILL SURVIVE?

*Stefan Paulus*

1996
Llewellyn Publications
St. Paul, Minnesota, USA 55164–0380

Scripture quotations are from *Today's English Version*—Copyright © American Bible Society 1966, 1971, 1976, 1992—with permission.

FIRST EDITION
First Printing, 1996

**Cover design by Tom Grewe**
**Cover photo: Images copyright © 1995 PhotoDisc, Inc.**
**Editing, interior design, and layout by Darwin Holmstrom**

Library of Congress Cataloging-in-Publication Data
Paulus, Stefan, 1956–
    Nostradamus 1999 : will you survive? / Stefan Paulus. — 1st. ed.
        p. cm.
    Includes bibliographical references and index.
    ISBN 1–56718–515–0 (pbk.)
    1. Nostradamus, 1503–1566.   2. Prophecies (Occultism)   3.
Twenty-first century—Forecasts.  I. Title.
BF1815. N8P38 1996
133.3—dc20                                     96–20696
                                                              CIP

This book is fervently dedicated to the hope that it is wrong. May the events envisioned never occur, and the devastation it foresees never come to pass.

# CONTENTS

WORLD

X

# EUROPE

# WESTERN ASIA

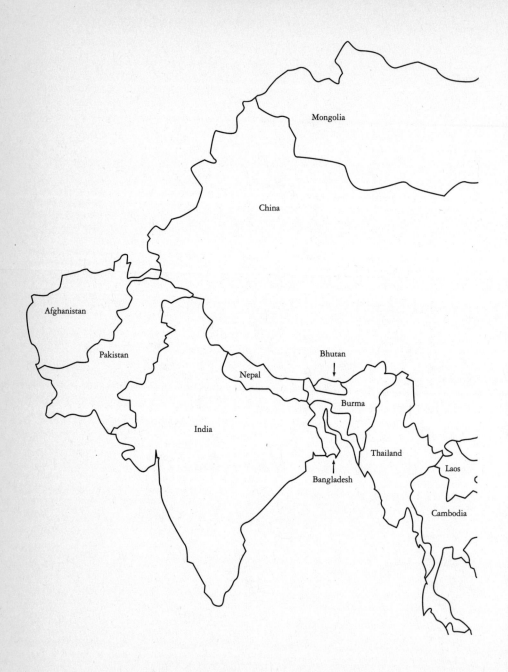

# AFRICA

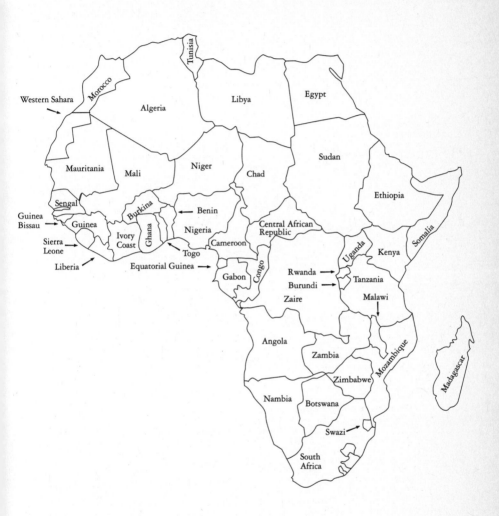

# MIDDLE EAST

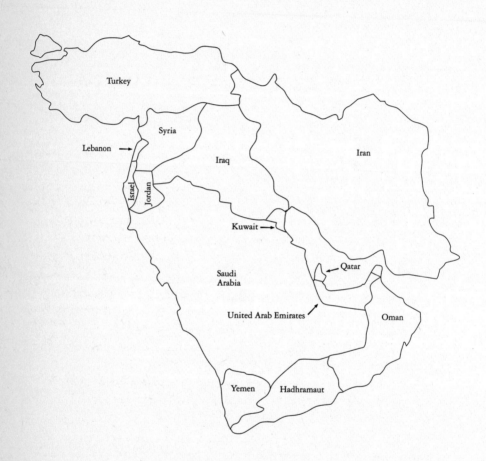

# INTRODUCTION

The book you hold in your hands is unique among all the works ever written on the prophecies of Nostradamus. There has never been another book written on the predictions of this 16th century prophet that contains any, let alone all, of the following elements:

1. The disregard of quatrains that are clearly in the past, leaving a group of predictions that are, thus far, unfulfilled.

2. An attempt to sequence those remaining quatrains into their original, chronological order, an order that was deliberately shuffled by Nostradamus in order to avoid persecution by the French Inquisition. When these shuffled quatrains are re-sequenced into their original order, a clear picture of what could occur in the near future appears in much the same way as an assembled jigsaw puzzle provides a clearer picture than does a jumbled pile of individual puzzle pieces.

3. A clear explanation of what Nostradamus' very last prediction with a specifically mentioned date, the seventh month of 1999, might mean.

4. The correlation of Nostradamus' predictions with Biblical prophecies, particularly those from the Book of Revelation. More specifically, this is the only book written that compares Nostradamus' predictions with unfulfilled prophecies from the Bible, then explains how those predictions and prophecies can be fulfilled in ways compatible with modern scientific knowledge.

5. The correlation of Nostradamus' predictions with the environmental devastation being wrought in the world today, particularly in worldwide food production capabilities and the impending famine that the world will face in the early years of the next century.

6. The correlation of Nostradamus' predictions with the resurgence in Islamic fundamentalism sweeping the globe. Also, no other book has compared his predictions with Islamic end-time beliefs and prophecies from the Koran, nor how those prophecies might be fulfilled within the next generation.

7. Finally, while many commentators on Nostradamus' works have vaguely described his vision of a future apocalyptic war, only this book fully explores the link between Nostradamus' prophecies and a detailed, battle-by-battle vision of what a near-future World War III might entail.

Before proceeding with the first quatrain, there are several items that must be noted. First, Nostradamus deliberately confused the order of his quatrains, apparently by writing each quatrain, unnumbered but in chronological order, on a separate sheet of paper and then throwing all of the individual papers into the air. After this thorough mixing he then numbered them in the order in which he picked them up. Since an attempt to restore that original order is presented in this book, a new numbering system besides the one that Nostradamus used is needed for simplicity's sake. As a result quatrains are numbered first, in parentheses, according to their order of appearance in this book. This new numbering system allows for a much simpler means of referring to quatrains in other parts of the book. However, the numbering system that Nostradamus used is also maintained for those readers wishing to cross-reference this author's interpretations with those from another source. Therefore, the first quatrain to appear is labeled (1) Century 10, Quatrain 72, the second one as (2) Century 3, Quatrain 95, and so on.

Second, since Nostradamus was a Catholic Frenchman, he saw his prophetic responsibilities as being primarily for his country and his church. Except for those quatrains that specifically mention another country, it should be generally assumed that the country referred to in any of the quatrains is France. Those quatrains that have been attached to items like California earthquakes by other interpreters are most likely being taken out of context.

Third, it is clear in many places in Nostradamus' writings that he foresaw a future era of great evil and destruction throughout Europe, particularly France. It thus seems likely, since Nostradamus saw himself as a prophet of warning for France, that a large number of his prophecies refer to that specific time of danger in France's future, when death and destruction will be great and his country will be at its greatest need.

Fourth, while he felt the need to disguise his quatrains to avoid persecution in his lifetime, Nostradamus must have left some key that would allow for their eventual understanding before the time of France's greatest danger. That key is the interlocking themes found in the quatrains themselves. For instance, there are many quatrains that deal with the appearance of a comet; other themes found in those comet-quatrains include (to name a few) famine, flooding, and war. Since there are then other quatrains that link those themes with still other themes, a picture is formed in a way that is very similar to the assembling of a jigsaw puzzle. The end result is the linking of roughly 200 quatrains into a single image.

Fifth, there is one quatrain that links a specific date with what seems to be the appearance of a comet. That date is the seventh month of 1999. It is that quatrain that allows the body of roughly 200 linked quatrains to be tied to a specific date. It is there that the story begins. . . .

# THE COMING
# OF THE GREAT
# KING OF TERROR

**(1) Century 10, Quatrain 72**

| | |
|---|---|
| The year 1999,<br>    the seventh month,<br>From the sky will come<br>    a great King of Terror:<br>Resuscitating the great<br>    King of the Mongols,<br>Before and after Mars<br>    to reign happily. | *L'an mil neuf cent nonante*<br>    *neuf sept mois,*<br>*Du ciel viendra un grand*<br>    *Roi d'effrayeur:*<br>*Ressusciter le grand*<br>    *Roi d'Angolmois,*<br>*Avant après Mars regner*<br>    *par bonheur.* |

Here is the last of the specifically dated prophecies of Nostradamus. Some of the prophecies that mention specific years were successes, while others were complete failures (see appendix A). However, if there is any possibility that he could see the future, if there is any possibility that a significant event will occur in the year 1999, then an effort must be made to find out what Nostradamus foresaw when he wrote this quatrain.

Is there any possibility that Nostradamus might be correct, that he actually saw something significant occurring in 1999? Has he had any other successes? An answer may be found in the following quatrain, the latest prophecy of this 16th-century mystic to be fulfilled.

1

**(2) Century 3, Quatrain 95**

| | |
|---|---|
| The Law of More people will be seen to fall: | *La loi Moricque on verra défaillir:* |
| After a different one a good deal more seductive: | *Après une autre beaucoup plus séductive:* |
| Dnieper first will fall: | *Boristhenes premier viendra faillir:* |
| Through gifts and language to another more attractive. | *Par dons et langue une plus attractive.* |

Sir Thomas More published a book during Nostradamus' college days by the name of *Utopia*, and Nostradamus was doubtless familiar with it. As another name for utopia is paradise, and since communism's claim throughout its history has been that it was a "worker's paradise," the connection of the first line with the Soviet Union is clear. Note also that Nostradamus predicted that the Soviet Union would "be seen to fall," a fact not lost on the many Nostradamian commentators who for many years have predicted the breakup of the Soviet Union and the end of communism there. Not only did Nostradamus predict the fall of communism, but in the second line here he also predicted that the new republics would embrace another form of government ("a different one"). This form of government is democracy, which is a "good deal more" attractive ("seductive") than communism on the surface. (Never mind that there has never been a democracy that lasted more than a few hundred years at most—internal decay, especially irresponsible fiscal policies, eventually dooms democratic governments!)

Besides accurately predicting the fall of communism and the turning to democracy in the former USSR, Nostradamus also predicted in this quatrain that the country bordering the Dnieper River ("Dnieper first will fall") would be responsible for it. This river runs through the heart of the Ukraine, and its capital, Kiev, is located on its banks. Why Nostradamus should have picked the area that is the Ukraine today for anything important must indicate some prophetic power, since in his day this area was part of the furthest reaches of the Polish-Lithuanian empire, a poor, sparsely populated region with no potential for influencing the affairs of any government.

But in fact it was the Ukraine, as the second largest republic (after Russia) in the USSR that played a large part in the breakup of the country. The Ukrainians also ruined the creation of a strong

Commonwealth of Independent States (CIS), allowing for further dissolution of the Soviet empire.

The last line of this quatrain indicates that this transition from communism to democracy was to be made peacefully, by diplomacy with foreign countries ("languages") and Western pledges of "gifts." Amazingly, this is exactly how Ukraine achieved its independence.

Having established that Nostradamus has had a very recent successful prediction to go along with his others throughout the centuries, attention can again be turned to Quatrain (1). How should this quatrain be interpreted? The first line gives a date: the seventh month of the year 1999. But is the month necessarily July? Look at the prophecy in the original French. While the word *sept* in French means "seven," possibly indicating the month of July, "sept" could also be interpreted as an abbreviation for the month of September. Besides, September was originally the seventh month, the name literally meaning "seventh month." It became the ninth month only 9-11 after Julius Caesar and his successor, Augustus, created and named the months of July and August after themselves, displacing the last four months of the year by two months each. Thus the intended month could be either July or September. More about this later.

The second line indicates something "great" coming from the sky, causing terror on a large, perhaps worldwide, scale. But what can this be? It appears to be something visible to the entire world, and visible for a long enough period of time to create terror. Fear can be created quickly, but terror takes time to develop. The length of visibility and degree of terror precludes any man-made event; the only possible one is nuclear war, and that would involve many "kings of terror," not just one. Besides, as terror requires time to build to a peak, the fifteen minutes or less warning of incoming nuclear warheads does not suffice. Among all of the natural events, the only possible one is a great 7 comet, and the cause of the terror in mankind will be the knowledge that it will make a near approach to the Earth.

The third line of this quatrain implies that the comet will be associated with significant changes in the political structure of the nations of the world; specifically, it will cause a resurgence in power of the Asian states, particularly Mongolia. The "Great King of the Mongols" was Genghis Khan, the first, and greatest, ruler of the Mongol Empire. He was born in obscurity in 1162, in what is today

3

far-northwestern China, and he died in the year 1227. The years between those dates marked the life of the ruler of one of the greatest empires the world has ever known. Twenty-five years after becoming a simple tribal chief, Genghis was master of most of the then-known world. Shortly after his death the Mongolian Empire extended from Korea to Germany and Italy, from northern Russia to India and Iraq. Within thirty years of standing on the shores of the Adriatic Sea, Mongol armies were in Japan and Java. But they were more than just conquerors. As perpetrators of genocide, they were the most efficient mass-murderers since the ancient Assyrians, and their record was not surpassed until the massacres of Hitler and Stalin in the twentieth century.

Genghis Khan waged his wars of conquest in terms of an order received from Tengri (Eternal Heaven—yet another historical instance of an individual committing atrocities in the name of God). Genghis saw the Mongol Empire as not merely a state among states but a world empire in the making. The building of that empire was the will of Tengri, who gave to Genghis, and to his descendants, the right to rule over the entire world. At its peak the Mongol empire reached westward into present-day Germany and the Italian border with Croatia. Had the Mongols actually undertaken an invasion of Germany and Italy, it is difficult to imagine them being repelled by the forces of a divided and disorganized Europe, especially since the Mongol troops in Europe alone outnumbered the combined forces of all of the kings of Western Europe put together. Additionally, the Mongols were better trained, used superior tactics, and had never been defeated.

This Mongol invasion of Western Europe, however, was not to be. In March, 1242, news reached the Mongol army that Ögödei, Genghis Khan's son and successor, had died a few months before. This stopped the Mongol army from operating further west and caused them to return to Mongolia in anticipation of a successor dispute. After that the Mongol empire was more concerned with internal problems than with conquest and they never ventured farther into Europe than Russia.

The last line of Quatrain (1) mentions "Mars," the Roman god of war. Nostradamus implies that war will both precede and follow ("before and after") the events of 1999. While he does not mention in this quatrain precisely which countries will be involved, he implies protracted war, similar in nature to the Mongol conquests. The man responsible for this war will come from either present-day Mongolia or northwestern China, the same area from which Genghis Khan came. If some other comparisons with the Mongols hold, then several other conclusions may also be reached. First, this is to be a religious war, the invaders claiming the authority of God as permission for starting the war. Second, their empire will come together quickly, probably within a decade at most. Third, genocide, the murder of entire cultures, will be a frequent occurrence in this war. One might even call it World War III. Fourth, this campaign will reach out from the depths of Asia into the heart of a disorganized Europe. Finally, the attacking armies from the East will greatly outnumber the defenders of Western Europe.

As interesting as this quatrain is, it is still just one quatrain, and some of the language is subject to various interpretations. For instance, the matter of which month is still not determined. Are there any other quatrains which correlate with this one? Consider the following:

### (3) Century 5, Quatrain 32

| | |
|---|---|
| Where all good is, everything right with the Sun and the Moon | *Où tout bon est, tout bien Soleil et Lune* |
| Is abundant, its ruin approaches: | *Est abondant, sa ruine s'approche:* |
| From the sky it advances to vary your fortune, | *Du ciel s'avance varier ta fortune,* |
| In the same state as the seventh rock. | *En même état que la septième roche.* |

Examine the last line since it is the key to understanding this quatrain. What is the "seventh rock"? A comet is not actually a rock, it is essentially a snowy dirt-ball which roams through the solar system in orbit around the Sun. Unlike the planets however, cometary orbits frequently cross the orbits of the planets in long elliptical or near-parabolic orbits. Quatrain (1) predicted a comet in the "seventh month." Thus, the last line here is best understood as another object, appearing together ("in the same state") with the comet, during the seventh month, which could be either July or September.

These two quatrains also share a common thought besides the "seven" theme; both also contain the words "from the sky." In the third line note that both of these objects (the comet and the "seventh rock") appear "from the sky" rather than "in the sky." The implication is that these two "objects" will actually approach the earth from out of deep space rather than from the atmosphere. This will occur during a time of, to paraphrase the first two lines, "All good and

5

abundant on the earth." While many might not consider themselves to have an abundance of goods, if Nostradamus could actually see the late twentieth century, what else could he have concluded from his sixteenth-century perspective? Anyone whose residence has clean running water and indoor plumbing, electrical lighting, central heating and air conditioning, a refrigerator, television, radio, and a telephone, has a higher standard of living than even the wealthiest people in the world had a mere century ago. And besides those creature comforts, western civilization also has an abundance of food, clothing, and health care that is unequalled in all history.

Also, note that the comet is not the direct cause of the destruction; the mysterious second object, "the seventh rock" is responsible. Just what this mysterious object is will be explained in a later quatrain. The following quatrain helps to confirm the date:

**(4) Century 2, Quatrain 46**

| | |
|---|---|
| After great trouble for mankind, a greater one prepared | *Après grand trouble humain, plus grand s'apprête* |
| The grand mover the centuries renews: | *Le grand moteur les siècles renouvèle:* |
| Rain, blood, milk, famine, iron and pestilence, | *Pluie, sang, lait, famine, fer et peste,* |
| In the sky fire seen, a long spark running. | *Au ciel vu feu, courant longue étincelle.* |

The last line is fairly clear, "a long spark running" in the sky can only be a comet. This was a fairly common expression of Nostradamus' time. The first part of the first line refers to World War II, certainly the greatest "trouble" for mankind in this century, a war that claimed 50 million lives and destroyed much of Europe and Asia. The last part of the first line indicates that World War III is coming, and that it will be "a greater one" than World War II. The entire second line is a colloquialism indicating that this "great trouble" will occur near the changing of a millennium, i.e. around the year 2000. In line three, iron is symbolic for weapons, in short, war. Pestilence, blood, and famine are self-explanatory. The significance of rain and milk is, as of yet, unclear; a possible explanation for their significance will be given later in this chapter.

The appearance of a comet in 1999 has now been linked with a "ruin" that comes from the sky, war, famine, and disease. But in exactly which month will this occur: July or September? The answer is found in the following quatrain:

**(5) Century 3, Quatrain 34**

When the eclipse of the Sun
    will then be,
In broad daylight
    the monster will be seen:
Everyone will differ
    on the interpretation,
High price unguarded:
    none will have prepared.

*Quand le défaut du Soleil lors sera,*
*Sur le plein jour le monstre sera vu:*
*Tout autrement on l'interprétera,*
*Cherté n'a gardé:*
    *nul n'y aura pourvu.*

Solar eclipses are a frequent phenomenon, occurring somewhere on Earth every six months or so. However, only 28% of all eclipses are total eclipses, and the average length of time between total solar eclipses in any given location is roughly 410 years. In the years since Nostradamus' death there have been only a handful of total eclipses occurring anywhere in France, so the possible occasions for the fulfillment of this quatrain have been very limited thus far. Interestingly, the next major solar eclipse of this century will be on August 11, 1999, and it will pass right through the heart of France. Most reputable commentators believe Nostradamus, as a Frenchman, wrote about France unless a country was otherwise specified. Since no country is named, this would appear to refer to a total eclipse in France.

During this eclipse Nostradamus predicts that a "monster" will be visible. But is this monster a comet? Johannes Hevelius' book, *Cometographia*, published in the free city of Danzig, (now Gdansk, Poland) in the year 1668, includes drawings of several different types of cometary forms seen between 1577 and 1652, which is the period slightly after Nostradamus' death. Several of the comets are labeled "monstriferous" comets. In particular, figure K in his book shows three comets labeled as "monstriferous." So it is clear that Nostradamus intended a comet when he wrote "monster." This "monster" will be seen during the eclipse, but apparently is invisible both before and after. If the "monster" is a comet, then it will approach Earth from behind the Sun, becoming visible only when the Sun is eclipsed by the Moon. This occurrence is not at all unusual. Comet 1948 XI was discovered on November 1, 1948, during a total eclipse of the Sun in Nairobi, the capital of Kenya. It was reported to have been as bright as Venus and to have had a long tail behind it. After the eclipse ended, the comet was again concealed by the glare of the Sun and did not become visible again until five days later, after it moved away from the Sun.

The third line of quatrain (5) indicates a multitude of opinions about the significance of the comet. What claims will be made? Some will see it as just a natural event of the solar system, others as a sign from God, and still others as a sign of the approaching end of the world, since it will occur near the end of the second millennium. The last line shows that few will be prepared for the calamity to come. The sight during the eclipse will be awesome enough to cause panic buying of supplies. Money itself, and the earning of it, will be secondary to acquiring stockpiles of food, water, clothes, weapons, etc.

This quatrain also answers the question, in which month the "ruin" will occur. Since the comet will not be seen from Earth until August, the "ruin" must occur in September, not July. Just what that "ruin" will consist of will be explained later. But, before going further with Nostradamus, some background information on comets is necessary.

Most comets are not discovered until they cross the asteroid belt, which lies between the orbits of Jupiter and Mars. Why? It is at this distance that water begins to vaporize and the comet forms a coma, its fuzzy appearing head. At this distance a bright comet appears to the naked eye as a fourth or fifth magnitude star (the lower the number the brighter the star). On a clear night the unaided human eye can see a star of sixth magnitude. This "star" is surrounded by a haze due to formation of the coma. Comets are rarely discovered before they form their coma, and if the comet is lost in the glare of the Sun as it approaches the Asteroid belt to form its coma, it may go unobserved. There are, in fact, many instances of comets being discovered during total eclipses of the Sun, comets that were previously invisible due to the Sun's glare. In this respect the previously mentioned Comet 1948 XI was by no means unusual. But still, is it not unusual for a comet to be discovered this close to the Sun? No, in fact most comets are discovered after they have reached perihelion (their point of closest approach to the Sun) and are racing back out of the solar system.

Will space-age satellites and deep space probes discover the comet before it appears during the total eclipse of the Sun? Perhaps the government will find it, but that doesn't mean they will inform the general public. Also, consider what happened in 1979. In August of that year the U.S. Naval Research Laboratory, through the use of an Air Force satellite, photographed the previously unknown comet 1979 XI as it crashed into the Sun, *but the comet remained unreported for two and a half years,* until the researchers actually had a chance to look at the film!

Nostradamus wrote another quatrain that also indicates that the comet will approach the Earth from behind the Sun:

### (6) Century 6, Quatrain 6

| | |
|---|---|
| There will appear | *Apparaîtra vers le Septentrion* |
|    towards the North | *Non loin de Cancer l'étoile chevelue:* |
| Not far from Cancer | *Suze, Sienne, Boëce, Eretrion,* |
|    the bearded star: | *Mourra de Rome grand,* |
| Susa, Siena, Boeotia, Eretria, |    *la nuit disparue.* |
| The great one of Rome will die, | |
|    the night over. | |

"Bearded star" was another common expression in Nostradamus' time for a comet, the "beard" being the comet's tail, and the "star" its bright coma. At the time of the August 1999 total solar eclipse, the Sun will be nearly out of Cancer and moving into Leo. If, as this quatrain states, the comet will appear "not far from Cancer," then it must approach the Earth from behind the Sun. Within a few weeks the Earth's orbit around the Sun will swing it into a nearly head-on path with the comet, so the near-encounter will occur at a great speed. A rough estimate of that speed will be calculated later. It is also notable that the comet, being near Cancer, will approach the Sun in the ecliptic plane, the same plane in which the planets lie. A comet with an orbit ninety degrees from the Earth (approaching from the pole) will cross Earth's orbit in only one or two places at most, and even then only if it is exactly 93 million miles from the Sun. However, a comet orbiting in the plane of the planets may spend a great deal of time crossing the Earth's orbit. The first line also indicates that the comet will be more visible from the northern hemisphere ("there will appear towards the north"), a sensible observation since during summer in the northern hemisphere the Sun is high in the sky, almost overhead, and the comet will be easily visible when it reappears a few weeks after the eclipse. Those people living in the middle latitudes of the southern hemisphere, with the Sun low in the northern sky, will have a poorer view of the comet since it will be near the horizon.

9

The third line is difficult to interpret as it lists only the names of places without any apparent activity occurring. Nostradamus' explanation of their importance was constrained to some extent by rhyme and by verse length, so the significance of these places is open to interpretation. Erika Cheetham, in her book *The Final Prophecies of Nostradamus,* adds without explanation, "will tremble," to her interpretation at the end of the line. This seems reasonable, and that interpretation will be used here, too. Why is it reasonable? Consider the locations mentioned. Susa is in northwest Italy, Sienna in central Italy, Boeotia was a province in southeastern Greece and Eretria is on the island of Euboea, just east of Boeotia and northeast of Athens. These areas are all very seismically active and are close to the border of the African and European tectonic plates.

The exact African-European tectonic plate boundary is difficult to determine due to thrusting of the overlying crust, unlike southern California where the San Andreas fault marks the junction of the two colliding plates very clearly. At a speed of about four inches a year, the African plate is sliding northward into, and under, the European plate. This collision has produced the Alps and Pyrenees mountains, the volcanoes Vesuvius and Mt. Etna, and an earthquake region similar to ones on the west coast of the entire North and South American continents. Thus the logical reason to link diverse areas such as Susa, Siena, Boeotia, and Eretria together is that an earthquake of massive proportions will cause large sections of the African plate to slip under the European plate.

During this earthquake the Pope will die ("the great one of Rome will die"), obviously along with many other people. Incidentally, the theory of plate tectonics has been accepted by the scientific community only within the past twenty-five years, and yet Nostradamus here places the length of the fault with uncanny accuracy. How could he have done this without some knowledge of the future?

There are still more quatrains relating to events surrounding the time of the comet's appearance:

**(7) Century 2, Quatrain 41**

| | |
|---|---|
| The great star for seven days will burn, | *La grande étoile par sept jours brûlera,* |
| The cloud will cause two suns to appear: | *Nuée fera deux soleils apparoir:* |
| The big mastiff all night will howl | *Le gros mâtin toute nuit hurlera* |
| When the great pontiff changes countries. | *Quand grand pontife changera de terroir.* |

"The great star" refers to the comet, and the "cloud" will be its fuzzy-appearing coma. For "seven days" it will "burn" bright enough in the sky to give the illusion of a second sun (Examine the French! An alternate interpretation is "The great star for *September* days will burn," possibly indicating that the comet's closest approach to the Earth will occur during the month of September.) Again, note that this is to be a daylight comet, approaching from the same sector of the sky as the Sun. If it approached from the other direction, it would be visible during the night, not the day. The brightness and the apparent size of the comet also indicate a close approach to the earth. The proximity of the comet to the Earth at this time shows that this quatrain should be dated after the August 1999 eclipse, but before the "ruin" of Quatrain (3) occurs. Why it must occur before the "ruin" will be explained later. The "big mastiff" is generally interpreted by Nostradamian scholars as a symbol for Great Britain, the "howling" indicating a time of severe national distress in that country. The earthquake of southern Europe mentioned in the Quatrain (6) will not only kill the Pope, but is somehow connected with the Papacy itself moving out of Italy and into another country.

As detailed and fascinating as this quatrain is, is it really possible? Could a comet really make the sky appear to have two Suns? After all, even a large comet is only a few miles across. And what could this possibly have to do with a national emergency in Great Britain, the Papacy leaving Italy for another country, and a massive earthquake throughout southern Europe? Before answering those questions, some more background information on comets is needed.

The last truly brilliant comet was the Great Daylight comet of 1910, sometimes confused with Halley's Comet, which appeared later that year. It was clearly visible during the day (hence its name) and outshone all heavenly bodies except for the Sun and moon. Its tail actually stretched halfway across the sky.

Another remarkable comet was the Great Comet of the year 1402, generally regarded as the finest comet ever seen. Records indicate it was visible in daylight for eight days, and was so bright that it may have even cast a shadow! The comet of 1577 was as bright as the moon, and like the moon, could even be seen through thin clouds at night. In 1811, a comet appeared that had a coma that was actually larger (not just apparently larger) than the Sun itself, and many,

11

many times the diameter of the Earth. The Great Comet of 1843 had a tail over 200 million miles long, far enough to reach from the Sun to more than 58 million miles past the orbit of Mars! Tebbutt's Comet (1861 II) was as bright as Saturn and its tail stretched 120 degrees across the sky, two-thirds of the way from horizon to horizon. It was so large and bright that the head of the comet was mistaken by many for the rising moon! Other brilliant, large comets appeared in 1861 and 1882, as well.

Comet Hyakutake was easily visible in March 1996 to the naked eye and was the finest comet seen at that time in the last twenty years, but it does not qualify as a spectacular comet. Comet Hale-Bopp, due in April 1997, is predicted to be the most brilliant comet since the Great Comet of 1843, but predicting the brilliance of comets in advance is a tricky business. In the mid 1970s similar predictions were made about Comet Kohoutek, which turned out to be something of a dud. If Hale-Bopp is also something of a dud, and barring the appearance of any other very bright comets between 1997 and 1999, then in August of 1999 the only individuals alive who will have ever seen a truly brilliant comet will be well into their nineties. In contrast, the century before 1910 contained no less than five spectacular comets. Over the past few centuries there was a general expectation that a very bright comet would appear every ten years or so. The Great Comet of 1729 was visible to the naked eye, even though the closest it came to the Sun was just inside the orbit of Jupiter. Had it come near the Earth, it would have reflected enough light from the Sun to read a newspaper in the middle of the night!

The lack of truly brilliant comets since 1910 is very unusual over the past millennium. Even the long awaited appearance of Halley's Comet in 1986 turned out to be a disappointment, as it provided its least spectacular sky show in over 2,200 years of recorded sightings. In the distant past the Roman historian Pliny even noted the appearance of a comet that was too bright to be looked at directly. In answer to the question posed a few paragraphs ago, yes, it is quite possible for a comet to give the sky the appearance of having a second sun. However, the comet must be at least slightly dimmer than our sun, since it generates no light of its own, reflecting only the light of the Sun itself.

Interestingly enough the coma of a comet reaches maximum size at roughly 1 AU (astronomical unit), which by definition is the same distance at which the Earth orbits the Sun. At the point that a comet crosses the Earth's orbit, a coma the size of the Earth itself is fairly common, and as previously noted, a coma the size of the Sun itself is quite possible. Lexell's Comet (1770 I), at the time of its closest approach to the Earth, had a coma that appeared to be nearly five times the diameter of the full moon! A daylight comet with a coma the size of the earth or larger making a near-earth approach would be a spectacular sight, indeed. And since the majority of known comets have near-parabolic orbits with their perihelion (their point of closest approach to the Sun) at roughly 1AU, the Great Daylight Comet of 1999 could well be swinging by the Earth when it is just about as far from the Sun as the Earth itself, with its coma at its maximum size, probably measuring at least as big as the Earth, and possibly much bigger.

As unusual as a great daylight comet with a near-Earth approach might be to those living today, this event would not be at all unusual. A comet will come as close to the Earth as the moon (roughly 240,000 miles) on an average of once every 2,000 years. Compare that with Comet Hyakutake, which at its closest approach to Earth was still 9 million miles away. Once every million years or so a comet with a diameter of one kilometer (five-eighths of a mile) actually impacts on the Earth, thus the chances of a one-kilometer comet hitting in any given year is one in a million. In a 1992 report, NASA estimated the chances of the Earth being struck by a comet, asteroid, or large meteorite in a lifetime at only 1 in 10,000! The report indicates that this could "possibly end civilization as we know it" and perhaps even "threaten the survival of the human species." Compare this with the possibility of being struck by lightning (1 in 9,100), being murdered this year (1 in 12,000), dying in a fire this year (1 in 40,000), dying in a single car ride (1 in 4,000,000), and being killed in an airplane crash (1 in 4,600,000). Imagine! It is nearly *500 times* more likely that the Earth will be struck by a large space object during a lifetime than it is that an individual will die in an airplane crash! Yet, many take the possibility of dying in an air crash very seriously. The reason catastrophe from comets and meteorites is not taken seriously is because it occurs so infrequently. Yet, this rarity is more than compensated for by the immensity of the destruction that cometary impacts bring.

Eleanor Helin, a planetary scientist at NASA's Jet Propulsion Laboratory in Pasadena, California, estimates there is a significant chance that an asteroid the size of a football field could hit Earth within the next century. Should it hit near an urban area, city and suburbs would both be completely obliterated. Close encounters with space objects are not all that rare; there are at least fifty-six meteorite craters classified as "large to very large" in just the continental United States and Canada alone, and *that* does not even account for those that exploded high in the atmosphere, devastating the land surface but leaving no crater!

The last line of quatrain (7) predicts the Papacy moving to another country. The only suitable reason is the degree of destruction that will occur in Italy. There is also a historical precedent for the Papal Seat being elsewhere besides Rome. In 1309 Pope Clement V, who reigned during the years 1305–14, took up residence in Avignon, France, due to wars in Italy and political instability. After this time all the Popes were French, lived in Avignon, and were strongly influenced by the French government until Gregory XI returned the Papacy to Rome, in 1378. Nostradamus makes several references to the moving of the Papacy to France again, apparently for the same reasons that Clement V moved from Italy. Those quatrains will be covered in a later chapter.

There are still a few more quatrains related to the appearance of the comet:

### (8) Century 2, Quatrain 62

| | |
|---|---|
| Mabus then will soon die,<br>   there will happen<br>Of people and beasts<br>   a horrible defeat:<br>After that everyone<br>   struck the vengeance seen,<br>Hundred, hand, thirst, hunger<br>   when will run the comet. | *Mabus puis tôt alors mourra, viendra*<br>*De gens et bêtes une horrible défaite:*<br>*Puis tout à coup la vengeance on verra,*<br>*Cent, main, soif,*<br>   *faim quand courra la comète.* |

Here is another quatrain that links the appearance of a comet with destruction and war. There are very few diseases that are capable of killing both humans and animals in large numbers, so the destruction ("a horrible defeat") will most likely result from either war or extreme changes in the environment. "Mabus" is unidentified at this time and is generally considered to be an anagram for a person of future importance, but a location is also possible. If so, Mabou Harbor, in Nova Scotia, Canada, may be specially marked for destruction (the anagram rules that Nostradamus used allowed not only for the scrambling of letters, but for the substitution of a letter as well). This possibility is intriguing since Nova Scotia was an early French colony, settled within fifty years after Nostradamus' death. Other potential geographical locations include Tabus, Turkey; Babus, Afghanistan; and Mabui, a small mountain on the Philippine island of Biliram. If Nostradamus intends a group of people, the Mabas are the most likely candidate. They are a mixed Negroid, Sudanic people of Muslim culture today living in eastern Chad, in central Africa. Chad is a former French colony, and the Mabas have already fought a "jihad" (religious holy war) with the French in this century. While the possibilities are almost endless, there is no certainty at this time what Nostradamus intended with the term "Mabus." It will certainly become clearer when, as the last line states, the comet appears. (Author's note: as this book was going to press, an article appeared in the July 1996 issue of *Reader's Digest*, titled "Alarm Bells in the Desert," that identified the former U.S. Ambassador to Saudi Arabia as none other than Ray Mabus. Does this prophecy refer to him? For his sake, one can only hope not.)

The third line includes "everyone struck the vengeance seen." What the Earth will be struck by will be made clear in the next few quatrains. Here Nostradamus indicates, to paraphrase the quatrain, that the "strike" will come "with a vengeance."

Exactly how close will the comet come to the Earth? Nostradamus answers that question in the following:

### (9) Century 2, Quatrain 47

| | |
|---|---|
| The enemy great old mourning dies of poison, | *L'ennemi grand vieil deuil meurt de poison,* |
| The sovereigns through infinites subjugated: | *Les souverains par infinis subjugués:* |
| Stones raining, hidden underneath the fleece, | *Pierres pleuvoir, cachés sous la toison,* |
| Through death articles in vain are cited. | *Par mort articles en vain sont allégués.* |

Who the "great old. . . enemy" might be cannot be predicted at this time. The second line predicts the defeat ("subjugated") of at least two countries ("sovereigns") through large numbers of invading troops ("infinites"), rather than through superior technology, conjuring up an image of Genghis Khan and his Asian hordes. The "articles" of the last line are probably the articles of the Geneva Convention regarding army conduct during war. Nostradamus predicts that they will be ignored ("in vain are cited"), and atrocities will be common.

All of this, however, is rather vague and could be applied to any period of time or any war, except for the third line. "Fleece" was a common expression for the tail of a comet, and the only way it can "rain stones" is if the Earth actually passes *through* the tail. The question is, which tail? Many comets have two types of tails, comprising a double tail. One is elongated and straight and consists of ionized gases. It is known as the gas or the ion (plasma) tail. The other is known as the dust tail, which is more strongly curved in shape and hazier in appearance. Also, a comet may have more than one dust tail. While the visible ion tail of most comets is still a better vacuum than can be produced in scientific laboratories, the visible dust tail can contain significant amounts of dust and small stones ejected from the nucleus due to solar radiation pressure and the solar wind (a stream of charged particles emanating from the Sun). Hence, the third line of this quatrain appears to describe a huge meteor shower as the Earth passes through the dust tail of the comet.

The Earth has passed through the tail of comets before, most notably in 1861. It also encountered the edge of Halley's tail in 1910, and that of Comet Suzuki-Saigusa-Mori in 1975. It is interesting that Nostradamus understood that the tail of a comet contained dust and stones. This was not completely understood by even the scientific community until this century. If not as a prophet, then he should be honored as a genius for his understanding of planetary geology and astronomy, in addition to being renowned in his own time as a medical doctor.

There is yet another quatrain about the comet:

**(10) Century 2, Quatrain 43**

| | |
|---|---|
| During the bearded star's appearance, | *Durant l'étoile chevelue apparente,* |
| The three great princes will be made enemies: | *Les trois grands princes seront faits ennemis:* |
| Hit from the sky, peace earth trembling, | *Frappés du ciel, paix terre tremulente,* |
| Pau, Tiber overflowing, serpent on the brink placed. | *Pau, Tymbre undans, serpent sur le bord mis.* |

The "bearded star" is, of course, the comet. Who "The three great princes" of the second line are cannot currently be guessed at, but apparently they will be leaders of three countries. During the appearance of the comet something of significance will fall from the sky and impact onto the Earth ("hit from the sky"). This is the mysterious object previously described in quatrain (3) as "the seventh rock." It is associated with an earthquake in Pau in southwest France and such a severe earthquake in Italy that the Tiber River overflows its banks. What the "serpent" of the last line might be is unclear.

The key to understanding this quatrain is "hit from the sky." Hit by what? The answer is found in the next quatrain:

**(11) Century 1, Quatrain 69**

| | |
|---|---|
| The great mountain round of seven stadia, | *La grande montagne ronde de sept stades,* |
| Afterwards peace, war, famine, flood, | *Après paix, guerre, faim, inondation,* |
| It will roll far away sinking great countries, | *Roulera loin abîmant grands contrades,* |
| Even antiquities, and great foundation. | *Mêmes antiques, et grande fondation.* |

What could this "great round mountain" be? The fact that it is round suggests that it might be spherical in shape. This rules out any object, such as a mountain, that is attached to the Earth, as a mountain would be more appropriately described as having a conical shape. The most likely candidate is a rock, one of fairly sizable proportions. The only place to find objects of this size that could relate to the rest of the quatrain is in outer space, in which case the object described here is a meteor. The Earth, then, is to be hit by a meteor, and as quatrain (10) related the "hit" to the comet, and quatrain (9) spoke of "stones" in the tail of the comet, the "round mountain" of quatrain (11) must be contained within the tail of the comet. Here Nostradamus gives the circumference of the meteor: seven stadia measures nearly 4,250 feet.

After the impact there will be a brief period of "peace," followed by "war" and "famine." But what does Nostradamus have in mind by "flood"? An oceanic impact is implied, which is not surprising, since almost three-quarters of the Earth's surface is covered with water. A meteor strike of this size into an ocean would create a huge tsunami, which is described here in the third line. The tsunami "will roll far away," probably around the entire globe, and flood "great countries,"

17

including some countries that have histories going back many centuries ("Even antiquities"), as well as the greatest powers in the world ("great foundation").

With the knowledge that the meteor is coming, would it not be a simple matter to simply blow it up before it reaches the Earth? Why not simply destroy it, or at least deflect it, while it is still a long way away? The answer is that, sadly enough, neither the Russians nor the Americans possess the tools to do it. To deflect a comet, meteor, or asteroid sufficiently so that it does not strike the Earth requires the use of nuclear weapons millions of miles away from the planet. At this time neither superpower possesses the launch vehicles to deliver the warhead to that distance. Also, there is the matter of timing the explosion. Intercepting Scud missiles during the Gulf War with Patriot missiles was difficult enough; space objects are far larger, far heavier, and far faster than Scud missiles. Even if the missiles could be brought to that distance it is likely that the explosion could not be timed precisely enough to do any good. Besides, the comet will not even be seen until August, and the meteor will impact in the following month. There will simply not be enough advance warning to prepare a warhead and launch vehicle even if the government had one.

Since even a fair-sized comet has a nucleus only a few miles across, is it realistic for a "rock" in the tail of a comet to be a quarter-mile in diameter? Yes, there are many historic instances of large bodies in the dust tails of comets. While some may be meteors captured by the comet's small gravitational field over the millennia, most seem to be chunks of the comet itself. For instance, in 1908, Comet Morehouse had sizable fragments leave the nucleus and become part of its tail. These fragments then began emitting tails of their own, which lasted for a few days each. If not for the presence of the tails these fragments might have gone unnoticed. How many other comets emit chunks of material that do go unnoticed? Many astronomers believe that probably most comets, if not all of them, routinely shed large pieces of debris during their orbit around the sun.

The multitude of meteor showers visible in the sky are essentially the remnants of the dust tails of past comets. As further examples: in 1846 Biela's Comet divided in half; the second comet of 1882 (1882 II) split into at least five individual nuclei; in 1889 Brooks 2 threw off at least four satellite comets after passing through the satellite system

18

of Jupiter; in 1916 Taylor's Comet (1916 I) split; the twelfth comet discovered in 1947 (1947 XII) divided in half; Comet Ikeya-Seki (1965 VIII) threw off several fragments; in 1976 Comet West, while still 30 million kilometers from the Sun, split into four fragments. Astronomers are still not always sure why comets spew large chunks of matter into space, but the occurrence is fairly common. Recently, in July 1992, Comet Shoemaker-Levy (1993e) passed within 100,000 miles of Jupiter and split into at least twenty sizable fragments, most of which collided with Jupiter in a series of spectacular explosions during their next approach to the planet in late July 1994. Some of the explosions generated by the collisions were massive; the largest explosion produced a fireball larger than planet Earth! In all history, this is the first time mankind has witnessed a comet impacting another planet; it is a warning of what will someday happen in the future of Earth, and a reminder of what has happened many times in Earth's past.

In the commentary on Quatrain (5), reference was made to the comets that Johannes Hevelius described as "monstriferous," apparently the type of comet that Nostradamus predicted as the one to come. Two of the comets labeled as "monstriferous" in his drawings show disconnected gaps in their tails that appear to indicate fragmentary cometary pieces, each sporting their own tail. By referring to Hevelius' "monstriferous" comets as the type of comet to come, Nostradamus warns that large bodies will be present in the tail of the Great Daylight Comet of 1999 as well.

Assuming an oceanic impact of Nostradamus' meteor, how disastrous will the collision be? To answer this question, the amount of energy involved must be calculated. This can be roughly estimated, provided that the speed and the mass of the meteor are known. A comparison can then be made with past collisions of interplanetary matter with the Earth, and with the energy involved in some naturally occurring events.

Dividing the circumference of the meteor (4,250 feet) by the constant Pi (3.14) gives a diameter slightly over 1,350 feet, a little more than a quarter of a mile, or just over four-tenths of a kilometer. Assuming the meteor is a perfect sphere (several assumptions must be made in the following calculations) gives a volume of $3.67 \times 10^{13}$ cubic centimeters (that's 1,300,000,000 cubic feet!) Since the meteor appears to be a fragment of the comet, it may have a density equal to the nucleus of the comet itself. However, there is still considerable uncertainty as to the density of cometary nuclei. During Comet Halley's 1910 visit, the density of its nucleus was calculated as being twice that of water, or 2 grams per cubic centimeter (by definition water has a mass of 1 gram per cubic centimeter). During Halley's 1986 passage, the density was re-estimated at somewhere between 0.2 and 1.5 grams per cubic centimeter, using data provided by space probes from the European Space Agency, Japan, and the Soviet Union. A density of less than 1 gram per cubic centimeter would allow the comet to float if it could be gently placed in a large enough body of water. However, Nostradamus' description of the meteor as a "round mountain" and "the seventh rock," rather than a fluffy snowball, appears to indicate a denser, more stony, composition than the values obtained during Halley's 1986 passage. A denser composition is also suggested since the meteor actually reaches the surface of the planet. Less dense objects tend to explode in the atmosphere rather than actually impacting with Earth. A density of 2 grams per cubic centimeter will be used in these calculations. Multiplying the volume ($3.67 \times 10^{13}$ cubic centimeters) by the density (2 grams per cubic centimeter) gives a mass of $7.34 \times 10^{13}$ grams.

The calculation of the speed of the comet and the trailing meteor also involves some estimation. The speed of the Earth as it moves through space in its orbit around the Sun is 30 km/sec (almost 19 miles per second). The speed of comets at 1 AU (the Earth's distance from the Sun) is 42 km/sec (26 miles per second). The impact could occur at any speed from 12 km/sec (7.4 miles per second), in the event the meteor overtakes Earth in a rear-end collision, to 72 km/sec (45 miles per second) in a head-on collision. While a glancing blow to one degree or another is likely, since the Earth's orbit will carry it forward towards the approaching comet a collision at speeds above the median speed of 42 km/sec is likely, and a speed close to the maximum of 72 km/sec is possible. An impact speed of 60 km/sec will be used to calculate the energy involved in this impact. At this speed the meteor will travel completely through the atmosphere in less than one second. Even the ocean will not be enough to stop it, for in only a fraction of a second the meteor will pass through the entire depth of the ocean, finally exploding on the underlying crust.

The energy released in the impact is determined by multiplying one-half of the mass by the square of the velocity. Note that variability in the velocity, which is squared, is far more important to the total energy than changes in mass.

Kinetic Energy= ½ mv²
Plugging in the numbers yields:
KE=½ x 7.34x10$^{13}$ gm x (6.0x10$^6$ cm per second)²
which reduces to the following:
KE=1.32x10$^{27}$ gram-centimeters²

A gram-centimeter-squared is also known as an erg. An erg is a very small unit of energy in the metric system, completely unfamiliar to the everyday life of most people, but it can be converted into units that are more familiar and understandable. Today's nuclear explosions are measured in millions of tons of TNT, or megatons. While the nuclear explosion that destroyed Hiroshima was the energy equivalent of only fifteen thousand tons of TNT, 10$^{27}$ ergs is the equivalent of roughly 2,000 *million* tons of TNT, or more than 130,000 Hiroshima-sized bombs! An impact by a mostly stony meteor measuring two city blocks long and traveling at 60 km/sec would create an explosion the equivalent of setting off 130,000 Hiroshima-sized bombs instantly in the same location. This explosion would take place on the bottom of the ocean floor.

Another example of the damage that can be caused by meteor impacts can be found in the March/April 1992 issue of *Final Frontier* magazine, in an article titled "Will We Be Ready. . . When Worlds Collide." It describes an asteroid with a diameter of a quarter of a mile (the same size as the one predicted by Nostradamus), that came within 400,000 miles of the Earth. Had an impact actually occurred, this article also estimates an explosive force of more than 130,000 Hiroshima-sized bombs.

The idea of an explosion of 2,000 megatons of TNT is mind-numbing. Some comparisons with the energy-yields of other natural events would be helpful. At sunrise on June 30, 1908, either a very small comet or a meteor entered the atmosphere and exploded at a height of about four miles over the Tunguska River in a remote region of Siberia. All of trees directly underneath the site of the explosion were left standing, but were driven into the ground some twenty feet in depth and stripped of all branches. Around the center of the site trees were blown down like toothpicks in a 750 square-mile area, over 15 miles from the

21

epicenter of the explosion. From the air the pattern of destruction resembled a giant wagon wheel. Fifty miles away survivors reported burns from the heat-flash of the explosion. Horses grazing over 400 miles away were knocked down, and the trans-Siberian railroad was almost derailed from the shock-wave of the explosion. The shaking of the ground and the shock-wave in the air were recorded on seismographs and barometers around the entire world. The glow in the sky was so brilliant that many Europeans, even as far away as London, could read their evening papers outdoors well after sunset without the use of streetlights!

Recently, researchers in Antarctica reported finding a thin layer of dust in Antarctic ice that was deposited in 1908. The dust is rich in pure Iridium, indicating extraterrestrial origins since on Earth Iridium is always found in alloy form with Osmium and Platinum, and implying a link with the Tunguska Event, as it came to be known. All this from an object only 160 feet in diameter, moving at a speed of 31 km/sec. The impact of the meteor in Nostradamus' prediction will release over *600 times* the energy of the Tunguska Event.

There have been several other large meteor collisions in the recent geological past. Duncan Steel, from the Anglo-Australian Observatory, and Peter Snow, a New Zealand physician, have identified a crater that appears to be from a Tunguska-sized air-burst explosion over New Zealand. Using local Maori records, the researchers estimate an impact date of roughly 800 years ago.

Wakefield Dort, a University of Kansas geologist, has located a badly eroded crater one mile in diameter in the middle of Nebraska. By examining the sediments that have filled the crater Dort estimates that the impact occurred less than three thousand years ago.

Barringer Meteor Crater in Arizona, near Flagstaff, is another famous impact crater. About 25,000 years ago an iron asteroid carved out a large hole in the slowly eroding rock of the Arizona desert. The dry Arizona climate makes this the best preserved meteorite crater in the world. While slightly smaller in size than the Tunguska meteor (about 100 feet in diameter) the nickel-iron core of this meteorite increased the mass significantly. Its mass has been estimated at 6.3 x $10^{10}$ gm, and its speed 16 km per second. While most of the meteorite vaporized upon impact, about 30 tons of fragments have been collected. The crater it left is three-quarters of a mile wide and 600 feet deep. The energy released in this explosion is estimated at 1,000

Hiroshima-sized bombs. The explosion to come will still be over *130 times* more powerful than the one that carved out Meteor Crater.

Large meteoric collisions with the Earth are not that rare; what is rare is that they do not occur more often. Two University of Arizona astronomers have even estimated that fifty house-sized asteroids pass between the Earth and the orbit of the Moon *each day*.

How do these explosions compare with the impact at the end of the Cretaceous Period 65 million years ago, an event that is now being blamed for the extinction of the dinosaurs? The estimated size of that object is a little over 6 miles in diameter, making it much bigger than the one predicted by Nostradamus. The energy release of that explosion has been estimated at 100 million megatons of TNT. This is 50,000 times the energy release that the event of 1999 will have. The impact of a quarter-mile diameter meteor is not likely to extinguish large numbers of plant and animal species, but the human race is already doing a pretty good job of that. Besides, any ecosystem teetering on the brink of collapse may not be able to tolerate the stresses caused by environmental changes, or by a desperate humanity hoping to survive in the aftermath. Should a meteor with a diameter of one-quarter of a mile actually strike the Earth in 1999, widespread ecologic disaster is a certainty.

While the above information on meteor collisions helps put the energy involved somewhat into perspective, the picture may still be somewhat fuzzy for many readers. Comparisons with the two greatest destructive forces of Mother Nature, volcanoes and earthquakes, may help.

Perhaps the most famous volcanic eruption in the recent past was at Krakatoa, located in the Sunda Strait, south of Sumatra and west of Java, Indonesia. On August 27, 1883, a series of four violent explosions literally blew the volcano, and much of the island it occupied, out of existence. The third, and largest, explosion was heard as far away as Singapore, western Australia, and Rodriguez Island, which is located nearly 3,000 miles away in the Indian Ocean. This explosion blew away the entire northern two-thirds of the island. The shock wave in the air reached the opposite side of the Earth nineteen hours later, and then continued on, back to Krakatoa. In all, there were seven recorded passages of the shock wave over the surface of the Earth.

Island-based volcanoes, undersea earthquakes and ocean-impacting space objects can all create *tsunamis* (from the Japanese words *tsu* for harbor and *nami* for wave). Tsunamis occur when the Earth's crust on the ocean floor moves, causing shock waves in the water above. In mid-ocean tsunamis are relatively shallow, perhaps one to two feet high, but as much as 100 miles long. A change in height that small over that large of a distance make tsunamis imperceptible to ships in the mid-ocean. However, as the waves near shore the leading edge of the wave slows down but the rear continues at full speed, causing the wave to mount up to enormous heights. The initial tsunami from Krakatoa was over 120 feet high and spent much of its force on Java and Sumatra, where entire towns were washed away and over 40,000 people were killed. The portion of the tsunami that passed through the channel into the open sea still created a wave over three feet high in Ceylon (now Sri Lanka), and thirty-two hours later the wave washed ashore in France, still a few centimeters high.

In the sky over Krakatoa, ash and gas were pushed fifty miles up, to the very limit of the atmosphere. Prior to the eruption, the volcano had a peak of 2,640 feet above sea level. After the eruption the peak had collapsed to 1,000 feet below sea level. The total energy released was no more than 150 Megatons. The meteor impact will still be at least *thirteen times* as powerful as this. Even more important, Krakatoa released its energy in a series of explosions, over a period of time. The disastrous effects of a meteor impact, in which all of the energy is released instantaneously, will be far greater. For instance, the Mauna Loa volcano, in Hawaii, erupted in 1950, with a similar energy release to Krakatoa, but all of the energy was released slowly in the form of heat, and the destructive effects of this eruption were minimal.

While Krakatoa's eruption blasted 5 cubic miles of rock into the atmosphere, and the Mt. Pinatubo eruption of 1991 lifted 30 million tons of particles into the stratosphere, enough to cancel out the greenhouse effect for several years, neither of these eruptions is the most powerful of the past two hundred years. That honor belongs to the volcano Tambora, on the island of Sumbawa, also in Indonesia. Between April 5 and 10, in the year 1815, repeated eruptions sent somewhere between 25 and 40 cubic miles of debris into the sky, blowing away over 3,600 feet from the top of the volcano. Ten thousand died in the initial eruption, but more than 80,000 died later from hunger and disease as the ash fall killed off vegetation across Sumbawa, Lombok, and the neighboring islands.

Tambora's eruption also had a major effect on world climate the following year. Fruit did not ripen in New England. There was snow in Pennsylvania in June. In Europe things were no better. London had almost continuous rain from May to October, and the temperature averaged between 3-6 degrees Fahrenheit below normal. Poor harvests in Wales and Ireland led to severe food shortages. Throughout the northern hemisphere, 1816 was known as the "year without a summer," and the following winter as "eighteen hundred and froze to death." Why did this happen? While exact figures cannot be ascertained, it is estimated that atmospheric dust from the Tambora eruption may have cut down the Sun's heat and light by 20%. By comparison, the eruption of Krakatoa and the 1912 eruption of Mt. Katmai in Alaska reduced solar radiation reaching the Earth's surface by only 10%.

Large volcanic eruptions that affect the weather of the entire planet are by no means rare. The previous century, in 1783, Benjamin Franklin noted a partial obscuring of the Sun during the summer and a very cold following winter. Showing keen insight, he attributed it to a volcanic eruption in Iceland.

Recent geologic history seems to indicate that once or twice each century a large volcanic eruption slightly cools the planet for a few years. How much dust is needed for this cooling to occur? Actually, very little, as the upper atmosphere is very sensitive to dust. A reduction in solar radiation by 20% would require only 1/1600 of a cubic mile of very fine-grained dust in the stratosphere, fifteen miles or more up. The finer the grain of the dust, the slower it settles out of the atmosphere.

The presence of a large amount of fine-grained dust in the stratosphere has the possibility to create an ecologic disaster. For instance, if the dust could be resupplied on a regular basis, then temperature reductions of ten degrees Fahrenheit on a worldwide basis are possible. In comparison, ten thousand years ago much of North America and Europe were under an ice sheet one mile thick, but the average worldwide temperature was only about five degrees cooler than it is today. One of the consequences of the meteoric impact will be a nuclear winter lasting for a few years, possibly even longer. If the aftermath of the Tambora eruption is any guide, the harvest from the summer of the year 2000 will be disastrous, and the winter of 2000-2001 will be extremely severe. The resulting food shortages will be worldwide and without precedent in human history. More about this in the third chapter.

Even Tambora, however, was not the biggest eruption of the last two thousand years. Somewhere around 150 A.D. the Taupo volcano, in New Zealand's North Island, erupted in eight separate events, depositing more than 6 cubic miles of debris over almost all of the North Island, covering 20,000 square miles more than 4 inches deep in volcanic ash and rock. And further back in history an even greater eruption occurred in the United States when in southern Oregon Mt. Mazama erupted, sending a magma flow over 30 miles away. The ash from that eruption settled over the entire northwestern United States and as far away as Saskatchewan, Canada. The collapse of the volcanic peak afterwards left a caldera six miles across and one-half mile deep, today known as Crater Lake. In the more distant past the volcano Toba, on the Indonesian island of Sumatra (apparently a popular area for massive volcanic explosions), exploded 74,000 years ago, leaving a 500 square mile lake in the crater of what was once a mountain peak. Toba is estimated to have lifted over 11 billion tons of ash and sulfurous gases 20 miles into the sky. This eruption is even blamed for triggering an ice age. It is interesting to note that the Earth routinely creates its own nuclear winters, even without cometary or meteoric impacts.

Besides volcanoes, earthquakes are the only other natural events that release tremendous amounts of energy. For example, in 1755, a large shift at the junction of the African and European plates in the Atlantic Ocean off the coast of Portugal resulted in the so-called Lisbon earthquake, which killed 60,000 people in Lisbon alone. The quake produced a 30-foot uplift in the seafloor, which in turn produced several tsunamis. The first, and largest, was over 50 feet high and was responsible for much of the damage and death toll in Lisbon. But that was not all. The tremors were felt throughout most of Europe and North Africa. The quake also caused the death of 10,000 in Morocco; again many from a tsunami. The city of Algiers was almost completely obliterated. In Luxembourg, 500 soldiers died when their barracks collapsed. Even in England great cracks developed in the ground.

In Scandinavia and Scotland, water in large lakes sloshed back and forth, overflowing their shores even though the tremor could not otherwise be felt. This response in large bodies of water is known as a *seiche* and it occurs when very long period earthquake waves cause large bodies of water to resonate. A very large earthquake can even make the entire planet resonate like a struck bell. On August 15, 1950, an 8.4 magnitude earthquake in Assam, India, killed 30,000 people and caused reservoir levels in England, halfway around the world, to fluctuate sharply. Likewise, a large meteor impact will probably result in seiches worldwide. Even the Great Lakes of the central North American continent, far removed from an oceanic impact site, might see serious damage from seiches days, even weeks, later as the vibrational energy resounding through the Earth is slowly dissipated.

On March 27, 1964, Good Friday, another large earthquake struck, this time off the coast of Alaska. While loss of life was relatively light with only 114 dead, the pattern of destruction is interesting. The Lisbon earthquake occurred well before the industrial revolution. The Alaska earthquake shows what a large quake can do to a modern city. In Seward, for example, the earthquake ruptured pipelines at a major petroleum storage plant and created massive explosions and fires. Since earthquake waves travel through the dense rock of the ocean floor at speeds nearing 1,000 miles per hour while the tsunami waves are carried along at less than 500 miles per hour, the tsunami always arrives after the earthquake. In this case the burning petroleum from the quake had time to spread over the harbor, setting the water on fire. The tsunami that followed lifted the burning oil and carried it deep into town, burning everything below the high-water mark of the tsunami. The entire industrial district was destroyed, including the railroad yards, powerplant, and twenty-six giant petroleum storage tanks. Seven hours later, when the tsunami reached Crescent City, a coastal city in northwestern California, it still had enough punch left to cause a fire at another oil storage depot.

Imagine what a huge meteor-induced earthquake from an oceanic impact could do to coastal port facilities all around the rim of the ocean in which it occurs. Picture what the following tsunami could do to spread the fires that are certain to occur afterwards. Uncontrolled fire is the greatest risk of a large earthquake. It is what turns an otherwise moderate disaster into one of historical proportions. The famous San Francisco earthquake destroyed only 20% of the city—it was the fire that followed that consumed the city and caused most of the casualties. The fire grew to such a size that it became a "firestorm" as the rising heat generated hurricane-force winds that sucked all loose objects (including people) into the inferno. Without that fire, the San Francisco quake would barely rate a footnote in today's history books.

Another quake, off the coast of Chile on May 22, 1960, created tsunamis over 30 feet high into the coast of Chile, but when it reached the Hawaiian island of Hilo 15 hours later, it came ashore at almost 40 feet. How is this possible? The shape of the seafloor just offshore significantly affects the size of the tsunami. Harbors, bays, and rivers can serve to funnel the onrushing water and concentrate the force. The tsunami created by the 1964 Alaska earthquake actually reached up 1,000 feet high when it was funnelled down a fjord, ripping every tree off the mountainsides. Yet harbors, bays, and river mouths are also the preferred locations for shipping facilities, oil storage tanks, and refineries, as well as industry of all types. A meteor-generated tsunami in mid-ocean would wreak havoc in every port on that ocean.

How large would the tsunami be? A one-size-fits-all approach cannot be adopted since many of the factors affecting size are determined by seafloor depth and shape as the tsunami approaches land, but some estimates can be made. The comet/meteor impact that caused the Cretaceous event 65 million years ago left evidence behind that leads geologists to believe that the tsunami created was *three miles high!*

In their excellent book *Comet*, Carl Sagan and Ann Druyan quote from the book *Project Icarus*, which was an outgrowth of a 1968 student engineering project at the Massachusetts Institute of Technology. The project estimated the consequences of a large meteor strike in the mid-Atlantic, 1,000 miles east of Bermuda. The calculated energy release from their meteor was 500,000 megatons of TNT, making the explosion roughly 250 times the size of the disaster predicted for 1999. Nevertheless, the results of their calculations are very instructive. The group estimated that a tsunami would hit Boston, over 1,500 miles away, with a 200 foot high wall of water. This wave would come ashore at a speed of roughly 70 miles per hour, and since the water in even a moderate sized tsunami totals nearly 2,000 tons per foot of shoreline, the destruction of coastal facilities would be complete. Nor would the Atlantic Ocean be the only site of damage. The authors of *Project Icarus* estimated that even places in the Pacific Ocean would see 100-foot-high tsunamis.

If a quarter-mile in diameter meteor should land in the mid-Atlantic how high would the initial tsunami be? 50 feet? 100 feet? Perhaps 200 feet or more in a few especially unfortunate places where the water will be funnelled into a Bay or river mouth? At this time there is no way to know for sure. But imagine the massive oil-refining and petro-chemical complexes of the Mississippi River near the Gulf of Mexico, one of the critical industrial areas of the United States, being struck by "only" a 100 foot-high wall of water moving at 70 miles per hour. Ruptured pipelines would spread flammable material over many square miles. A single spark from any source could be disastrous.

Just as important as the height of the tsunami, however, is how far inland the water penetrates. As an example, a December 1992, earthquake in Indonesia generated a tsunami 80 feet high that penetrated as far as 1,000 feet inland. Other tsunamis have carried ocean-going ships as far as three miles inland. Anything and everything within one to perhaps as much as three or even four miles of the coastline surrounding the impact site will be completely destroyed. In the lower Mississippi the destruction may extend upriver for many miles from the Gulf, and perhaps as much as two or three miles on each side of the river. A single fire might turn into a firestorm, a fire that would prove impossible to extinguish. The firestorm would rage for weeks, possibly months, until every possible source of fuel in the region has been exhausted. Since a large portion of the petrochemical industry of the entire United States is located in the Mississippi delta, the loss of those facilities would result in the crippling of the entire U.S. economy.

The Richter scale is the standard by which earthquake strength is measured. Named for the American seismologist Charles Richter (1900-1985), the Richter scale estimates total energy released in an earthquake by the amplitude of the seismic waves at various points around the Earth. If the amount of energy released from Nostradamus' projected meteor impact was all released in seismic waves instead of an explosion, what number would this impact rate on the Richter scale? $1.32 \times 10^{27}$ ergs translates to greater than a 14.0 on the Richter scale! In comparison, the 1906 San Francisco earthquake rates a 7.9 on the Richter scale, the 1755 Lisbon earthquake is estimated at 8.6, and the 1964 Alaska earthquake at 9.2. The 1960 Chile quake registered at 9.5 on the Richter scale, which is probably about as big as a non-meteor induced earthquake can get.

The destructive power of a magnitude 14 earthquake is simply unimaginable. However, comparisons between earthquakes and meteor strikes are very limited. Since almost all earthquakes occur in the cold, brittle rocks of the crust, they are usually not more than 12.5 miles deep; below that the rocks are too fluid to crack. However, the shallowest earthquakes are still at least 3 miles deep, because above that depth enough stress cannot be built up in the rocks to cause an earthquake. Thus, in any earthquake there is at least 3 miles of insulating rock between the site of the energy release and the surface of the Earth, which is quite different from a meteor strike, where the energy release occurs on the face of the planet.

Moving at a speed of nearly 40 miles per second, the meteor will travel completely through the atmosphere and the ocean in less than a second, exploding on the crust at the bottom of the ocean. Parts of the meteor might even penetrate a few miles into the crust itself. Tsunamis that occur from earthquakes are due to changes in seafloor height that accompany the quake. As noted during the Lisbon quake a change in seafloor height of 30 feet caused a tsunami that was over 30 feet high. Changes in seafloor height after a meteor strike of this magnitude might be measured in *thousands* of feet!

Another factor limiting energy comparisons of earthquakes with meteor collisions is the way in which energy is dissipated. Earthquakes tend to disperse their energy along the length of a fault, while meteor-strikes concentrate their energy with pinpoint precision. As noted previously, the eruptions of Krakatoa and Mauna Loa released the same amount of energy, but concentrating that energy in time and space made for far more destruction at Krakatoa. The pinpoint, instantaneous release of energy will result in a far larger, far more destructive tsunami than any same-energy-release earthquake could ever generate, even at an intensity level of greater than 14 on the Richter Scale.

How bad will the damage from Nostradamus' meteor be? It could put more dust, not to mention water vapor and sea salts, into the stratosphere than the eruption of Tambora did, while at the same time creating the most violent earthquake ever seen. The destruction on land, even thousands of miles away, is simply incomprehensible. Tsunamis are likely to fall on every shore surrounding the ocean in the 50-200-foot range, possibly even larger in industrial districts located in river mouths and other areas "protected" from the open sea that might serve to funnel the force of the water. Distance provides no safety with tsunamis; remember, the 1960 Chile earthquake caused a larger wave in Hawaii than it did in Chile!

In addition to the damage from the earthquake and tsunami, the ensuing firestorms will be widespread, pushing tremendous amounts of soot into the upper atmosphere, soot that will further serve to block sunlight and cool the planet. A recent analysis of soot deposited at the time of the Cretaceous Event shows that the ensuing firestorm burned up roughly one-third of the vegetation of the entire planet!

The above information on historical meteor impacts, volcanoes, and earthquakes helps provide some perspective of the massive energies involved, but all of these examples are only pale reflections of what a collision with a meteor might really bring. Since Nostradamus is calling for this disaster, does he say where? A hint can be found in the following quatrain:

**(12) Century 9, Quatrain 31**

| | |
|---|---|
| The trembling of land at Mortara, | *Le tremblement de terre à Mortara,* |
| Tin St. George half sunk, | *Cassich saint George à* |
| Peace drowsy the war will awaken, | *demi perfondrez,* |
| In the temple at Easter | *Paix assoupie la guerre éveillera,* |
| abysses open. | *Dans temple à Pâques* |
| | *abîmes enfondrez.* |

Mortara is in northern Italy, thirty-five miles southwest of Milan. "Tin St. George" is a reference to Great Britain and its patron saint, St. George. "Tin" refers to the Scilly Islands, off the coast of England, which are also known as the Tin Islands. In the first two lines of this quatrain Nostradamus makes another reference to an area located on the African-European plate border that will suffer an earthquake ("the trembling of land at Mortara"), and this time links the earthquake with a flood that covers half of England. While Scotland and Wales have mountainous regions, much of England is fairly flat and near sea level. In fact, most of the English people live at elevations less than 300 feet above sea level. Also, England is a fairly narrow island country and it is impossible to get farther than 70 miles from the sea. In the event of an impact fairly close to Great Britain, the tsunami could literally drown half of the country. Nostradamus is hinting here that the meteor will strike in the northern half of the Atlantic Ocean. Hitting near the undersea border of the European and African tectonic plates, the shock will serve to bounce those

31

plates, allowing them to temporarily unlock and slip past one another. The resulting secondary earthquake (the impact being the initial quake) will unlock the boundary of the two tectonic plates throughout their length, and the quake will be felt in southern France, northern Italy and Greece.

The last two lines of quatrain (12) are difficult to understand. The third line might be understood better as "after drowsy peace, war will wake up and come upon mankind." The last line is even more difficult to understand. Since this is supposed to occur in September, how can Easter be involved? It is possible that Nostradamus is referring not to the feast of Easter but to a physical building (church?) that contains "Easter" as part of its name. Another possibility is that he is indicating an event that will occur some months later, perhaps a late, large, aftershock earthquake. Since in the third line he indicates a war, which may not start for months, even years, after the impact, it is very possible that in the fourth line he is referring to an event that will occur the following Easter. His intention cannot be precisely determined at this time.

Two previously discussed quatrains, (7) and (10), also indicate an impact site in the Atlantic Ocean. In quatrain (7) England, "the big mastiff. . .will howl" because the tsunami will have washed away half the country. "The great pontiff," the Pope, may change countries because the secondary earthquake along the European-African plate border, along with the tsunamis likely to be generated in the Mediterranean Sea by that secondary quake, will destroy large parts of Italy in general, and Vatican City in particular. However, other quatrains indicate that the Pope will "change countries" as a result of the war that will follow the meteor impact. More about this in a later chapter.

In quatrain (10) again note the relationship of an earthquake in Pau, France, and a seiche in the Tiber river in Italy with the appearance of the comet. Is this likely with an impact into any ocean other than the Atlantic? A site in the Mediterranean Sea could not generate a tsunami that would half-flood England, and other oceanic sites are probably too removed to inundate England that badly. Nostradamus predicts that the meteor will strike in the Atlantic Ocean, either on or near the undersea junction of the European and African tectonic plates, which is near the Azore Islands.

As discussed briefly already, one of the major effects of the dust thrown into the atmosphere will be a significant reduction in the amount of sunlight reaching the Earth. Just as the 1815 Tambora eruption created a miniature nuclear winter, the winters of 2000-2001 and, possibly, 2001-2002 will be severe. Nostradamus has a quatrain describing those winters:

**(13) Century 10, Quatrain 71**

| | |
|---|---|
| The earth and air will freeze so much water, | *La terre et l'air geleront si grand eau,* |
| When they will come for Thursday worship: | *Lorsqu'on viendra pour Jeudi vénérer:* |
| That which will be will not ever be as fair as it was, | *Ce qui sera jamais ne fut si beau,* |
| From the four parts they will come to honor it. | *Dès quatres parts le viendront honorer.* |

The first line describes the bitter winters to follow the impact. The third line is difficult to interpret. It appears to mean that life after the meteor will never be as luxurious, as lavish, or as materially wealthy as it was before. The "four parts" of the last line refers to the "four corners" of the Earth, meaning the entire planet, which will "honor" the memory of the "good old days" before the meteor impact.

The most interesting part of quatrain (13) is the "Thursday worship" theme. No major religion conducts worship services on Thursday. For Christians, Sunday is the holy day, Saturday is the day of worship for Jews, and Friday is holy for Moslems. If Nostradamus intended actual religious services on Thursdays, then a new world religion is required. While this is possible, it is unlikely, since none of his other writings deal with this subject. It is possible that Nostradamus is making an obscure reference to the United States, with its Thanksgiving Thursday holiday. The United States may be asked, after the impact, to open its food storage bins and feed the world. In this case the other nations will be worshipping, in a sense, at the bread altar of the U.S. While possible, this seems unlikely since the United States will be quite incapable of dealing with its own problems, let alone those of the rest of the world. Still another possibility is that Nostradamus intends an obscure reference to Jupiter. All of the days of the week are named after ancient gods. Thursday, Jeudi in French, is the day named after Jupiter, the Roman king of the Gods. In English, Thursday is named after the Norse god Thor. Among their other duties, both Jupiter and Thor were responsible for wielding the thunderbolts from the heavens. Nostradamus may be describing the meteor strike as being like a thunderbolt thrown from the heavens, wielded by Jupiter, with sudden disaster the result. It is also possible he intends Thursday as the day of the meteor's impact, in which case a worldwide annual day of mourning on the anniversary of the impact is quite understandable. This would also nicely explain the "Thursday worship" and "from the four parts they will come to honor it" themes.

Nostradamus has another quatrain about a nuclear winter:

**(14) Presage 124**

| | |
|---|---|
| The grains not to abound too much, of all other fruits force, | *Les bleds trop n'abonder, de toutes autres fruits force,* |
| The summer, spring wet, winter long, snow, ice: | *L'été, printemps humides, hiver long, neige, glace:* |
| In arms the East, France itself will reinforce, | *En armes l'Orient, la France se renforce,* |
| Death of cattle much honey, the seat to the besieged. | *Mort de bétail prou miel, aux assiégés la place.* |

Since a "spring wet" and "summer" was also seen in western Europe in the year 1816 following the 1815 Tambora eruption, this quatrain probably belongs in the spring and summer of the year 2000. The "winter long" of 2000-2001 will be associated with an "arms" race in "France" and the "East." This "winter long" will be severe enough to cause the "death of cattle" and honeybees throughout France. In a severe winter this would be likely. For example, in April 1993, the worst blizzards in over thirty years resulted in the death of more than *one million* cattle in Mongolia; a very severe nuclear-type winter would prove disastrous to the domesticated animals of Europe. Grain harvests will also be poor, just as they were in 1816, and the "fruit" most in abundance will be "force" and violence, probably in a struggle for food and other vital resources. The latter part of the last line suggests that the "arms" race will end in war, which will include a siege of the papal seat in Vatican City. An attack on the Vatican, as described here, also fits with quatrain (7), which described the movement of the Papacy to another country.

It is in the cross-linkages of Nostradamus' quatrains, such as those described above, that Nostradamus leaves the clues to the proper interpretation of his predictions. The same theme found in two different quatrains allows them to be connected, just as the same picture on two different jigsaw-puzzle pieces allows them to be connected. The quatrain with a specific date, the seventh month of 1999, then allows the whole body of work to be tied to a specific date.

For those having difficulty picturing the predicted events, the next few pages will sequence them in chronological order:

During the total eclipse of the Sun in France on August 11th, 1999, a comet will be seen. It may or may not have been previously identified by satellites, but Nostradamus predicts that this will be its first naked-eye view from Earth. After the eclipse it will disappear into the Sun's glare once more, only to reappear a few days or weeks later. Its approach to Earth will be close enough that the sky will actually appear to have a second sun, caused by the reflection of the Sun's light off the comet's massive coma. The Earth will actually pass through the comet's dust tail sometime during September 1999. Contained within the dust tail will be many cometary fragments, some large, others small. One fragment, roughly one-quarter mile in diameter, will strike the Earth, possibly on a Thursday, at an estimated speed of 60 kilometers (37 miles) per second. The projected impact site is in the Atlantic Ocean, east of the Mid-Atlantic Rise, at or near the junction of the African and European tectonic plates, east of the Azore Islands.

The fireball from the explosion will quickly rise to the very top of the atmosphere and then spread laterally. The fireball could easily be fifty, perhaps even a hundred, miles in diameter. The explosion of only a one-megaton nuclear weapon generates temperatures of 100 million degrees at its center, so this temperature is a minimum that can be expected. Everything within many hundreds of miles will instantaneously ignite from the flash of the explosion, and any satellites overlooking the area will be destroyed. The shock wave in the atmosphere will crumple any aircraft within thousands of miles that might happen to be in the air.

The initial earthquake wave will race out at speeds approaching 1,000 miles per hour. The vertical movement in the Earth's crust close to the epicenter of the explosion will be thousands of feet high; by the time the shock wave reaches coastal areas it is likely to still be several feet high. As this shock wave races under coastal cities, the buildings there will have to climb the shock wave and then ride it on the downhill slope again, much as little toy buildings lying on a sheet that is shaken. Many, if not most, of the man-made objects will collapse, and small fires will begin in many areas. The Atlantic coastal areas of all of Western Europe, Africa, and the east coast of North and South America will be severely damaged, possibly completely destroyed, by the strongest earthquake ever known. The pattern of damage will be similar in nature to other quakes: collapsed buildings, incapacitated roads, bridges, and railroad tracks, fractured natural gas and oil pipelines, ruptured oil and chemical storage tanks, and worst of all, fire.

The tsunami will follow soon afterwards. Locations 1,000 miles from the epicenter of the impact will have a one-hour gap between the quake and the tsunami; in places 4,000 miles away the time gap will be four hours. The extent of damage from the quake, especially the rupture of water mains, will dash any hopes of extinguishing whatever fires may have started. Within an hour the fires will be well established, and few will have burned themselves out within four hours, so the tsunami will serve to spread the fire everywhere it strikes. The force of the tsunami will further ravage the coastlines, but the damage will be different from that of the earthquake waves in one important respect. The topography of the undersea continental shelf just offshore greatly affects the concentration of the energy of a tsunami. Bays and river-mouths will serve as magnifiers of the tsunami. Unfortunately, these are the precise locations that ports, with their railroads, oil storage depots, refineries, power plants, and heavy industry of all types, are located. Thus the destruction of weather-protected port facilities is likely to be amplified by the tsunami, and the fires already present will be enlarged immensely by water spreading the burning debris and petroleum products. The fires are likely, in many locations, to turn into firestorms, similar to the ones that Allied bombers created in Dresden and Tokyo during World War II that destroyed both cities. Impossible to fight, the fires will die out only after exhausting every source of fuel in entire cities. Nostradamus notes that England, a country of coastline with little interior and essentially no high ground, will be especially devastated.

While the initial tsunami will be the worst, many more, over a period of days, or even weeks, will follow. Even the ice cap at the North Pole presents no obstacles to the tsunami as a typical tsunami in mid-ocean is only a foot or two high, but many miles long. It is only as it reaches shore that it bunches up again into a huge wave.

Therefore, the wave will pass under the North Pole and re-emerge in the northern Pacific undiminished, with enough punch to ravish the Pacific rim countries as well, perhaps as far as the north coast of Australia. It is also possible that the southern-moving part of the tsunami will disrupt the Antarctic ice cap. Should that disruption cause a large part of the Antarctic ice sheet to slide into the ocean, a permanent raising of sea level of at least several feet will occur.

As if the original earthquake will not be enough, very strong secondary quakes will occur throughout the border of the African and European plates as the shock wave of the impact frees the African tectonic plate to slip under the European plate. Southern France, northern Italy, Greece, and northern Africa in particular will suffer massive destruction from these tremors and subsequent tsunamis.

Hurricanes, perhaps many, will further harass the impact survivors. Over the impact site the hot ocean water will create a massive hurricane. Recent research indicates that if an area of ocean thirty miles in diameter could be heated to 120 degrees Fahrenheit, which is exactly what could be expected with a large meteor-induced explosion, then the hurricanes spawned from that site would not be ordinary hurricanes, they would be hypercanes. The storm itself would be only 10 miles in diameter, and the eye of the hypercane only 100 yards in diameter, but winds would top out at *500 miles per hour*! Shortly after forming, this hypercane would begin to drift westward, off the super-heated ocean water, and would probably deteriorate to just a very strong hurricane. Within a day or two another hypercane would then form over the impact site. This process would continue until water cooled sufficiently that only ordinary hurricanes could form, so it is likely that large storms would be generated off the impact site for at least several weeks.

An additional problem posed by hypercanes is their height. It is estimated that they will reach as high as 35 miles into the atmosphere, well into the stratosphere, carrying water vapor and sea salts high into the atmosphere. These salts would further serve to block the sunlight reaching the planet, and it is also possible that the chlorine from the sea salts would destroy the ozone layer.

Even if these hypercanes quickly deteriorate into just ordinary hurricanes, then there will be many storms as large as hurricanes Hugo and Andrew, forming on almost a daily basis as the planet attempts to dissipate the massive amount of thermal energy released into the Atlantic. Smaller heat waves and tropical storms will last for several months, perhaps even a year. Both the frequency and intensity of storms throughout the world will be without precedent. The "rain" discussed previously in quatrain (4) appears to refer to the time period after the impact in which storms, and rain, will be almost continual. The "milk" from that same quatrain might represent the whitish coloring of the salty precipitate as it settles out of the sky.

Following this period of storms of massive strength and unprecedented frequency will be a period best described as a nuclear winter, as the dust lifted from the initial explosion into the upper reaches of the atmosphere spreads worldwide, significantly reducing the amount of sunlight and heat reaching the Earth. This "winter" will be far harsher than the 1816 "year without a summer," already noted. The harvests in the years of 2000 and 2001 will be poor throughout temperate climates worldwide. The years following those will also see poor harvests due to a lack of petrochemical-based fertilizer and insecticides, along with a lack of seed from previous poor harvests. This will be discussed in more detail in the third chapter.

At the impact site the crust will rebound immediately afterwards, much as a raindrop that falls in a puddle causes an inward and upward surge in the water. A buried meteor crater, measuring 22 miles in diameter, is located in the cornfields of Iowa. It came from a meteor one mile in diameter. Ray Anderson, a geologist with the Iowa Department of Natural Resources, notes that the impact caused deeply buried granite to instantly rise 20,000 feet and form a permanent dome. Given an impact site near the Mid-Atlantic rise, where the crust of the Earth is thin and vulcanism is already occurring, and given a possible penetration of the meteor several miles into the crust of the Earth, a residual large, active volcanic island is possible. Some scientists even believe that Iceland may have been formed in this manner at some time in the distant past. Should that volcano stay beneath the surface of the sea, then yet another heat source will be present that will contribute to the development of hypercanes. Should it rise above the water, then there will be yet another factor adding dust to the atmosphere and contributing to global cooling.

The toll of the impact on human civilization will be enormous, ending modern civilization and returning the world to a standard of living at least as far back as just before the industrial revolution, and possibly more appropriately to the middle ages. The great global economy touted by economists recently has a danger that is little recognized. Had this impact occurred 100 years ago its influence on civilization would have been far less. Why? During the 1800s the population of the United States was over 90% rural in nature. Most people provided for their own food, shelter, energy, and clothes. Compare this to today, when less than 5% of the population is rural, and most of that 5% do not maintain gardens, orchards, or even small animals. After the impact, the disruption of transportation systems, especially shipping and air transport, means that there will be no global economy.

What effect will the loss of the global economy have? Take the city of Chicago, for instance. Far removed from the impact site, it should be structurally intact. However, the city runs on oil pumped from the ground tens of thousands of miles away, refined thousands of miles away, in cars manufactured in Asia and Europe. Food is no better. With potatoes from Idaho, wheat from Nebraska, meat from Texas, citrus and vegetables from California and Florida, or even worse, Mexico and Chile, the loss of oil production and refining facilities will lead to fuel shortages that will cripple transportation and may make it very difficult for the city to feed itself after a few weeks. In today's world, few of the basic needs are produced locally. Whether it be clothes from China or computers from the Philippines, steel from Brazil or machine tools from Germany, oil from Saudi Arabia or bananas from central America, the United States economy is desperately dependent on a global economy. Any serious hindrance to transportation *from any cause* would cripple every industrialized society in the world, but particularly the United States. The currently interdependent world economy is unique in history, and has many benefits, but has an unrecognized weak spot, as well. The Achilles Heel of the world economy is the absolute dependence on inexpensive transportation of goods.

After the impact, with port facilities destroyed throughout the Atlantic, and possibly the Pacific as well, world trade will come to an instant halt. Even if the Pacific Ocean is spared, the earthquake may well cause landslides from the unstable mountains overlooking the Panama Canal to close the canal, or the tsunami may destroy its eastern entrance, likewise closing the canal. Also, a major earthquake in southern Europe and a subsequent Mediterranean tsunami may close the Suez Canal. It is very possible that the countries bordering the Atlantic Ocean will be completely cut off from those of the Pacific, and all possibility of help.

Those happy to not be living in a such a big city as Chicago and who feel safer in their distant suburbs would do well to consider how well they will be able to exist without gasoline. Will they be able to walk to work? How about getting to the shopping centers? And even if they do, will there be anything in the stores? And what about getting to a doctor or hospital? In all of history, suburbs as bedroom communities for the cities have existed only since World War II, when cheap energy and the automobile made long distance commuting possible. Even without a close encounter with a meteor, the world is approaching the time when energy will become gradually more expensive, in real dollars. As this happens suburbs will no longer be economically viable. They will become the slums and the cities, thanks to cheaper mass transportation systems, will be rejuvenated. Suburbs, on the scale that they exist today, have been present for not quite fifty years. Perhaps in another hundred years they will cease to exist, except as a footnote in history books.

The loss of supertankers in the Atlantic, the destruction of port facilities, and the loss of the Suez Canal (if not by disaster, then by Muslim terrorists seeking to drive the final nail in the coffin of western civilization) will decimate Europe and America, which are both heavily dependent on the Middle East for oil. The North-Sea fields will not be operational, to say the least, and the Alaskan North Slope will be scarcely better off. Without oil, cars, trucks, trains, and airplanes are useless.

Besides the lack of fuel, airplanes face another problem. . . dust. At the end of June, 1982, a British Airways Boeing 747 was flying from Singapore to Australia, at a height of 37,000 ft. A dark cloud in front of them turned out to be the dust cloud of the Indonesian volcano Galunggung. Upon flying into the cloud all of the engines failed and the pilot could not restart them until the plane had fallen to a height of 12,000 ft. Two weeks later, a Singapore Airlines 747 on the same route stalled three engines inside another ash plume from the same volcano. Jet engines simply do not do well in dusty conditions, as the dust clogs the fuel lines and abrades the turbines. Air travel across the Atlantic will be prevented for at least a few weeks, long enough for civilization to collapse, so that when air travel is again possible, few will care about crossing the ocean.

Along with the destruction of advanced transportation systems will come the destruction of one of the other great advances of the twentieth century. . . global communications. The impact will not only push immense dust clouds into the upper atmosphere, it will also eject *billions* of pieces of rock into Earth orbit. These rocks will, within a few years at most, destroy all of the communication, weather, and military satellites in orbit. For instance, of the spacecraft sent to observe Halley's Comet in 1986, three suffered damage, two of them extensive damage, from collisions with dust. The dust particle that damaged the Giotto spacecraft weighed no more than 0.17 grams! The number of particles this size or larger will be simply uncountable.

Without a meteoric impact mankind is in danger of losing the space frontier anyway. Space junk, consisting of debris from old satellites and discarded rocket boosters whose residual fuel causes them to explode, is quickly making Earth orbit a dangerous place. The U.S. Space Command in Colorado tracks about 8,000 objects in orbit the size of a baseball or larger, which is the smallest object that ground-based radar can track. This junk orbits the earth at about 24,000 m.p.h., nearly seven miles per second. However, as noted above, while radar can track only objects larger than four inches in diameter, smaller objects are still very dangerous. At seven miles per second a billiard ball, slightly smaller than four inches, packs the wallop of a bowling ball moving at 70 mph.

NASA estimates a one-in-thirty chance of a space shuttle colliding with space junk. In 1983, prior to its untimely demise, the ill-fated Challenger actually collided with a small piece of junk, a tiny fleck of paint. Yet, though very small, this paint chip still pitted the outer pane of the windshield so badly that it had to be replaced. One study estimated that there is a 1-in-100 chance that the Hubble Space Telescope could be destroyed by junk.

Consider this quote from University of Chicago physicist John Simpson: *"If junk keeps accumulating at the current rate, space missions may become impossible in 20 or 30 years."* NASA scientist Donald Kessler notes that a 2,000-pound spacecraft would burst apart if hit by a fragment weighing just two pounds. Such a collision would produce hundreds of smaller fragments, each capable of destroying another spacecraft. NASA has had to replace windows after about half of the shuttle missions due to collisions with space debris, and has made orbit corrections on several missions to avoid space junk. Eventually, orbiting space junk slows down and falls into the atmosphere, becoming another tiny meteor, but in the future, there could be enough collisions to produce new fragments at a faster rate than old fragments fall back to earth. In this case space junk would continue to grow, even without new spacecraft.

In the event of a large meteoric impact on the Earth, billions of meteorite-generated small rocks thrown into near Earth-orbit would, in at most a few years, destroy every satellite in space. The debris would linger for many years, perhaps centuries. Mankind's reach for the stars is about to be put on hold for a few generations. With the loss of communication satellites and the cutting of the transoceanic cables by the tsunami, the information age will come to an end along with the transportation age.

A collapse of transportation and information systems will result in a general business collapse. For instance, Louis Rukeyser (of PBS' *Wall Street Week* fame), in the May 1992 issue of *Individual Investor*, writes: "Historically, companies that experience a computer outage lasting longer than ten days never fully recover. About 50% go out of business within five years. . . . The average company loses 2-3% of its gross sales within eight days of a sustained computer outage like those set off by Hurricane Hugo or the 1990 earthquake in San Francisco." The computer outages from a meteor impact will last far longer than ten days, and businesses of all types will be bankrupted. The general business collapse will far exceed that of the late 1920s and 30s, and will be worldwide in nature.

The Great Depression resulted in the rise of totalitarian governments in Spain, Germany, Italy, and Japan among other countries. The economic collapse after the impact will be followed by a general political collapse in many countries, which will in turn be followed by a new wave of totalitarianism. Nostradamus has many predictions about a pan-Muslim totalitarian government rising from Islamic religious fundamentalism in the aftermath of the destruction brought by the comet. This theme will be addressed in great detail later.

Finally, the ecologic effects of the impact will be stunning as well. While it is unlikely that there will be large-scale extinctions of species throughout the world, extinctions in the Atlantic Ocean may well occur. Tsunamis are not just surface waves, they occur throughout the entire depth of the ocean, scouring the ocean floor. All aquatic life for thousands of miles within the epicenter will be crushed by the shock wave. The pollution resulting from burning coastal debris will poison coastal waters, where most marine life exists. Also, the fireball itself will result in the production of tremendous quantities of nitrous oxides that will fall out of the sky as acid rain, further poisoning the oceans, lakes, and rivers. It is estimated that the acid rain generated from the Cretaceous Event was sufficient to acidify the upper 100-300 feet of all worldwide water sources, poisoning the marine life. While the energies involved in the Cretaceous Event are much larger than what is to come, it is conceivable that the Atlantic Ocean, at least for a generation or two, could turn into a dead body of water.

It should be noted at this point that it is quite possible that Nostradamus is completely wrong, or that this author is mistaken in his interpretation of Nostradamus' work. Regardless, if a small chunk of comet or meteor/asteroid should, at any time, hit the Atlantic ocean, or rather, *when* a piece of space matter once again impacts the Earth, then the technical information of what would happen in such an event as described in the rest of this chapter is completely accurate. Also, since the following chapters of this book are based on what would likely occur in the aftermath of such a disaster, then Nostradamus could be entirely wrong and the rest of this book would still provide a fair assessment of the political, economic, military, and environmental aftermath of such an unprecedented disaster for the human race. The reader should note that planetary-scale catastrophic events do occur with some regularity, and eventually will happen again.

Many of those individuals living when planetary-wide disaster strikes will lose their lives, many more will lose all of their material possessions; but those who lose all their belongings, even their lives, will not have suffered the ultimate human tragedy. After all, what is life all about? Is the drive to acquire more money, stocks, bonds, newer cars, more jewelry, more clothes, more status, more of . . . well, anything, worth the cost? Does even prolonging life make it better or more worthwhile? Is it even *really* more important to live to ninety instead of fifty-five? One of saddest bumper stickers is the one that states "He who dies with the most toys. . . wins!" Life does not consist of material possessions! The purpose of life is not even to live longer! The point of life is to find out who put us here, and why, and then to carry out the purposes for which we are here. There is no religion in the world that believes that the most important purposes of life are to acquire more things and to live longer. Material goods can be taken away at a moment's notice, and besides, they are of no use in the grave. Even if Nostradamus, and this author, are wrong about the

43

events of 1999, death will come to all those reading this book within a few short years. What is even a long life of over one hundred years when compared with all eternity? In the Gospels Jesus compared a lifetime to the grass of the field—it grows and blooms in a day and then is gathered up and thrown into the furnace. It is vitally important that you, the reader, consider why you are here, what is the purpose of your life, and how you are going to spend it. Many spend their lives only in materialism, or in trying to live healthier and longer without ever considering why they should live longer or healthier. Dying at a ripe old age, with an abundance of physical possessions, after having lived a self-centered, materialistic lifestyle, never considering the purpose of life, is the greatest tragedy possible. Considering the number of people living that lifestyle today, the world may currently be experiencing a greater tragedy than if Nostradamus' comet really should appear.

# NOSTRADAMUS' BIBLICAL CORRELATIONS

Before continuing with Nostradamus' predictions of what will follow the appearance of the comet and impact of the meteor, some prophetic passages of the Bible need to be addressed. Besides his own visions of the future, Nostradamus also claimed to be inspired by the Bible. Specifically, in a letter to his son, Cesar, Nostradamus wrote: "For by the use of the Holy Scriptures, with the help of inspiration and divine revelation, and continual calculation, I have set down my prophecies in writing." Unfortunately, he was not specific as to exactly which portions of the Holy Scriptures he utilized. While there are many prophetic passages found throughout the Old and New Testaments, the Book of Revelation contains perhaps the bulk of the unfulfilled prophecies to come, certainly some of the most vivid and fascinating. Several chapters of the Book of Revelation do indeed provide support for Nostradamus' vision. For those who believe Nostradamus to be a charlatan, it is possible that he took the events of Revelation and adapted them to his own uses. While it seems unlikely, he may have taken Biblical prophecy and reworked it into his own quatrains, claiming the visions as his own. However, regardless of whether Nostradamus' predictions stand or fall, for Christians the prophecies of Revelation need no outside verification, they are truth and will be fulfilled when God sees fit to do so. They believe that, whether Nostradamus is right or wrong about the events of 1999, the predicted events contained within the Book of Revelation will happen, in God's time. It is the purpose of this chapter to explore the links between Biblical prophecy and the quatrains of Nostradamus that were discussed in the first chapter of this book.

There have been many interpretations of Revelation, and some of the more popular in the past few decades place the entire time frame of the book in a three-and-one-half-year period. Yet nowhere in the Bible does it state that the events depicted in Revelation all occur at the same time, and there are multiple passages throughout the Bible of so-called "split prophecies" in which two, or more, separate events are combined into a single story. For example, consider Jesus' own words, quoted from the twenty-fourth chapter of the Gospel According to Matthew (all scriptural references are from Today's English Version):

> Jesus left and was going away from the Temple when his disciples came to him to call his attention to its buildings. "Yes," he said, "you may well look at all these. I tell you this: not a single stone here will be left in its place; every one of them will be thrown down."
>
> As Jesus sat on the Mount of Olives, the disciples came to him in private. "Tell us when all this will be," they asked, "and what will happen to show that it is the time for your coming and the end of the age.
>
> Jesus answered, "Watch out, and do not let anyone fool you. Many men, claiming to speak for me, will come and say, 'I am the Messiah!' and they will fool many people. You are going to hear the noise of battles close by and the news of battles far away; but do not be troubled. Such things must happen, but they do not mean that the end has come. Countries will fight each other; kingdoms will attack one another. There will be famines and earthquakes everywhere. All these things are like the first pains of childbirth.
>
> "Then you will be arrested and handed over to be punished and be put to death. All mankind will hate you because of me. Many will give up their faith at that time; they will betray one another and hate one another. Then many false prophets will appear and fool many people. Such will be the spread of evil that many people's love will grow cold. . . ."

This part of Matthew's Gospel, and its companion passages in Mark and Luke, were written at least several years before the second Temple in Jerusalem was destroyed by the Romans in 70 A.D. The passage begins with Jesus predicting the destruction of the Temple. His followers ask the obvious question. . . when? However, they mistakenly assume that the destruction of the Temple is linked with

Jesus' Second Coming. Jesus' response covers both events and it was impossible before 70 A.D. to know that these events were separated in time by thousands of years. Another split prophecy is found in the ninth chapter of the Old Testament book of Daniel:

> . . .I was studying the sacred books and thinking about the seventy years that Jerusalem would be in ruins, according to what the Lord had told the prophet Jeremiah. . .

Here Daniel mentions a prophecy written earlier by the prophet Jeremiah, which appeared to describe a seventy-year captivity for the Jews in Babylon. While studying and praying about the meaning of this prophecy, the angel Gabriel appeared to Daniel and said:

> Seven times seventy years is the length of time God has set for freeing your people and your holy city from sin and evil. Sin will be forgiven and eternal justice established, so that the vision and the prophecy will come true, and the holy Temple will be rededicated. Note this and understand it: From the time the command is given to rebuild Jerusalem until God's chosen leader comes, seven times seven years will pass. Jerusalem will be rebuilt with streets and strong defenses, and will stand for seven times sixty-two years, but this will be a time of troubles. At the end of that time God's chosen leader will be killed unjustly. The city and the Temple will be destroyed by the invading army of a powerful ruler. The end will come like a flood, bringing the war and destruction which God has prepared. That ruler will have a firm agreement with many people for seven years, and when half this time is past, he will put an end to sacrifices and offerings. The Awful Horror will be placed on the highest point of the Temple and will remain there until the one who put it there meets the end which God has prepared for him.

What was originally given as a prophecy of a seventy-year exile of the Jewish people was later clarified as a prophecy lasting for "seventy weeks of years," or 490 years! Not only that, the 490 years are broken into four separate segments, lasting 49 years, 434 years, and two of three-and-one-half years each, with unmarked periods of time between each segment! Thus, interpreting in advance the correct time frames of future prophecies found in the Bible is extremely difficult, if not downright impossible. In hindsight, of course, it will all be perfectly clear. Strangely, many commentators still feel the entire Book of Revelation will be fulfilled in one three-and-one-half-year time period. The precedents established in Matthew and Daniel argue strongly that the events depicted in Revelation will occur over an extended time period. Some of the prophecies may occur many hundreds of years before the Second Coming of Christ, and the timetable of the entire book may yet involve even *thousands* of years.

Since there are prophetic passages of scripture with split fulfillments, can the same be said of Nostradamus' quatrains? For example, could the first two lines of a given quatrain refer to one event and the latter two lines to another place and time? Since Nostradamus, unlike the passages of the Bible noted above, left no indication that he ever intended any of his quatrains to be interpreted in this manner the answer would seem to be no. Besides, most quatrains are difficult enough to interpret as they are. If the splitting of quatrains is allowed then his predictions degenerate into hopelessly vague gibberish. While an angel-given precedent allows Biblical prophecies to have split fulfillments, neither precedent nor common sense allows for the splitting of Nostradamus' quatrains. In *Nostradamus: 1999* each quatrain will be treated as a whole.

Returning to the twenty-fourth chapter of Matthew, note Jesus' predictions of the following: the rise of false religions, wars, famines, earthquakes and religious persecution of his followers. These events are also common themes of Nostradamus' quatrains. Once again, it is these themes, interlinked with various locations and events, that create a pattern, a pattern that forms the later chapters of this book.

Should there actually be an Earth-grazing comet in 1999 and a subsequent meteoric collision, the earthquake of the twenty-fourth chapter of Matthew is easily explained as a direct result of the collision itself. The rise in false religion, persecution, war, and famine is also predictable in the desolation afterwards. If Nostradamus saw the future correctly, then part of the twenty-fourth chapter of Matthew will be fulfilled very soon. However, this does not include the Second Coming of Christ. In answer to his disciple's request of a date for his return he stated in this passage that "All these things are like the first pains of childbirth." Jesus obviously implied that the coming of these miseries upon mankind would not be soon followed by his return, just as the first pangs of labor are not immediately followed by birth. Confirmation of this is found by continuing in the twenty-fourth chapter of Matthew:

> No one knows, however, when that day and hour will come, neither the angels in heaven nor the Son; the Father alone knows. The coming of the Son of Man will be like what happened in the time of

Noah. In the days before the flood people ate and drank, men and women married, up to the very day Noah went into the boat; yet they did not realize what was happening until the flood came and swept them all away. That is how it will be when the Son of Man comes. At that time two men will be working in a field: one will be taken away, the other will be left behind. Two women will be at a mill grinding meal: one will be taken away, the other will be left behind. Watch out, then, because you do not know what day your Lord will come. If the owner of a house knew the time when the thief would come, you can be sure that he would stay awake and not let the thief break into his house. So then, you also must always be ready, because the Son of Man will come at an hour when you are not expecting him.

While Jesus states that no one knows the day or hour of his return, he does give some hints by comparing it to the time of Noah. What was that time like? Jesus describes it as "eating, drinking, and marrying," all of which imply a calm, peaceful existence, without any hint of impending doom. After a large meteoric impact it is highly unlikely that a life of peace will describe those left alive. Jesus predicts his return will occur while people are engaged in such simple acts as grinding meal and plowing fields, not coping with ecologic disaster or preparing for war. His description brings up thoughts of world peace, not war. In Noah's time no one expected imminent disaster; the return of Jesus will likewise be completely unanticipated. Another passage reinforcing the view that the Second Coming will be during a time of world peace is found in the fourth and fifth chapters of St. Paul's first letter to the Thessalonians:

> There will be the shout of command, the archangel's voice, the sound of God's trumpet, and the Lord himself will come down from heaven. . . the Day of the Lord will come as a thief comes at night. When people say, "Everything is quiet and safe," then suddenly destruction will hit them! It will come as suddenly as the pains that come upon a woman in labor, and people will not escape.

Contrast these two passages that both predict the return of Christ during a time of peace with the historically sharp rise in predictions of his return during times of turmoil and distress. Rare is the prediction of his return during a time of peace and prosperity, in spite of the Bible's own words! Just as His first coming occurred during the Pax Romana, a time of peace throughout most of the then-known world, the Second Coming will likewise occur during a period of external peace between countries, prosperity within countries, but internal evil in the lives of men and women. Even if Nostradamus is wrong, the current world trends described in the next chapter would seem to indicate that the several decades following 1999 will not be marked by either peace or prosperity. Those Christians anticipating that Christ will return during the appearance of the comet to take them to heaven in the rapture, avoiding the hell-on-earth to come, may be sadly disappointed.

Having established that prophecies often have split fulfillments and that the return of Jesus is not likely during or after the comet's appearance (but then again, he may return since no one knows the time!), attention can be turned to the Book of Revelation. The possibility of split fulfillments allows the luxury of not having to explain the entire book. Several chapters of Revelation describe physical events that correlate perfectly with Nostradamus' predictions for 1999 and beyond. Further support for these events is found in various Old Testament prophetic books. Still, great care must be taken when interpreting Revelation. It is the most obscure book of the New Testament, full of strange, symbolic language. The name *Revelation* means "disclosure" or, better, "divine manifestation." This disclosure is clearly to explain future events that are to take place on the Earth, while showing the sovereignty of God over it all. While the language and images make interpretation difficult, if it was completely incomprehensible, why write it at all? Clearly all are expected to try to understand the events predicted. In the first sentences of Revelation John states his purpose:

> This book is the record of the events that Jesus Christ revealed. God gave him this revelation in order to show to his servants what must happen....

Of what value is it to show what is to happen if it cannot be understood and acted upon? Despite the imagery and language, the events depicted in Revelation must be understandable as real, physical events, events which can be understood! The book continues with a greeting from John to seven churches in Asia Minor, probably churches over which he previously had been a bishop. This is followed by a vision of the resurrected Christ, and Christ's messages to those seven churches. Then a scene that takes place in Heaven is described. Following that is the first of a series of passages describing events to take place on the Earth, passages that bear a striking resemblance to those events described by Nostradamus in his quatrains. While reading the passages, try to consider how they might relate to Nostradamus' predictions. Later in the chapter an interpretation of all of these events will be provided. Beginning with the first verse of the sixth chapter:

Then I saw the Lamb break open the first of the seven seals, and I heard one of the four living creatures say in a voice that sounded like thunder; "Come!" I looked, and there was a white horse. Its rider held a bow, and he was given a crown. He rode out as a conqueror to conquer.

Then the Lamb broke open the second seal; and I heard the second living creature say, "Come!" Another horse came out, a red one. Its rider was given the power to bring war on the earth, so that men should kill each other. He was given a large sword.

Then the Lamb broke open the third seal; and I heard the third living creature say, "Come!" I looked, and there was a black horse. Its rider held a pair of scales in his hand. I heard what sounded like a voice coming from among the four living creatures, which said, "A quart of wheat for a day's wages, and three quarts of barley for a day's wages. But do not damage the olive trees and the vineyards!"

Then the Lamb broke open the fourth seal; and I heard the fourth living creature say, "Come!" I looked, and there was a pale-colored horse. Its rider was named Death, and Hades followed close behind. They were given authority over one fourth of the earth, to kill by means of war, famine, disease, and wild animals.

Then the Lamb broke open the fifth seal. I saw underneath the altar the souls of those who had been killed because they had proclaimed God's word and had been faithful in their witnessing. They shouted in a loud voice, "Almighty Lord, holy and true! How long will it be until you judge the people on earth and punish them for killing us?" Each of them was given a white robe, and they were told to rest a little while longer, until the complete number of their fellow servants and brothers were killed, as they had been.

And I saw the Lamb break open the sixth seal. There was a violent earthquake, and the sun became black like coarse black cloth, and the moon turned completely red like blood. The stars fell down to the earth, like unripe figs falling from the tree when a strong wind shakes it. The sky disappeared like a scroll being rolled up, and every mountain and island was moved from its place. Then the kings of the earth, the rulers and the military chiefs, the rich and the powerful, and all other men, slave and free, hid themselves in caves and under rocks on the mountains. They called out to the mountains and to the rocks, "Fall on us and hide us from the eyes of the one who sits on the throne and from the anger of the Lamb! The terrible day of their anger is here, and who can stand up against it?"

After this I saw four angels standing at the four corners of the earth, holding back the four winds so that no wind should blow on the earth or the sea or against any tree. And I saw another angel coming up from the east with the seal of the living God. He called out in a loud voice to the four angels to whom God had given the power to damage the earth and the sea. The angel said, "Do not harm the earth, the sea, or the trees, until we mark the servants of our God with a seal on their foreheads. . .

There follows a short description of angels symbolically putting God's seal on the forehead of his people, and then a few paragraphs describing a scene at the throne of God in heaven. As neither of these events will be observable to those living on Earth, they will not be discussed here. Continuing in Revelation, the story picks up again in the beginning of the eighth chapter:

When the Lamb broke open the seventh seal, there was silence in heaven for about half an hour. Then I saw the seven angels who stand before God, and they were given seven trumpets.

Another angel, who had a gold incense container, came and stood at the altar. He was given a lot of incense to add to the prayers of all God's people and to offer it on the gold altar that stands before the throne. The smoke of the burning incense went up with the prayers of God's people from the hands of the angel standing before God. Then the angel took the incense container, filled it with fire from the altar, and threw it on the earth. There were rumblings and peals of thunder, flashes of lightning, and an earthquake.

Then the seven angels with the seven trumpets prepared to blow them.

The first angel blew his trumpet. Hail and fire, mixed with blood, came pouring down on the earth. A third of the earth was burned up, a third of the trees, and every blade of green grass.

Then the second angel blew his trumpet. Something that looked like a huge mountain on fire was thrown into the sea. A third of the sea was turned into blood, a third of the living creatures in the sea died, and a third of the ships were destroyed.

Then the third angel blew his trumpet. A large star, burning like a torch, dropped from the sky and fell on a third of the rivers and on the springs of water. (The name of the star is "Bitterness.") A third of the water turned bitter, and many people died from drinking the water, because it had turned bitter.

Then the fourth angel blew his trumpet. A third of the sun was struck, and a third of the moon, and a third of the stars, so that their light lost a third of its brightness; there was no light during a third of the day and a third of the night also.

Then I looked, and I heard an eagle that was flying high in the air say in a loud voice; "O horror! horror! How horrible it will be for all who live on earth when the sound comes from the trumpets that the other three angels must blow!

Then the fifth angel blew his trumpet. I saw a star which had fallen down to the earth, and it was given the key to the abyss. The star opened the abyss, and smoke poured out of it, like the smoke from a large furnace; the sunlight and the air were darkened by the smoke from the abyss. Locusts came down out of the smoke upon the earth, and they were given the same kind of power that scorpions have. They were told not to harm the grass or the trees or any other plant; they could harm only the people who did not have the mark of God's seal on their foreheads. The locusts were not allowed to kill these people, but only to torture them for five months. The pain caused by the torture is like the pain caused by a scorpion's sting. During those five months they will seek death, but will not find it; they will want to die, but death will flee from them.

The locusts looked like horses ready for battle; on their heads they had what seemed to be crowns of gold, and their faces were like men's faces. Their hair was like women's hair, their teeth were like lions' teeth. Their chests were covered with what looked like iron breastplates, and the sound made by their wings was like the noise of many horse-drawn chariots rushing into battle. They have tails and stings like those of a scorpion, and it is with their tails that they have the power to hurt people for five months. They have a king ruling over them, who is the angel in charge of the abyss. His name in Hebrew is Abaddon: in Greek the name is Apollyon (meaning "The Destroyer").

The first horror is over; after this there are still two more horrors to come.

Then the sixth angel blew his trumpet. I heard a voice coming from the four corners of the gold altar standing before God. The voice said to the sixth angel, "Release the four angels who are bound at the great Euphrates River!" The four angels were released; for this very hour of this very day of this very month and year they had been kept ready to kill a third of all mankind. I was told the number of the mounted troops: it was two hundred million. And in my vision I saw the horses and their riders: they had breastplates red as fire, blue as sapphire, and yellow as sulfur. The horses' heads were like lions' heads, and from their mouths came out fire, smoke, and sulfur. A third of mankind was killed by those three plagues: the fire, the smoke, and the sulfur coming out of the horses' mouths. For the power of the horses is in their mouths and also in their tails. Their tails are like snakes with heads, and they use them to hurt people.

The rest of mankind, all those who had not been killed by these plagues, did not turn away from what they themselves had made. They did not stop worshiping demons, nor the idols of gold, silver, bronze, stone, and wood, which cannot see, hear, or walk. Nor did they repent of their murders, their magic, their sexual immorality, or their stealing.

The events that John (the writer of Revelation) has sketched as a group appear to end here. The next section, beginning with the tenth chapter, deals with an encounter between John and an angel. The encounter finishes with the Angel telling John:

Once again you must proclaim God's message about many nations, races, languages, and kings.

Why would the angel make the statement: "Once again you must proclaim. . ." unless the prior message had been completed? The angel implies that the prior vision of a connected series of events has been completed and the material following will consist of a new message for a different age. The Seventh Trumpet, and the rest of Revelation, will wait for another time to be fulfilled, perhaps even thousands of years from now. While it is quite possible for the entire book to be fulfilled at one time, the precedent established by other Biblical split prophecies argues for the likelihood of a long gap before completion of the predicted events. Nostradamus indicates, through correlation with the quatrains already clarified and those yet to be examined, that the fulfillment of at least some of the events of the Book of Revelation are to begin in 1999. Once again, though, note that the prophecies of Revelation stand on their own. Should Nostradamus be wrong, or this author's interpretations of Nostradamus' work be incorrect, in no way is the integrity, and eventual consummation of Holy Scripture compromised.

How does one organize and interpret this information from the Book of Revelation? An assumption is made here that having every item in chronological order was not important to John. Evidence to support this is found later in the book of Revelation. For instance, in a later vision, which is contained in the fourteenth chapter, a description of the "harvest of the Earth" is found. In this "harvest" all the good people are gathered into heaven and all the evil trampled "in the wine press of God's furious anger"; yet the sixteenth chapter consists of angels pouring out seven "bowls of anger" onto the people of the Earth to punish them. How can the book be in chronological order if the inhabitants of the Earth are being punished after the final judgment has already been given by God? Found in the eighteenth chapter is the fall of Babylon, likewise difficult to interpret if the inhabitants of the Earth are all either in Heaven or Hell. From these examples, as well as several others, the book cannot be considered to be structured in a strictly chronological order.

Besides the above examples, it should also be noted that in the Jewish apocalyptic literature of the times that chronological sequencing was not essential. It seems likely that John had a vision of huge magnitude and scope and sought to put what he saw into writing by grouping different events together. It also appears that the events from the beginning of chapter six through the end of chapter nine represent a cluster of events, but again not necessarily in chronological order. As noted previously, what John saw and described are real, physical events. An attempt will now be made to explain what those physical events might be, and to sequence those events into chronological order.

With the blowing of the second trumpet something resembling "a huge mountain on fire was thrown into the sea." Most Biblical expositors explain this event as a volcanic eruption near the sea. But read the passage again! The description is not of a volcanic eruption where something is thrown up into the sky and then *falls* into the sea—it is a description of something appearing to be on fire that is thrown into the sea.

If not a volcanic eruption, then what might this "huge mountain on fire" be? All meteors have the appearance of being on fire as they fall through the atmosphere and have their outer layers burned off, and the speed of their passage certainly gives the illusion of their having been thrown, as well. Anyone witnessing such an event without knowing what it was might easily describe a large meteor's passage through the atmosphere as resembling a mountain on fire.

The second trumpet also includes: "A third of the sea was turned into blood, a third of the living creatures in the sea died, and a third of the ships were destroyed." The loss of large numbers of fish during a large meteor impact was discussed in the first chapter and is easily understood, and the tsunami is capable of destroying any ships near port, but how can the sea turn into blood? The blood could be symbolic for death, but if the impact re-distributes a great deal of iron, or any other reddish-colored rocks, from the Earth's crust into the seawater, then the water could take on a red, bloody appearance. Since it is the iron in hemoglobin that gives blood its reddish color, poets might even comment on the stirred-up, reddish rocks from sea giving the appearance of the Earth "bleeding" from its meteor-induced wound. Note that the "mountain on fire" is related to the destruction of one-third of the ships on that sea, the death of one-third of the fish, and one-third of the sea being turned into blood. While a meteoric event is quite capable of this level of destruction, a volcanic eruption, even a very large one, is not.

The twenty-first chapter of Luke also describes the comet and meteor: ". . . there will be strange and terrifying things coming from the sky." Can this be anything other than a comet and a large meteor? Is there any other possible explanation for a terrifying object coming from the sky! This passage is very similar to the previously discussed passage from the twenty-fourth chapter of Matthew. Luke also links the appearance of the comet with the rise of false religion, war, revolutions, earthquakes, famines, and plagues throughout the world.

The opening of the sixth seal is related to several events. A "violent earthquake" will occur and the Sun will become "black like coarse black cloth, and the Moon turned completely red like blood." Can an earthquake darken the Sun and Moon? While earthquakes can raise dust into the air, the amount is relatively small, certainly not enough to darken the Sun and Moon. However, if the earthquake is caused from a meteoric impact, then the tremendous amount of dust thrown into the atmosphere could easily obscure them both. Besides, how can the Sun, which creates its own light, be darker than the Moon, which only reflects light? The change cannot be in the intrinsic brightness of the Sun, for then the Moon would dim proportionally and would still be darker than the Sun. The only possible explanation is that a filter of some sort, like atmospheric dust, changes the appearance of the Sun and Moon to those living on Earth. For a day or two after an impact into the Atlantic Ocean a viewer in New York City (or at least what is left of it), when viewing the expanding dust cloud, would note the rising Sun to be completely obscured while the Moon, if setting in the west, would have only a reddish tinge. A western European viewer would note the same effect with a setting Sun and a rising Moon. Note that the prophecy is fulfilled even if it occurs only for one night, at only one location on the Earth. The prophecy does not state that the blackened Sun and reddened moon must be visible worldwide, nor does it specify a length of time. The Sun and Moon will be farthest apart from each other in the sky, i.e. a full moon, around the 23rd of September in 1999. Incidentally, that date also happens to be a Thursday. Refer back to quatrain (13) for a possible indication that the impact may occur on a Thursday. Is it possible that September 23, 1999 will be the impact date?

Also contained in the opening of the sixth seal is: "The stars fell down to the earth, like unripe figs falling from the tree. . . ." John's so-called "stars" are meteors, "shooting stars" in our own vernacular. Since Nostradamus' quarter-mile-wide meteor is part of the dust tail of the comet, other smaller meteors will light up the sky as well. A tremendous meteor shower, perhaps even a meteor storm, may occur. During meteor showers these heavenly objects can be seen lighting up the sky at a rate of roughly one per minute, but during meteor storms, which occur several times a century when the Earth passes through a relatively dust-dense portion of an old comet orbit, meteors can light up the sky as often as sixty times per second. On rare occasions these meteors can even reach the ground, much like hail (More about this in quatrain (16) in the next chapter). Watching this, John must have been hard pressed to explain what he saw. The best example his first-century experience could provide him with was the sight of unripe fruit falling to the ground during a strong wind.

The opening of the sixth seal also includes: "The sky disappeared like a scroll being rolled up, and every mountain and island was moved from its place." Again, a very large earthquake is described, related to the disappearance of the sky. Also note that the earthquake will be felt on every mountain and island on the entire planet, implying a quake of unprecedented intensity. What will cause the sky to disappear? A huge cloud of dust, slowly spreading across the upper atmosphere, would give the appearance of a daylight sky rolling up like a scroll of paper, or a carpet. On a clear, starlit night the effect would be even more pronounced as the stars winked out one by one. Mankind's response to these events, from the greatest to the least, will be one of fear. John describes their fear:

> "Then the kings of the earth, the rulers and the military chiefs, the rich and the powerful, and all other men, slave and free, hid themselves in caves and under rocks on the mountains. They called out to the mountains and to the rocks, "Fall on us and hide us from the eyes of the one who sits on the throne and from the anger of the Lamb! The terrible day of their anger is here, and who can stand up against it?"

The events depicted in the sixth seal are similar to other passages of scripture. For example, in the thirty-fourth chapter of Isaiah is written:

The LORD is angry with all the nations and all their armies. He has condemned them to destruction. Their corpses will not be buried, but will lie there rotting and stinking; and the mountains will be red with blood. The sun, moon, and stars will crumble to dust. The sky will disappear like a scroll being rolled up, and the stars will fall like leaves dropping from a vine or a fig tree.

This passage from Isaiah correlates precisely with that from Revelation. In addition, Isaiah links with these events the destruction of armies, implying a very large war. How can this be anything but another world war?

In the third chapter of the book of the Old Testament prophet Joel is found the following: "The sun and the moon grow dark, and the stars no longer shine."

Actually, there are several themes found in Joel that correlate with the events predicted by Nostradamus and described in Revelation. The major themes of Joel are drought, famine, a massive plague of locusts, a war that apparently involves the conquest of Israel, and the eventual restoration of Israel yet one more time. All those who believe that since Israel has been re-established as a nation, Jesus can return at any time should note that Joel predicts Israel will go into captivity at least one more time! But before these events take place, God sends a warning that they are coming. From the second chapter of Joel:

I will give warnings of that day in the sky and on the earth; there will be bloodshed, fire, and clouds of smoke. The sun will be darkened, and the moon will turn red as blood before the great and terrible day of the Lord comes.

Once more war is linked with the darkening of the sky. The impact will result in the death of many ("bloodshed") and the "fire" will be the firestorm generated from the meteoric impact. These "warnings" in the sky (loss of light) and on the earth (impact crater, fire, and smoke) are to precede the other events (famine, drought, locusts, war) sketched by Joel. Observe that all this is to happen "before the great and terrible day of the Lord comes," a clear indication that the Second Coming will not immediately follow these events. The reader is encouraged to study the short book of Joel in its entirety.

Another passage from the Old Testament, in the eighth chapter of Amos, also describes the darkening of the Sun and Moon. The passage begins with a condemnation of those that cheat the poor and needy, and continues:

The LORD, the God of Israel, has sworn, "I will never forget their evil deeds. And so the earth will quake, and everyone in the land will be in distress. The whole country will be shaken; it will rise and fall like the Nile River. The time is coming when I will make the sun go down at noon and the earth grow dark in daytime. I, the Sovereign LORD, have spoken. I will turn your festivals into funerals and change your glad songs into cries of grief. I will make you shave your heads and wear sackcloth, and you will be like parents mourning for their only son. That day will be bitter to the end.

Note again the relationship of a severe earthquake with the noontime darkening of the Sun. Could anything other than a massive dust cloud, slowly spreading across the sky, accomplish this? Also note that this is to happen at noontime, again confirming that the comet and meteor will be approaching the Earth from the same sector of the sky as the Sun. Interestingly, while the passage from Isaiah describes God as being angry, Amos predicts that the source of God's anger, the reason for this punishment, is at least partly due to the cheating of the poor and needy by the wealthy of the world.

In the twenty-first chapter of Luke, in a companion passage to the twenty-fourth chapter of Matthew, Jesus instructs his followers:

There will be strange things happening to the sun, the moon, and the stars. On earth whole countries will be in despair, afraid of the roar of the sea and the raging tides. People will faint from fear as they wait for what is coming over the whole earth, for the powers in space will be driven from their courses.

Could anything other than an Earth-grazing comet provoke such despair and fear? Could anything other than a meteor collision into an ocean cause the sea to roar and tides to rage? Could anything other than a comet and the meteor hidden in its tail be "powers in space" that "will be driven from their courses"? This passage is immediately followed by a passage predicting the return of Jesus, but as has already been shown, God's method of timekeeping and event-sequencing is not necessarily what humanity thinks it should be!

With the blowing of the fourth trumpet the scene shifts from the time period immediately after the meteor collision to a time several weeks, possibly several months, later. "A third of the sun was struck, and a third of the moon, and a third of the stars, so that their light lost a third of its brightness." As the dust cloud spreads and becomes worldwide it will also thin. John indicates that the amount of sunlight

59

reaching the Earth will be reduced by roughly one-third. In comparison, the Krakatoa eruption reduced sunlight worldwide by only 10%, and even the great Tambora eruption that significantly reduced global temperatures the following year is estimated to have reduced sunlight by only 20%. Shortly after the eruption of Mt. Pinatubo in 1991, Patrick McCormick, an atmospheric scientist at NASA's Langley Research Center in Virginia, flew over the island of Barbados, in the Caribbean Sea, at a height of 20,000 feet. There he and his group measured a reduction in sunlight reaching the Earth of as much as 33% in some wavelengths. As this cloud continued to spread out and thin, the effect was, of course, less pronounced, but here John indicates that after the cloud thins that the sum total of all visible light will be diminished by one-third.

The blowing of the fourth trumpet continues with: "there was no light during a third of the day and a third of the night also." Why should this be so? At four o'clock in the afternoon sunlight has to pass through twice as much atmosphere, and twice as much dust, as it does at noon. As the Sun moves closer to the horizon this effect is even more pronounced. At dawn and dusk this additional atmosphere serves to filter out the shorter wavelength blue light, while the longer wavelength red light passes more easily. This is the reason for the normal redness of the Sun at sunrise and sunset. After the impact the additional dust in the air will filter out even the red light near the horizons. John's "one-third" is probably an estimate and not an exact number, but if he intended exactly 33%, then sunrise will occur when the Sun is 30 degrees above the eastern horizon and finally able to pierce through the dust cloud, and it will set 30 degrees above the evening horizon in the west.

The fourth trumpet concludes with: "O horror! horror! How horrible it will be for all who live on earth when the sound comes from the trumpets that the other three angels must blow!" In the years following the cometary impact, things will get worse, not better. As previously noted, the seventh trumpet will wait for a time many years after the conclusion of this particular vision before it will be fulfilled. The fifth trumpet speaks of a volcano and an insect plague, the sixth trumpet of war. As both of these events will follow the expansion of the dust cloud, this is apparently one instance in which John recorded the parts of his vision in chronological order.

The blowing of the fifth trumpet is linked with several events. It begins with another description of the meteor and events already described: "I saw a star which had fallen down to the earth. . . The star opened the abyss, and smoke poured out of it, like the smoke from a large furnace; the sunlight and the air were darkened by the smoke from the abyss." John's description of the impact site appears to indicate that the meteor will actually penetrate into the crust of the Earth, opening a crack from the depths below. The smoke pouring out of the abyss may be steam from the ocean itself as it slowly dissipates the heat of impact, but it is also possible that the meteor will completely penetrate the Earth's crust. As noted in the first chapter, the crust is thinner in the oceans than over the continents, and even thinner still near geologic rift zones such as the Mid-Atlantic Rise. A crust-piercing meteor near a location already forming volcanoes, such as at the Mid-Atlantic Rise, could easily result in an instant volcanic island.

Still in the fifth trumpet John continues with: "Locusts came down out of the smoke upon the earth, and they were given the same kind of power that scorpions have. . . ." In the climactic disruptions that are certain to follow any sudden, major change in the environment, large-scale death in the animal community is inevitable. Predators, since they reproduce more slowly, recover from reduced numbers much more slowly than prey, so the years following the meteor strike will likely be marked by insect plagues of all types. One specific insect which John refers to as a "locust" will emerge "out of the smoke," i.e. as the dust cloud settles back to Earth in the years following the impact. This "locust" plague will affect the people "who did not have the mark of God's seal on their foreheads." John is probably describing non-Christian countries rather than individuals here. The number of insects capable of carrying this out in the Middle East, India, southeast Asia, and China are probably uncountable. (This, of course, assumes that western society is a Christian culture, an assumption that even a casual observer may have difficulty believing!) The plague of these locusts is not indefinite, lasting only "five months." Presumably the "locusts" exhaust their food sources by that time, or perhaps, like most insects, they are relatively short-lived. Also possible is that the disease they inflict will last for only five months.

Continuing in the fifth trumpet is a physical description of these locusts: ". . .looked like horses ready for battle. . . on their heads they had what seemed to be crowns of gold. . . faces like men's faces. . .hair like women's hair, teeth like lions' teeth. . . chest covered with what looked like iron breastplates. . . tails and stings like those of a scorpion." Does this sound incredible? Perhaps too bizarre to be possible? Before the invention of magnifying glasses and microscopes this passage must have given fits to commentators, but John's description is not unreasonable for the magnified view of many insects.

The blowing of the third trumpet is associated with: "a large star, burning like a torch, dropped from the sky. . .," perhaps another reference to the meteor as it passes through the atmosphere, or possibly a description of the comet itself. Here it results in "A third of the water turned bitter, and many people died from drinking the water, because it had turned bitter." What will poison the water? While cometary debris contains fairly large quantities of organic material, such as cyanide, most of this is likely to be destroyed in the heat of the impact explosion, and it is doubtful if the total amount is much more than is contained in the air over any large city on a smoggy day. Heavy metal poisoning from the ash fallout is also possible, but not likely, given the relatively small amount of material, the area the material will be spread over, and the poor solubility of most metals in water. The explosion and the resultant fireball from the impact will generate tremendous quantities of nitrous oxides in the atmosphere, later precipitating out as acid rain. Sufficient quantities might be generated to acidify the above-ground aquifers of a third of the world, giving the water a bitter taste. This, however, is not likely to sufficiently poison drinking water so that many might die. Another candidate is petrochemical poisoning of rivers, lakes, and streams from ruptured underground lines and storage facilities caused by the impact-generated earthquake and subsequent tsunami. Under normal circumstances municipal water treatment plants can filter out these contaminants, but only when present in small quantities. Besides, any area with ruptured pipelines and storage tanks is unlikely to have a functional water treatment and distribution system. The populace will be forced to drink directly from poisoned, above-ground water sources. It is very interesting that the last possibility, hydrocarbon poisoning, was impossible prior to the rapid growth in the petrochemical industry over the past fifty years.

In the blowing of the first trumpet: "Hail and fire, mixed with blood, came pouring down on the earth." The hail will be created from the massive amount of water vaporized at the time of the meteor impact, then suddenly cooled in the upper levels of the atmosphere. Large hailstones require thunderstorms with large updrafts to keep them aloft. Each successive passage of the stone through warmer and cooler portions or the storm adds a layer of ice to the hailstone. A large meteoric impact, as already discussed, would result in huge weather disturbances, and violent storms without precedent, over the ensuing weeks and months. Violent storms such as hurricanes, typhoons, and tornadoes occur as a self-regulating mechanism of the planet to distribute heat to the upper latitudes from the equatorial regions. The tremendous amount of energy released from the impact, especially if the impact site is near the equator, will create violent storms throughout both the northern and southern hemispheres. Large and frequent hailstorms will be common.

The "fire" of the first trumpet is also easily explained as hurricanes of fire itself will form in the aftermath of the meteor's explosion, causing fires hundreds, perhaps even thousand of miles away. Large quantities of soot found in the dust layer associated with the meteor-related extinction of the dinosaurs 65 million years ago indicates that the fireball from that event triggered massive worldwide forest fires. Some researchers even think that one-third of all forests throughout the world burned in gigantic firestorms. Similar, but on a smaller scale, fires can be expected after another meteoric collision. It is also possible that John's "fire" is a reference to the tsunami-spread coastal firestorms.

The "blood" mentioned in the first trumpet could refer to the people killed in the explosion or it could refer to the red-colored sediments cast into the atmosphere from the bottom of the sea. As fallout, the ash, perhaps along with small stones, will maintain its red color as it is deposited worldwide. John describes the physical devastation simply as "A third of the earth was burned up, a third of the trees, and every blade of green grass." The destruction of a significant portion of the world's forests from fire is understandable, but can "every blade of green grass" be destroyed? Possibly John is referring only to a single country or continent. If he intends the entire globe, then perhaps massive heat waves after the explosion are responsible, or perhaps petrochemical complexes will feed firestorms throughout many parts of the world. Worldwide drought is also a possible cause, in which case the "burning out" is not a physical burning, but a withering from lack of moisture. The surviving trees, being deeper rooted than the grasses, will stay green during droughts that turn grasses brown.

Support for the idea that large-scale drought will follow after the initial storms is found in the first verse of the seventh chapter: "After this I saw four angels standing at the four corners of the earth, holding back the four winds so that no wind should blow on the earth or the sea or against any tree." After the massive heat waves and storms following the impact subside, perhaps as long as a year later, the climate will change again. With sunlight significantly reduced and a falling temperature, evaporation from the oceans will become significantly reduced. Yet it is evaporation from the oceans that produces low-pressure systems, the systems that eventually generate rainfall on the land masses, and it is the Sun's warmth heating up the continental interiors that draws in the rain. Less evaporation means weak low-pressure systems, producing little or no rain. Cooler interiors create smaller draws on those low-pressure systems, and what rain will occur is likely to stay at sea or near the coasts.

It is the interaction of high- and low-pressure systems that produces wind. Some time after the impact the weak high and low pressure systems will result in a sharp drop in wind speed, perhaps worldwide. Drought, particularly in the continental interiors far from the oceans, will be widespread. Yet it is precisely the continental interiors where the great grain-growing areas of the entire planet are located.

The recent past includes a small example of what might be expected from a reduction in the intensity of sunlight due to the presence of atmospheric dust. The 1982 monsoons in India were very weak for reasons no one quite understood. But recent research by Alan Strong, an oceanographer at the U.S. Naval Academy, has linked the lack of rain in India with the April 1982 eruption of the Mexican volcano El Chichon. The sulfuric acid cloud generated by the eruption stayed near the equator and gradually spread over the Indian subcontinent. While the acid cloud reflected only a small amount of sunlight back into space, it was sufficient to prevent India from heating up enough to draw in the moisture-laden air from the Indian Ocean, which resulted in an unusually weak monsoon season. Magnify this small blockage of sunshine many times and spread it around the entire planet, and the result will be dramatically reduced winds and rainfall worldwide. This effect will be especially pronounced in the major growing regions of the continental interiors.

What effect will reduced sunlight, a worldwide drop in temperature, and drought have on food production? The answer is found in the opening of the third seal:

> . . .there was a black horse. Its rider held a pair of scales in his hand. I heard what sounded like a voice coming from among the four living creatures, which said, "A quart of wheat for a day's wages, and three quarts of barley for a day's wages. But do not damage the olive trees and the vineyards!"

In John's time a day's wage could buy 10–15 quarts of wheat, not just one. A quart of wheat was roughly what the average laborer consumed in a day. Implied in this passage is an unprecedented scarcity of food, with a major increase in price. The price will rise so high that the average worker will spend his or her entire salary on food just to stay alive. Parents trying to keep children fed in many parts of the world will find the task difficult, if not downright impossible. However, all is not completely lost. The grapes and olives represent perennial, deep-rooted plants which are able to survive a year or two of drought. Even if their crops fail, the plants themselves will survive. This luxury does not apply to grains, which require successful annual harvests for seed the following year as well as for food. Since grapes and olives are also more expensive foods than grains, John may also be hinting that the poor of the world, who rely more on cheaper foods, may suffer more than the rich with their more expensive diets.

Large-scale famine will serve as a trigger for worldwide wars. Take any densely populated country—India, for example. India's population is more than all of Africa and South America combined, roughly three times that of the United States; yet its land area is only one-third the size of the U.S. A large famine there will result in the starvation deaths of tens of millions. The temptation to use military force to take food from neighboring countries will be tremendous. Even if millions of their soldiers die in a war, if they are able to take food from neighboring countries then the death toll might still be lower than sitting home waiting to starve. This situation is likely to be repeated in countries throughout the world.

In Revelation the war after the famine is described in the first seal: "Then I saw the Lamb break open the first of the seven seals. . . I looked and there was a white horse. Its rider held a bow, and he was given a crown. He rode out as a conqueror to conquer." Some commentators feel the rider of the white horse is Jesus, and his riding out is a symbol of the preaching of the Gospel. But how can this be, since Jesus is the "lamb" that breaks the seal? He is the one who will send out the white rider! How can he send himself out? Besides, the Gospel has been preached for centuries: sending out a rider to proclaim its message now makes no sense. What the rider represents is clearly stated. He rides out "as a conqueror to conquer." Why the white color? Implied is the perception of purity and holiness that white represents. This "conqueror" will be one who claims to represent God himself, one who will organize a holy war in God's name. However, it is not necessary that he actually be holy, just appear to be. It is not even essential that this "conqueror" be a good man, a man blessed by God who will eventually see paradise. After all, in the Old Testament God sent the Assyrians and the Babylonians to punish his own chosen people when they would not repent and turn to him. He used wicked, evil people to accomplish his will. The rider of the white horse may, in fact, actually be a very evil individual, perhaps even the Antichrist himself. Nostradamus has much about this "conqueror," and the subject will be addressed fully in the fourth chapter.

The breaking of the second seal also describes widespread war, apparently a war that the rider of the white horse will bring: "Another horse came out, a red one. Its rider was given the power to bring war on the earth, so that men should kill each other." Red has been the symbol for both blood and war for thousands of years. Even the ancient Romans named Mars, the red planet, after their god of war.

With the blowing of the sixth trumpet, John becomes much more specific about where World War III is to begin: "The voice said to the sixth angel, 'Release the four angels who are bound at the great Euphrates River!' The four angels were released; for this very hour of this very day of this very month and year they had been kept ready to kill a third of all mankind." The Euphrates River is part of present-day Iraq. Nostradamus has much to say about this war, which will also be addressed in the following chapters, but one item needs to be mentioned here. Many unfulfilled prophecies in the Bible refer to "Persia," which consisted of the modern countries of Iraq and Iran. The Bible and Nostradamus are both in agreement on the eventual unification of Iraq and Iran into a modern Persia. With the blowing of the sixth trumpet, John indicates that it will be a modern-day reunited Iran and Iraq, a new Persia, that will be responsible for starting World War III. If Nostradamus is right in his dates, then WW

III will begin in the early years of the next century. If Iraq and Iran have not united by 1999, which does not appear likely, they will do so in the years after the impact of the meteor.

Continuing with the sixth trumpet: "I was told the number of mounted troops: it was two hundred million." This number is very interesting. Revelation has numbers that are full of symbolism. For instance, the number three stands for perfection, as in the Trinity of God; four symbolizes the visible world, as in the four corners of the Earth; seven signifies fullness and perfection, as in the seven days of creation; twelve stands for the twelve tribes of Israel and, by extension, all of God's people, and one thousand represents a full period of time. But is 200,000,000 a symbolic number? John clearly states that this book was meant to be understood and to show events that are to come, so without any possible symbolic application two hundred million is not a symbolic number, but a real number. It is the number of troops that the new Persia will commit to battle during the Third World War.

Throughout all recorded history no country ever raised an army of two hundred million, let alone one of "mounted" troops. However, the population explosion of the latter part of the twentieth century, especially notable in the countries of Asia, now means that China, or possibly a unified Moslem state, could raise armies of that size by early in the next century. Also note that these are mounted troops. How could any army ever expect to seat that many men on horses? The answer is found in the "cavalry" units of today. These so-called "mounted troops" have no horses. Instead today's cavalry consists of trucks, armored fighting vehicles, and tanks. What John is trying to communicate is that the armies will ride, not walk to war; and they will ride in machines, not on horses. He describes their colors (possibly the flag of the new Persia?) as being "red as fire, blue as sapphire, and yellow as sulfur." He then launches into a description of the so-called "horses" that carry the mounted troops: "The horses'" heads were like lions' heads, and from their mouths came out fire, smoke, and sulfur." This would be an amazing animal indeed, but it sounds remarkably like a tank. While a tank's muzzle (its "mouth") might not look like the head of a lion, it certainly sounds like one when it fires. And the "fire" (muzzle flash), "smoke" (self-explanatory), and "sulfur" (smell of gunpowder) coming "from their mouths" are easily understood. Also, note that the colors of the fire (red), smoke (possibly blue), and sulfur (yellow) are possibly the same colors as those of the flag of the new Persia. Since a flag is symbolic for a country and since the colors mentioned are the colors of war, John may just be indicating that this will be a very war-like nation. The fact that these "horses" will be weapons is reinforced as the sixth trumpet continues:

> A third of mankind was killed by those three plagues: the fire, the smoke, and the sulfur coming out of the horses' mouths. For the power of the horses is in their mouths and also in their tails. Their tails are like snakes with heads, and they use them to hurt people.

The "horses' mouths" has already been explained as most likely being the muzzle of a tank barrel. The "tail" would appear to be artillery pieces in tow. John writes that one-third of mankind will die in this war. A United Nations report issued in 1992 projected world population in the year 2000 to be 6.2 billion people. Thus, in the early part of the next century, even after allowing for a death toll in the hundreds of millions as a result of the meteor and its aftermath, World War III will still kill roughly two billion people.

One of the countries conquered by the new Persian armies will be Egypt. (Nostradamus also addresses the conquest of Egypt. Once again, it will be covered later!) Linked with the darkening of the Sun and Moon, in the thirty-second chapter of Ezekiel is written the following prophecy addressed to Egypt:

> When I destroy you, I will cover the sky and blot out the stars. The sun will hide behind the clouds, and the moon will give no light. I will put out all the lights of heaven and plunge your world into darkness. I, The Sovereign LORD, have spoken.
> Many nations will be troubled when I spread the news of your destruction through countries you never heard of. What I do to you will shock many nations. When I swing my sword, kings will shudder with fright. On the day you fall, all of them will tremble in fear for their own lives.

Note the implied swiftness and violence of the fall of Egypt during World War III, provoking great fear among those who know that they will be the next target. As it has throughout history, Egypt occupies a pivotal geographic position. Once Egypt falls, the armies of the east will be able to quickly gain control of all of North Africa and threaten the entire Mediterranean Sea.

With the breaking of the fourth seal John relates the following: "I looked, and there was a pale-colored horse. Its rider was named Death, and Hades followed close behind. They were given authority over one-fourth of the earth, to kill by means of war, famine, disease, and wild animals." Does this "one-fourth" contradict what was just discussed, namely the death of one-third of mankind? No, look closely at the prophecy! In this instance John is discussing the land mass of the Earth, not its population. While many geographical areas are possible, the rise of a unified Muslim state and a religious war against a Christian Europe indicates that the Middle East, part of western Asia, and the European continent will be at least some of the battlegrounds. Twenty-five percent of the surface of the Earth will be struck by war. In comparison, during World War II, combat actually touched less than ten percent of the land surface of the Earth; so World War III must involve far more land area than just the Middle East, western Russia, and Europe. Indications that this is to be a religious war against Christianity are found in the fifth seal:

> Then the Lamb broke open the fifth seal. I saw underneath the altar the souls of those who had been killed because they had proclaimed God's word and had been faithful in their witnessing.

This seal attests to the religious persecution that this war will involve. Who would want to kill Christians for their religious beliefs? The only possibility is another competing religion seeking the extermination of Christianity, either through converts or through massacre. In today's world the only imaginable groups are all of an Islamic extremist nature, headquartered primarily in Iran. Similar "be baptized or die" episodes occur in the history of many religions, including Christianity. These Iranian-based terrorist groups have already shown themselves capable of atrocities. Given a chance, many would engage in a religious holy war against Christians. If able, they would martyr Christians who refused to renounce their faith.

What will be the response of the people of the world to all of these disasters, all the death and destruction? John provides an answer to that, too, at the end of the ninth chapter, the concluding verses of this section in the Book of Revelation:

> The rest of mankind, all those who had not been killed by these plagues, did not turn away from what they themselves had made. They did not stop worshiping demons, nor the idols of gold, silver,

bronze, stone, and wood, which cannot see, hear, or walk. Nor did they repent of their murders, their magic, their sexual immorality, or their stealing.

This is amazing! Mankind will not change! If these events were supernatural in nature, as most commentators on Revelation assert, then repentance would come easily. But when it can be explained away by "it was a meteor, those things occur every so often," or "wars are bound to happen," then those unwilling to see the hand of God in human history will continue in their ways and will see no reason to repent. These last few verses also imply that this section of the Book of Revelation must describe real, physical events. If this were not so why would John be surprised over a lack of repentance?

# AFTER THE DISASTER

3

$W$ hat will be the environmental and geopolitical state of the world in the years following the meteor impact? To fully understand the situation, both the indirect and the direct effects of the meteor need to be compounded onto the current unprecedented environmental stresses that homo sapiens are placing upon the Earth, but for all practical purposes there will be only one fact to consider. That fact will be the hunger present through most of humanity. Quatrain (8) linked hunger with the appearance of the comet, and quatrain (11) predicted famine after the meteor impact. Here is another quatrain linking the tsunami with famine:

### (15) Century 6, Quatrain 5

So great a famine through
    wave pestiferous,
Through long rain the length
    of the pole arctic:
Samarobryn one hundred leagues
    from the hemisphere,
They will live without law
    exempt from politics.

*Si grande famine par onde pestifère,*
*Par pluie longue le long*
    *du pôle arctique:*
*Samarobryn cent lieues de l'hémisphère,*
*Vivront sans loi exempt de politique.*

A "league" in Nostradamus' time was a loosely defined unit of distance that varied from 2.5 to 4.5 miles. Since the only way to get "one hundred leagues from the hemisphere" is to go straight up,

71

Nostradamus is predicting here that mankind will be 250-450 miles above the surface of the earth, roughly the height used by the space shuttle! Along with his other credits, Nostradamus apparently predicted space travel as well! "Samarobryn" of line three is an anagram, possibly for a person, that has not been solved yet. The "wave" mentioned in the first line is, of course, the tsunami, here seen traveling into and under the North Pole, emerging again in the northern Pacific. The key to the last line is "They will live without law," a clear indication of the anarchy that will be present as central governments break down all over the world.

To summarize this quatrain Nostradamus predicts that a spacecraft (either manned or perhaps a weather satellite) will observe the tsunami as it spreads under the north polar ice cap, emerging in the Pacific Ocean. The destruction it will bring will result in "famine" and civil anarchy ("they will live without law"). "Politics," and political life in general, will end as humanity scrambles to cope with unprecedented disaster. Incidentally, in the 16th Century it was not known that there was no land under the North Pole, so without being able to see the future, how could Nostradamus know this? How could he have guessed at space travel during a time when most intellectuals still believed the sky was fixed and unreachable? Whether Nostradamus' predictions, as interpreted in this book, are right or wrong, he deserves immense credit as a man of sharp intellect and keen foresight.

There are now three quatrains linking hunger and famine with the comet, meteor, and tsunami. This is enough to make famine a major Nostradamian theme related to the events of 1999. Is famine on a large scale likely following a meteoric impact? While there have been episodes of localized starvation over the past few decades, mostly in Africa, how is it possible that large numbers of people around the world might starve to death? Before continuing with Nostradamus' quatrains, a clear picture must be painted of the food-producing capabilities of the planet in the years before the impact.

There are four biological systems that provide the basic framework on which every economy in the world is based. Those systems are the oceans and seas, the forests and woodlands, grass and pasture lands, and croplands (especially lands used for growing grain). The oceans provide fish, a high-quality protein food; the forests furnish wood for fuel, housing, and paper, as well as a small quantity of food in the form of fruits and nuts; the animals that graze on grasslands supply meat, dairy products, leather, and wool; and the croplands are the primary food source, in addition to supplying commercial items such as fibers and oils. The health of these four systems is absolutely crucial to the world economy, and the best measure of how wealthy the planet is. What good is it to build faster airplanes, more powerful computers, taller skyscrapers, and bigger gambling casinos if the biological infrastructure that permits the very existence of human life itself fails? If these systems collapse, then everything built upon them will collapse as well. Sadly, for much of humanity these systems are already failing and will be either at or near the point of collapse by 1999. Each system will now be examined in detail.

# OCEANS

In 1987, the coral reefs that surround the island of Puerto Rico began to blanche white. This bleaching is common and temporary, occurring during periods of stress, such as a very low tide, pollution, water that is too warm or to cold, or silt runoff from nearby land. Marine scientists expected the bleaching to resolve in short order, but it did not. Instead, coral bleaching was noticed soon afterwards in the entire Caribbean Sea, and then throughout the tropical corals of the entire world. While the cause has still not been proven, pollution, human exploitation, and possibly global warming are all suspected to play a role.

In 1992, Clive Wilkinson of the Australian Institute of Marine Science estimated that mankind has caused the death of as much as 10% of coral reefs worldwide. He also predicted that, at current rates of destruction, at least another 60% could be lost in the next 20-40 years! Aside from their natural beauty and wonder, corals reefs are important food producers. Reefs produce 10 to 100 times more fish than an equivalent area of open ocean, and fully 10% of all the ocean fish caught in the world are harvested from reef ecosystems. Many countries are heavily dependent on the fish caught from the reefs for food. For example, Pacific Islanders rely upon ocean fish as the source of the vast majority of their animal protein. It is also an important protein source for Southeast Asia, east Africa, and the Caribbean. Destruction of the coral reefs will probably result in a significant protein reduction for people in those regions, even if their growing populations could suddenly stabilize at current levels.

While the coral reefs may be the most visible example of future falling fish production, they are not the only one. The United Nations Food and Agriculture Organization (FAO) estimated in the early 1990s that of the seventeen fishing zones in the world, four were being overfished, and production in those zones will fall, perhaps precipitously. For example, in 1968 there were 1.6 billion pounds of cod caught off the coast of Labrador and Newfoundland. In July of 1992, when the Canadian Minister of Fisheries and Oceans banned cod fishing, there were only 44 million pounds of codfish left in the entire sea off of Newfoundland! There has been little improvement in cod stocks since the banning, and some experts think that it may be decades before cod fishing is once again allowed in the region.

While the tale of the Newfoundland fishing industry is distressing, it is not unique. Most of the other thirteen fishing zones that are not being overfished are already being utilized at their maximal production level. Between 1950 and 1988 the world's total fish harvest increased 4% annually. Over the next four years it actually fell a total of 7%. Very simply, the oceans of the world are already providing all of the food that they can supply. The best that can be hoped for is a levelling off in production, but with the ongoing coral reef destruction, and current overfishing, further declines are almost certain.

# FORESTS

While it is difficult to capture the gradual loss of productivity of the seas on film, deforestation is much easier to document. As a result, most individuals are aware of the clear-cutting of the Brazilian rainforest, but may not be aware of how global the problem has become. Global forested area has been shrinking gradually for several centuries, but the rate of shrinkage increased with the worldwide economic boom after World War II, and again increased during the decade-long economic surge in the 1980s. As a result, in 1984 the world was losing 11 million hectares (a hectare is roughly 2.25 acres) of tropical rain forest a year. By 1992 that loss had increased to 17 million hectares a year, and was still rising. Seventeen million hectares is slightly larger than the entire state of Georgia, and this represents just the tropical rain-forest losses. When the loss in temperate rain forests is added, the total increases even more. In just a twenty-year period, from 1970 to 1990, the net loss of forests worldwide was nearly 200 million hectares, an area surpassing the entire United States east of the Mississippi River! Since 1950, 20% of the world's total tropical rain forests have been cut down, and the demand for wood is still growing. The loss of trees, combined with surging population growth (world population continues to grow by nearly 100 million people every year), will lead to a 20% shrinkage in world forested area per person during the decade of the nineties alone.

Why are the forests being cleared? There are several reasons. In Brazil, and many other countries, the trees are being cleared for farming and ranching operations. Is it possible to increase food production in the years after the comet and meteor by clearing forests and planting more crops? Well, consider what is happening in Brazil. The soil there, as in most tropical countries, is notoriously thin; most of the nutrients being in the decaying vegetation in the top inch of the soil only. When this thin nutrient layer is exposed to the direct rays of the harsh tropical sun, the soil quickly bakes into a useless hardpan, suitable only for making bricks. The soil becomes so hard and nutrient-depleted that even weeds have a hard time growing in it. Tropical rain forest soils can support ranching for no more than ten years, and farming for no more than five years, before becoming unproductive and then being abandoned by their owners as a wasteland. No more than ten years after being a lush tropical rain forest, the land becomes a barren, tropical desert. Land that has been forested for millions of years is being turned into desert daily throughout the tropical world.

Agriculture, however, is not the only reason forests are shrinking. Another reason for tree cutting is to obtain firewood for fuel. For two-thirds of the Third World, including China, India, Andean South America, and most of Africa, trees are still the primary energy source. Populations that once could meet their firewood needs by picking up only dead wood have mushroomed to the point where living trees must be cut as well. In 1980, over one billion people were cutting firewood faster than nature could replace it. By the year 2000 that number will be close to two-and-a half billion. Two-and-a-half billion! In only a few years! What will they do when even the live wood finally runs out? How will they live? Where will they go? Will they live? Two-and-a-half billion people!

Forestry problems are not limited to Third World countries. Acid rain is significantly slowing growth rates of trees in industrialized countries as well. For instance, the U.S. forest service found that the size of annual growth rings of yellow pine trees declined between 30-50% in the years from 1955 to 1985. Yellow pine is one of the major forest species in the southeastern United States, covering more than 40 million hectares. Nor is slowing growth the only problem. In 1975, 9% of the trees in those yellow pine forests were dead. However, by 1985, just ten years later, the number of dead trees totaled 15%. Forestry experts are reporting similar, or even worse, findings for all of Europe and the republics of the former Soviet Union, so productivity of existing forests throughout temperate forests appears to be falling. Despite massive tree replanting by forestry companies in the United States (the acreage of forests in the U.S. is now larger than at any time this century), forests worldwide are shrinking rapidly in size and slowing in productivity. In a world of shrinking forests and growing demand for wood and wood products, the possibility of converting more timberland to cropland is limited at best. When also considering slowing growth in the remaining forests, and accelerating population growth, the wooded lands are facing a future crisis very similar to what the seas are facing.

# GRASSLANDS

Grasslands consist of animal grazing lands that are too nutritionally or water poor to support crops. Because the soil has lower levels of nutrients and moisture, it deteriorates much more quickly than cropland when abused. Unfortunately, abuse is a mild term for what is occurring in pasturelands throughout much of the world. In most Third World countries the feed needs of the animals far exceeds what the grasslands are capable of providing. The result is overgrazing which, if severe enough, can turn a verdant pasture into desert within a few years. For example, overgrazing in the sub-Saharan country of Mali, in combination with overcutting of forests, has caused the Saharan desert to expand southward over 350 kilometers (220 miles) in just twenty years. Imagine, a desert moving south at an average of eleven miles a year!

In 1990, world grasslands averaged 0.61 hectares per person. During the nineties alone that figure will decrease 20%, along with the 20% per capita drop in forested land. Once again, the two primary reasons are an expanding population and overuse. Overgrazing of grasslands, however, is much more serious than overfishing. Even severely overfished areas can be restocked and eventually become productive within a few decades. Overgrazed grasslands, however, turn into desert. And once pastureland has become desert it is essentially not recoverable as grazing land ever again. Turning pasture into useless desert is fairly easily accomplished in many parts of the world, but turning desert back into any type of productive land is, for all practical purposes, impossible.

# CROPLANDS

Healthy, productive croplands are the key link in the chain of food production. And of all the types of crops grown on farmland, the grain crops are the most important. Half of all calories consumed by humanity come directly from grains, and a good portion of the rest by eating meat, milk, and eggs from grain-fed animals. Given the strategic importance of grainlands it is of critical importance that a determination be made about their long-term health and stability.

How is the health of croplands measured? The simplest and most direct measurement is the amount of topsoil present, and since numerous studies in the United States have shown a direct relationship between the amount of topsoil present and productivity, this is probably the most accurate measurement as well. For every inch of topsoil eroded, production falls roughly 6%. Unfortunately, the world's farmers, in the decade of the '80s, lost in excess of 250 billion tons of topsoil. How much is 250 billion tons of soil? It equates to fully half the total amount of topsoil on croplands in the United States, all of the soil on Australia's wheatland, or one inch off half the cropland in China! And this occurred in just one decade! In the 1970s a similar amount of topsoil was lost, so that the total loss of soil from 1970 to 1990 was equal to the amount on all of India's croplands. Since the end of World War II, fully 20% of the world's total topsoil, soil that took millennia to build, has eroded away. Given current trends, what will soil quality be in another fifty years?

During the nineties, the amount of cropland per person worldwide is expected to shrink by nearly 2% every year, yet another instance of a 20% decrease per capita for that decade alone. Additionally, fertility, and thus productivity, on existing land continues to fall. For instance, in Ontario, Canada, soil that in 1950 had an organic matter content of 10% (organic matter contains all of the living material in soil) now has an organic matter content of only 3%, and that number is still falling. Yet farmers in 1992 managed to feed 1.6 billion more people than they did in 1972, even with 500 billion tons less topsoil. The twin trends of a gradual loss of farmland fertility due to erosion and a burgeoning population are on a collision course. Environmentalists saw that collision occurring in the 1970s; when large-scale famine did not occur they were discredited. Nevertheless, eventually these two trends will lead to large-scale famine at some point. There is simply no more farm land available anywhere on Earth, fertility and productivity are falling on existing farms, and the population of the world is increasing by 100,000,000 every year, nearly a quarter of a million people each and every day.

Even worse than the continuing erosion is the indifference of governments throughout the world to the problem. The United States is the only country making a significant effort to reduce its erosion problem. Between 1985 and 1990 the U.S. cut soil erosion by one-third, and probably reduced it another third between 1990 and 1995, but in most Third World countries the problem is actually worsening. And despite the critical relationship between topsoil and soil productivity, most countries have no idea how much topsoil they possess, how quickly it is eroding, and how soon their cropland will become barren.

Nature forms topsoil from decaying grass, crop residues, leaves, and the natural weathering process of rocks. An inch of topsoil can take as little as 100 years to as much as 1,000 years to accumulate, depending on conditions. Yet, under conditions of extreme erosion, such as in Oklahoma in the 1930s, or those of sub-Saharan Africa today, that topsoil can completely erode away in just a few years. While less acute, erosion is present to some extent in even the most fertile farmlands. The U.S. Department of Agriculture has estimated that 25% of all farmland in the United States cannot support farming indefinitely due to erosion problems. That land will eventually need to be retired from farming and put to other uses, either as forest or pastureland. Topsoil, the lifeblood of the land, is today bleeding away far faster than it is being generated all over the world.

The deterioration of grasslands, croplands, and forests has greatly speeded the spread of deserts. Every year, 6 million hectares of new desert are formed, mostly in Africa and Asia. Six million hectares is an area nearly half the size of Kentucky, turned irreversibly into desert each and every year. In an additional 20 million hectares, slightly larger than the state of Missouri, the land deteriorates every year to the point where farming or grazing are no longer profitable and the land is abandoned. In total, 35% of the Earth's surface either is a desert already, or is in the process of becoming one. Furthermore, these areas undergoing desertification are home to nearly one billion people.

Where are those areas becoming desert located? The one billion people living on land turning into desert reside primarily in Africa and Asia. Unfortunately, those are the same areas that are already experiencing food shortages, shortages that the meteor impact will turn into famines. But what about the rest of the world? Will Europe and North America face food shortages as well? Since the meteor impact will significantly slow, possibly even halt, world trade, even a severe decrease in harvests will leave the grain exporting countries of the world with probably enough to eat.

Who are the current grain exporting countries? For the several hundred years prior to the middle of this century, local economies were self-sufficient in food production with the exception of North America, which was a net food exporter, and Western Europe, which was a net food importer. Over the last 40 years, however, the picture has changed greatly. North America is now the breadbasket of the world, exporting well over 100 million tons of grain annually, an increase of 500% since the end of World War II. Interestingly enough, Western Europe is fast becoming the second leading grain exporter behind North America, ending hundreds of years of dependence on imported grain. While Australia and New Zealand are still large exporters of grain, Africa, Asia, and even Latin America are now large grain importers.

The harvests of 1988 are illustrative of recent grain production and consumption patterns. On the exporting side were North America at nearly 120 million tons of grain (despite the severe drought that year), Western Europe at just over 20 million tons, and Australia/New Zealand with nearly 15 million tons. On the importing side were Latin America at 11 million tons, Eastern Europe and the former USSR with 27 million tons, Africa at 28 million tons, and the rest of Asia (minus the USSR) at a phenomenal 90 million tons. Even worse, the tonnage of imports into Asia and Africa is still accelerating, much like the population growth curves of the individual countries that form these two continents.

With the destruction of port facilities and the loss of ocean-going ships it is unlikely that the hungry of Africa and Asia will attempt to take grain from Australia or North America, but Europe is a different story. While it may take years, it is even possible to walk to France from India, or even from China. In the aftermath of the meteor strike, hunger lasting for decades may be near-universal among the masses of Africa and Asia, while Europe, particularly Western Europe, will probably be better off. If war is to develop, it will most likely pit the food "have-nots" of Africa and Asia against the relatively grain-rich "haves" of Western Europe. However, before continuing with Nostradamus' account of how World War III will develop, he has some other quatrains describing the hunger. In the following quatrain Nostradamus predicts that even the Europeans will have food shortages:

**(16) Century 3, Quatrain 42**

| | |
|---|---|
| The infant born with two teeth in his mouth, | *L'enfant naîtra a deux dents en la goàrge,* |
| Rocks into Tuscany will like rain fall: | *Pierres en Tuscie par pluie tomberont:* |
| A few years after will be neither wheat nor barley, | *Peu d'ans après ne sera blé ni orge,* |
| To satisfy those who from hunger faint. | *Pour saouler ceux qui de faim failliront.* |

The second line, indicating that "Rocks will. . . like rain fall" is not as implausible as it appears. On July 24, 1790, a large number of meteorites fell near Agen, in southwestern France. Similar episodes occurred on December 14, 1807, near Weston, Connecticut, and over Siberia in 1947. In fact, the only conceivable reasons rocks might fall like rain are intense meteor showers, as when the Earth passes through the tail of a comet, a local massive volcanic eruption, or possibly even a splash of rocks from a meteoric impact. If not by meteor impact with a subsequent nuclear winter, then how else could this "rain of rocks" be linked with famine in Italy several years later? The real significance of this quatrain is that Italy will be in famine "a few years after" the impact of September 1999, possibly by 2001, almost certainly by 2002 at the latest. Also note how this quatrain correlates with John's prediction from Revelation of a meteor shower in which rocks would reach the ground like unripe figs falling from the tree

("The stars fell down to the earth, like unripe figs falling from the tree when a strong wind shakes it"). The child born with two teeth in his mouth is mentioned in another quatrain and will be discussed again in a later chapter.

Nostradamus has a quatrain about another of the reasons for the famine in Italy:

(17) **Century 4, Quatrain 48**

| | |
|---|---|
| The plain of Ausonia fertile, spacious | *Planure Ausonne fertile, spacieuse* |
| Will produce so many gadflies and grasshoppers: | *Produira taons si tant de sauterelles:* |
| The brightness of the sun will become clouded, | *Clarté solaire deviendra nubileuse,* |
| Devoured all, great pestilence to come from them. | *Ronger le tout, grande peste venir d'elles.* |

Ausonia was part of the Kingdom of Naples. The most notable plain near Naples in southern Italy is Campania, on the west coast. Here Nostradamus predicts an insect swarm that will devour the produce of the plain. In modern times there have been insect swarms in northern Africa that have been thick enough to completely obscure the Sun. Some of these swarms have even crossed the Mediterranean on rafts made of the dead carcasses of their brothers into southern Europe. The "great pestilence" that comes from them will probably be famine and the diseases that accompany it. If enough of the insects manage to cross the Mediterranean Sea for "the brightness of the sun" to "become clouded," then one can only imagine the scale of destruction in North Africa.

Why will there be such an increase in insects? As discussed previously, the nuclear winter after the meteor impact will kill off large numbers of creatures of all types. Furthermore, insects reproduce themselves at fantastic rates, hundreds, or even thousands, of times faster than their predators (birds, for instance). Until a natural balance is again established, locust-like plagues of all sorts of insects will be common, not only in Italy but throughout much of the world, as well. Ecological models show that establishing a new point of balance, or homeostasis, will take many years, perhaps even a decade or two, to reach. Until that point is reached, insect plagues may be common.

Nostradamus has yet another quatrain about famine:

**(18) Century 1, Quatrain 16**

Scythe to the pond joined
   towards Sagittarius
At its upper increase of exaltation,
Plague, famine, death
   from hand military:
The century approaches
   of renovation.

*Faux à l'étang joint vers le Sagittaire*
*En son haut AUGE de l'exaltation,*
*Peste, famine, mort de main militaire:*
*Le siècle approche de rénovation.*

At a time when Saturn ("Scythe") and the Moon ("the pond") are in the constellation of "Sagittarius," a "plague, famine," and war ("death from hand military") will occur. These events will take place near the end of "the century." Saturn entered the astrologically-defined borders of Sagittarius in February 1994, and left it in January 1996. That was close enough to the end of a century that it may apply to the end of the current one. If so, then a major war will break out before the new century begins, which is January 1st of 2001. This war will be associated with plagues and famines. Perhaps this will even mark the beginnings of what will come to be known as World War III, although it will not be called that until much later. This dating, however, assumes that Nostradamus either calculated the planetary motions correctly, or foresaw their positions by his ability to peer into the future. Most of his configurations are impossible to date accurately, for reasons that will be explained in a later chapter.

And still another quatrain about famine:

**(19) Century 1, Quatrain 67**

The great famine that
   I sense approaching,
Often turning, then
   becoming universal,
So great and long that
   one will come to pull
From woods roots,
   and infants from breast.

*La grande famine que je sens approcher,*
*Souvent tourner, puis être universelle,*
*Si grande et longue qu'on*
   *viendra arracher*
*Du bois racine, et l'enfant de mamelle.*

This quatrain is graphic enough to be self-explanatory. The only weakness is that Nostradamus does not link the "great famine" with any other event in this quatrain, which would allow for placing it here without any doubt. However, since he describes it as "The great famine" that will "become universal," it is placed here since that is exactly what can be expected after the impact of the meteor.

Assuming that this book is mistaken in its interpretation of Nostradamus (which is very possible), or even that Nostradamus was a fraud or lunatic (also possible), it is likely that large-scale famine awaits humanity sometime early in the next century. If world fertility rates hold at current levels into the next century, by 2025 the world will hold over 11 billion people, double its current number. Can they all be fed? Past and current famines in Africa require the answer to be: not always. Will the hungry sit quietly and starve or fight to live? The African famines of the past 25 years have been in poor countries with paltry military capabilities. What if the modern equivalent of the Irish potato famine strikes Russia, Pakistan, or India? Would a United States of over 400 million in 2025 sit quietly by if a drought crippled the Great Plains? Who will survive the wars that the "have-nots" will launch upon the "haves" in a time when the "have-nots" have nuclear weapons?

Quatrain (19) hints at cannibalism. There is another quatrain that describes it more clearly:

**(20) Century 2, Quatrain 75**

| | |
|---|---|
| The sound of the rare bird heard, | *La voix ouïe de l'insolite oiseau,* |
| On the stack of the chimney: | *Sur le canon du respiral étage:* |
| So high will the bushel of wheat rise, | *Si haut viendra du froment le boisseau,* |
| That man his fellow man will devour. | *Que l'homme d'homme sera Anthropophage.* |

This quatrain is essentially a restatement of the previous one. Food will be so scarce and expensive that cannibalism will occur. The record of cannibalism during times of severe food shortages is unfortunately long. Those that may have been known to Nostradamus include Italy in the year 450, England and Ireland between 695-700, Germany from 845-851, Scotland from 936-940, throughout all of Europe at various times from 950-1000, England during William the Conqueror's invasion of 1069, and all of Egypt from 1201-1207. In Egypt particularly, the initial horror of cannibalism was eventually met with acceptance; there were even many instances of human flesh sold in the marketplaces. Desperate times breed desperate behaviors. Lest the reader think that in the so-called civilized world of the twentieth century these events do not occur, some of the more current episodes of cannibalism include Napoleon's troops during their withdrawal from Moscow during their disastrous winter campaign, the famous Donner party, which was trapped for the winter in the Wasatch mountains of Utah in 1846, in Germany and along the banks of the Volga River after World War I, in the Ukraine from 1929-31 during Stalin's genocide of the Ukrainian people, and from 1941-44 in Leningrad while the Germans blockaded the city. In this last instance the violence was especially notable—many people were kidnapped off of the street and murdered so that they could be eaten. Even in the very recent past, sixteen Uruguayans survived an airplane crash in the Andes Mountains in 1972 by eating the dead. There should be no doubt that when large-scale famine returns to the world that cannibalism will be carried out by those desperate to survive by any means possible.

Before continuing with Nostradamus' quatrains, a final glimpse will be taken at the state of the world, on a continent-by-continent basis, in the years immediately following the comet's appearance.

# NORTH AMERICA

The entire eastern coast of the United States, and probably the gulf coast as well, will be devastated. The earthquake, tsunami, and subsequent firestorms will cause unimaginable destruction. However, the initial loss of life should be relatively light, due to the excellent highway systems in the United States and abundance of automobiles. Evacuating people 100 miles, just a short drive, should remove coastal dwellers from the immediate disaster. Even when allowing for massive traffic jams, the long period of the comet's visibility will allow for evacuation of all who want to leave. This, however, leaves the problem of what to do with tens of millions of homeless people. Also, the 500-mile-per-hour hypercanes that will form over the impact site will drift into the western Atlantic and Gulf of Mexico. These storms are still likely to pack winds of at least 150 miles per hour, and there could be a dozen of them. At least a few are bound to hit the U.S. coast, causing further destruction, perhaps even well inland. Huge thunderstorms, in unimaginable numbers, will form as the atmosphere seeks to disperse the heat from the suddenly blisteringly hot Atlantic Ocean. The amount of flooding will be incomprehensible; every part of the entire country may have not just a hundred-year-flood, but a thousand-year flood. Many, many, tornadoes, which are more frequent in the U.S. than in any country in the world anyway, will occur with daily frequency over the entire continent east of the Rocky Mountains. The number and intensity of storms will destroy large sections of the electrical distribution network throughout the country.

As the heat from the impact is gradually dissipated the climate will begin to cool. The dust-cloud induced nuclear winter that will begin roughly fifteen months after the impact will freeze the ground well below the level at which municipal water supplies are buried. The resulting burst pipes will cripple municipal water supplies throughout the nation; particularly in the Midwest, where brutally cold winters frequently occur anyway. By the way, In February of 1996 a week of very cold winter weather in Chicago drove the frost line down to the four-foot level. Had it stayed bitterly cold just a few more days the frost would have reached to five feet, the level at which water mains are buried in the city. If the frost had reached the mains, many, perhaps even thousands, of pipes would have burst, leaving the entire city without water. The public works department does not have enough equipment, workers, or supplies to cope with that number of broken mains, and it would have been at least several months before water could be restored to the entire city.

If the system of interstate natural gas pipelines are not severed in the earthquake or destroyed in the firestorms, they too will fail. The February 1996 cold snap resulted in so much gas being drawn off at the consumer end that the natural gas utilities had difficulty keeping enough pressure in the pipes to keep the system functioning. A nuclear winter could well cause the entire system to collapse; at the minimum a severe rationing plan will be in effect.

Few people appreciate how fragile modern civilization is, how easily it can be disrupted. The impact will not only severely curtail import and export activity, end global communications, and disrupt transportation within the country, thus crippling the U.S. economy, but it will also severely damage the distribution of electricity, natural gas, and clean water throughout much of the country. After the comet, diseases more typical of Third World countries, such as dysentery and cholera, will abound among those left homeless. At this point the reader should stop and consider how easily a space rock could change their life: no heat, no electricity, no water, probably no employment, rationed gasoline, violent weather, etc. And this will occur in those areas lucky enough to escape the worst destruction!

As the largest grain producer in the world, the U.S. also has enormous amounts of grain in storage, so starvation should not occur on a large scale, if the grain can be distributed. Remember, the famines in Africa over the past few decades have been due to transportation problems (usually trying to get through the middle of a war), rather than food shortages. Even with the likely severe crop reductions in the years following the meteor strike there should still be enough food stocks available to avoid large-scale famine. (Of course, the same cannot be said for those countries to which the U.S. currently exports grain!) The difficulty will be in the transportation of food from storage facilities to the hungry. Localized pockets of starvation are possible.

The armed forces will be no better off than the economy. By 1999, the United States Navy will have closed its port facilities on the Gulf of Mexico, leaving only three on the east coast for the Atlantic fleet. These are sure to be destroyed by the tsunami and subsequent firestorms. As it is also quite possible that the Panama Canal will be damaged, the U.S. Navy may effectively be without an Atlantic fleet, until it develops a port on one of the Great Lakes. Ships at sea will be able to ride out the tsunami, assuming they can avoid the fireball of the explosion, but how long can a navy function without a home port? Within a year or two the fleet will be transferred to the Pacific, anchored just off the eastern U.S. coast, or possibly moved to one of the Great Lakes.

Civil government will change dramatically. Democracies, by their very nature, are slow to react to sudden changes. The multiple crises that will be present will lead without doubt to the imposition of martial law throughout the nation. It is possible that it may be a decade or more before elections are once again held.

As discussed in the first chapter, the loss of high-tech satellites and communications will further serve to cripple military capabilities along with commerce and industry. In addition, an American population that is already becoming more isolationist in the 1990s will adopt not just an "America first" attitude but an "America only" attitude when confronted with the environmental and economic disasters to come. Not only will the United States be unable to project military power abroad—its citizens will demand that the government not get involved in foreign affairs until the domestic economy has been stabilized. Given the nature of the destruction, this is likely to take an entire generation, possibly even longer. Until that time, the U.S. will be a regional power only, with no influence in the events occurring in Africa, Asia, and Europe. Foreign affairs will be dominated by events occurring in Canada and Mexico, and the most important part of the military will be the Coast Guard and the Border Patrol. It is not even certain that the federal government itself will be able to survive. It is possible that a new constitutional convention will be called and a Second Republic will rise up from the ashes of the current United States of America. Since the Caribbean islands will be severely damaged by the tsunami, possibly even depopulated, the new United States might even include islands like Cuba and Jamaica, resettled by some of the homeless from the U.S. mainland.

All of the problems present in the United States will also be present in Canada, with one addition. Its more northerly latitude will make the nuclear winter especially severe, probably lasting through at least one summer, and many may die from it. Also, Canada may have complete crop failures from the cold for several years. Canada's very survival as a country may depend on its ability to pump oil and trade it for food with a suddenly fuel-short United States.

Mexico may be shielded somewhat from the tsunami by Florida (which may be completely flooded), but its Gulf coast is still likely to be devastated. In addition, Mexico is currently experiencing the population growth and environmental deterioration commonly seen in Third World countries. While Mexico can expect some shielding from the effects of a nuclear winter due to its more southerly latitude, economic disaster, epidemics, and famine will be widespread, even with what limited help the United States will be able to provide. The ability of the federal government to survive is questionable here, as well.

# SOUTH AMERICA

In the continent of South America, only Argentina is a significant net grain exporter. For the continent as a whole, grain production per person has been falling since the mid-eighties and the region is now heavily dependent on U.S. grain. Famine and disease will be rampant throughout the entire continent. Given the continent's history of unstable governments, revolutions and uprisings will be common. It is also possible that regional wars, between a food-rich Argentina and a starving Brazil, for example, may occur. The events here will be of little interest to the rest of the world for many years, and the countries of South America will likewise be incapable of influencing world affairs. As important as these events will be to those living there, since Nostradamus had nothing to say about events in South America they will not be mentioned again in this book.

## AUSTRALIA

Australia, New Zealand, New Guinea, and the major surrounding islands should be among the most stable places on Earth in the next century. Far removed from the impact site, relatively rich in food, and geographically separated from the starving masses of Asia, this region should survive with relatively little damage. There are, however, two dangers. The first is from the tsunami; distance alone does not necessarily provide safety from the raging water. As a result, while severe coastal damage is not likely, some damage is still possible. The second danger lies in the fact that Australia may not be quite far enough away from Asia. In the first and second decades of the next century food procurement invasions from Indonesia, India, or even China, are possible. But, once again, Nostradamus has no predictions about this area of the world and the future events of this region will not be discussed again in this book.

## AFRICA

In contrast to the relative stability of Australia, the countries of Africa are already among the sorriest places on Earth, and after the meteor impact things will get only worse. Since 1970, Africa's grain output per person has fallen 20%, and most of the continent, if not actually already starving, is at least hungry. Any further drop in food production here will trigger massive famine. Most, if not all, governments will collapse under the stresses of life after the meteor. The anarchy present in Somalia and Rwanda during the nineties is a good example of what will be present throughout all of sub-Saharan Africa a few years after the meteor impact. North Africa will scarcely be any better. With the exception of Morocco, all of the Mediterranean countries already import more than half of their grain, and they will be even more dependent on it in the early twenty-first century. With the inability of the U.S. and Europe to export grain to Africa, most of the continent will starve. The rest, especially in sub-Saharan Africa, will descend into anarchy or, at best, tribal rule.

# ASIA

The Asian continent has experienced explosive population growth in this century; over one-third of all the people in the world live in China and India alone. Also, Asia contains some of the worst environmental damage in the world. While shielded from the direct effects of the blast, the indirect effects, especially starvation, will put tremendous strain on every government. Local wars for control of food-growing regions will be common. Russia will experience the same intense nuclear winter as Canada, and given the country's other massive problems (for instance, in June of 1994, Boris Yeltsin announced that over half the country had income at or below the poverty level) Russia is not likely to survive as a country. Instead, the individual republics will probably splinter into ever smaller regions filled with warring ethnic groups. As the former Soviet Union disintegrates into small fiefdoms, the political situation will be very similar to what Genghis Khan faced during his conquests from Mongolia to Europe.

The following quatrain, describing the recent relationship of the United States and Russia, appears to be applicable here:

(21) **Century 2, Quatrain 89**

One day will be friends
   the two great masters,
Their great power will
   be seen to increase:
The land new will be
   at its upper peak,
To the bloody one
   the number told.

*Un jour seront demis les*
   *deux grands maîtres,*
*Leur grand pouvoir se verra augmenté:*
*La terre neuve sera en ses hauts êtres,*
*Au sanguinaire le nombre raconté.*

If the quatrain is applicable to the twentieth century, the "two great masters" of the first line must be the United States and Russia, without doubt the two greatest powers of this century. But while the two are no longer technically enemies, they are not "friends" either, are they? Well, in June 1992, George Bush and Boris Yeltsin signed a "charter of friendship." While the treaty carries no legally binding clauses, it was still an embarrassment to the U.S. State Department. A senior State Department official was quoted as moaning "It's still a friendship treaty. I don't know how we get into these positions." The third line is interesting. North America, even in Nostradamus' day, was referred to as "the new land." Did he foresee that the United States would reach its pinnacle of economic and military power in the early 1990s? Is it all downhill from here? The question of who "the bloody one" might be will be addressed in the next chapter. While this particular quatrain may well belong to another time and other countries, it does fit very well here.

Besides Russia, how well off will the other Asian countries be? Despite its own food problems, China, as the most independent, self-sufficient economy in the world, may well be the most powerful country in the world in the early years of the next century. To ease their famine, the Chinese will exploit the anarchy in Russia by expanding into the thinly-defended regions of Siberia, invade Vietnam and the other Southeast Asian countries, and possibly even India as well. Politically, the Chinese are already allies with Iran, and this relationship is sure to expand. More about this later.

India, with an exploding population and rapidly deteriorating forestland and croplands, is another region where civil war and anarchy is likely. Civil war with its Sikh separatists and substantial Muslim minorities is inevitable, and war with Pakistan is possible. The future for India is one of death on a massive scale from civil war, disease, and starvation. As a single, united country India probably will not survive.

Japan, the country with a meteoric rise to economic superpower status, will quickly fall to only a regional power, perhaps even a non-power, without enough food to feed its own population. Japanese grain production peaked in the seventies, and production has dropped more than 25% since then. In the eighties Japan was importing over 70% of its grain; it is the single largest grain importing country in the world. In contrast, China has been importing only 5% of its grain. In addition, Japan is a country destitute of raw materials. Its wealth comes entirely from the importation of raw materials and re-exporting finished goods at a profit. With world trade severely curtailed and seriously short of grain, Japan not only may not survive as an Asian power—it might even fall into anarchy, or civil war, and not survive at all.

The Muslim countries of Asia and Africa will have some unique problems, which will be dealt with in the next chapter. At this time, let it suffice to say that their infrastructure will be spared destruction from the tsunami, and they will be looking for ways to feed a hungry population and exploit the destruction and political turmoil present in the West.

# EUROPE

If the meteor should impact near the junction of the African and European tectonic plates near the Mid-Atlantic Rise, then Europe will bear the brunt of the force of the earthquake and the tsunami, and the results will be frightful. As discussed in quatrain (12), Nostradamus foresees Great Britain being "half sunk" by the tsunami. Should this actually happen, London would probably be completely destroyed. As the hill country of Scotland would offer some protection from the destructive water, the capital of the British Isles may move there. Support for this is found in other quatrains, discussed later in this book, in which Nostradamus mentions the leader of Great Britain as being from Scotland, rather than England. Could anything other than the complete destruction of London cause the capital to be relocated to Scotland?

Portugal, and to a lesser extent Spain, will also experience severe blast damage, and both countries will have their infrastructures crippled. Italy and Greece will be damaged not only by the initial collision, but by the subsequent secondary earthquake, and probable tsunami, along the African-European tectonic plate boundary.

All of the former Soviet-Bloc countries of Eastern Europe were left with economies that were, at best, inefficient, all have severe environmental problems, and all face a worsening future even without a cometary appearance. In the aftermath of the meteor impact they will have great difficulties just surviving. Economic and environmental disaster, famine, and plague will be common in Eastern Europe. The entire region may well collapse into small pockets of warring regional ethnic groups, much like what the Mongols found on their march across Europe centuries ago.

Despite the difficulties brought on by the comet, France and Germany should be in the best shape of all the countries of Europe. There are several reasons for this. First, their populations are stable in size or shrinking slightly. Second, they are now both prodigious food producers and should be able to weather the shortages brought on by the nuclear winter. Third, France and Germany are probably the only countries on Earth without significant soil erosion problems. Fourth, both are much less dependent on imported energy than the rest of Europe. France especially, due to its aggressive domestic nuclear energy program and low erosion rate, will survive with its power-generating systems and food production capabilities reasonably intact.

In summary, what will the geopolitical state of the world look like? Africa, Eastern Europe, and the states that made up the former Soviet Union will collapse into anarchy. The individual countries of North America, South America, and Australia will be completely absorbed in internal affairs and completely isolated from the events of Europe and Asia. In the Far East, China will be the only major power and will expand into Russia, Southeast Asia, and probably India as well. Their Muslim allies, especially Pakistan, will assist them in India. The rest of the Muslim states, with China securing the rest of Asia, will look with a hungry eye to a weakened Europe. In Europe, only France and Germany will resemble the countries that they are today, and the stage will be set for a showdown.

Quatrain (14) bears reviewing now, as it predicts the condition of France during the nuclear winter following the meteor impact. The small grain harvest and the violence ("force") of line one, along with a wet spring and summer fit well with what might be expected in the year 2000. Nostradamus indicates that the following winter will be "long" and hard, not only on humans, but cattle and honeybees as well. These events will be associated with an arms race between France, and unnamed eastern countries. The war will eventually carry to Rome, and the Papal seat, itself. While Nostradamus does not name the countries of "the East" that are arming themselves in quatrain (14), he does in another quatrain:

**(22) Century 3, Quatrain 60**

Through all of Asia a great
  military call-up,
Even in Mysia, Lycia and Pamphilia.
Blood spilled because
  of the absolution
Of a black young one
  filled with felony.

*Par toute Asie grande proscription,*
*Même en Mysie, Lysie, et Pamphilie.*
*Sang versera par absolution*
*D'un jeune noir rempli de félonie.*

Mysia, Lycia, and Pamphilia are all located in Asia Minor. Since the third line indicates the spilling of blood, the "great military call-up" will lead to war. The leader of the Asian forces is described as "a black young one filled with felony," with "black" better translated as "evil" rather than a reference to skin color.

The quatrain just prior to (22) in Nostradamus' numbering system provides a good continuation of the war theme:

**(23) Century 3, Quatrain 59**

| | |
|---|---|
| Barbarian empire | *Barbare empire par le tiers usurpé,* |
| through the third usurped, | *La plupart de son sang mettra à mort:* |
| The majority of his blood | *Par mort sénile par lui le quart frappé,* |
| brought to death: | *Pour peur que sang* |
| Through death senility by him | *par le sang ne soit mort.* |
| the fourth struck, | |
| For fear that blood by the blood | |
| be not dead. | |

While in this quatrain the nationality of the "Barbarian empire" is not identified, in other quatrains it is clearly described as having a Muslim origin. The first and third lines here contain very clear references to the Book of Revelation. The "third" in the first line is similar to the "third of mankind" killed in the war described in Revelation. In the third line "by him the fourth struck" is similar to John's description of the war touching upon one-quarter of the Earth. The continual references to "blood" in the second and fourth lines also indicate war. The "blood" of the second line refers to the relatives of the man implied in the second line of the quatrain, probably the "black young one filled with felony" from quatrain (22).

Who will belong to this barbarian empire that Nostradamus describes? How does it arise early in the next century? Why will this "empire" begin what can only be described as World War III? The next chapter will answer these questions by showing Nostradamus' vision of the rise of a united Islamic fundamentalist totalitarian power in the Middle East.

# THE RISE OF AN
# ISLAMIC STATE

The March 30, 1992, issue of *U.S. News & World Report* carried an article titled "Iran's New Offensive." The article describes how Iran was the only winner of the Gulf War, and their plans in the aftermath of the war. With the destruction of much of Iraq's military and civilian infrastructure, Iran is stepping forward into the power vacuum in the Persian Gulf. They are spending over $2 billion a year on weapons, weapons that are well above their defensive needs. In addition, they are involved in joint military ventures with China, who is likely to be their major arms supplier in the next century.

That Iran is arming itself for war is evident from the following military purchases it made in just a short period of time during the early nineties:

1. At the end of 1992, several hundred Scud ground-to-ground missiles were shipped from North Korea to Iran. This particular type of missile is known as the "No Dong" and has a range of 600-800 miles, capable of striking anywhere in Israel from Iran. Libya and Algeria are also interested in the missile, which would enable Libya to reach southern Italy. Since Libya has already test-fired missiles into Italian territorial waters, the Italians are obviously concerned. If a pan-Muslim fundamentalist government should emerge and the Libyans and Algerians ally themselves with Iran, then Iran will have launching sites in North Africa that are capable of striking Italy and Spain.

2. In the winter of 1993, Iran purchased state-of-the-art diesel-powered Kilo-class attack submarines from Russia. These submarines are super-silent as they possess a unique propeller design, making them very hard to detect with passive sonar. The propellers are of U.S. design and Japanese manufacture and are state-of-the-art on current U.S. attack submarines. The large Japanese international corporation, Toshiba, inadvertently sold the plans for the propellers to the Russians, and now the Russians are selling the submarines to the Iranians. Iran plans to base these subs at the Straits of Hormuz, a narrow sea-lane through which 14 million barrels of oil, one-third of the oil used in industrialized countries, passes every day. It would be a great irony if someday these submarines were to do great harm back to Japan, Russia, and the United States. Future deals are also possible as the Russians have already indicated they will continue to sell these submarines in order to obtain hard currency and to maintain jobs for thousands of shipyard workers. Libya, Algeria, and Syria have all indicated some interest in purchasing Kilo-class submarines (Algeria already owns some). In this deal the Iranians also purchased SU-24 fighter-bombers and MiG-29 fighters.

3. In the spring of 1993, Iran purchased weapons from both Russia and Ukraine. The key weapons purchased in this deal were cruise missiles, capable of hitting ships in the Straits of Hormuz only seventeen seconds after launch from Iranian soil. Not only do these missiles threaten oil tankers, they are capable of sinking U.S. aircraft carriers as well. The deal also included another fifty MiG-29s and other aircraft, over 200 battle tanks, and a modern air-defense-system.

Besides purchasing weapons, Iran is actively developing clones of Western weapons as well. For instance, in the late eighties it was widely reported that Iran had captured a band of Afghan rebels near the Afghanistan-Iran border. The rebels were armed with U.S.-made Stinger hand-held anti-aircraft missiles. These missiles were given to the Afghan rebels by the U.S. to help in their civil war against their Russian-led government. Iran confiscated and dismantled the weapons, and later shared the technology with China. It should be assumed that by now both China and Iran possess Stinger-equivalent weapons.

This sharing of military technology between China and Iran is not unusual. During the Nixon administration the United States gave China the technology to build nuclear power plants, plants that could also be used to produce weapons-grade nuclear material. During the eighties China then shared that technology with the Iranians. Iran plans to develop operational nuclear weapons with Chinese technology by 1997 at the latest, if they don't already possess them. The collapse of the Soviet Union has created many opportunities for Iran and other Third World countries interested in acquiring nuclear technology, and even already built weapons. The prospects are frightening. For instance:

1. The Republic of Kazakhstan was given control of over 1,000 nuclear warheads when they were given their independence from the USSR. In May of 1992, the Russian Foreign Intelligence Agency reported that "several" warheads had disappeared from the previous Soviet Semipalatinsk nuclear test site in Kazakhstan. They further reported that the cash-poor Kazakh government had traded the nuclear weapons to Iran for oil and hard currency, a report which Iran has denied.

2. At Chelyabinsk-70, the core of the former Soviet nuclear weapons complex, the $50 per month salary paid to top nuclear scientists does not even begin to cover their basic needs. The CIA reports that the scientists are now being drawn away by better job offers in China, Iraq, North Korea, India, Pakistan, and yes, Iran. The experts being recruited most heavily are those with expertise in improving the range and accuracy of long-range nuclear ballistic missiles.

3. In July 1993, the Finnish newspaper Iltalehti carried a story about an undercover investigation they had conducted in combination with British and German television reporters. Posing as nuclear weapon buyers they met with a dealer in Moscow. Since a sample he provided was later lab tested and proven to be weapons-grade plutonium, they believed his offer to be genuine. The dealer was quoted as saying: "You want to buy. We can sell. We can let you have as much plutonium as you want. We can deliver fifteen or sixteen kilograms of plutonium-239 in ten days." This amount of plutonium is sufficient to make 3-4 Nagasaki-sized simple fission bombs. Even worse, he even offered two complete intercontinental ballistic SS-20 missiles, including their operational nuclear warheads! Now, if these are the offers being made to individual Western Europeans, who obviously do not represent their governments, what kind of deals are countries like Iran getting? The

resources of a country, especially an oil-exporting country, are far greater than the resources of any individual. It should be assumed that Iran, by 1999, will possess sufficient quantities of nuclear warheads and delivery systems to wipe Israel off the face of the Earth within minutes. Some experts even believe that Iran may have developed that capability during 1995.

In the middle-nineties, Iran's only rival for dominance of the Persian Gulf is Saudi Arabia. At this time Iran is incapable of defeating the U.S.-backed Saudi army in an armed conflict, just as Iraq was incapable of holding Kuwait. However, should the United States be unable to project a military presence into the Middle East for any reason, it is unlikely that Saudi Arabia could stand alone against Iran. In the early1990s Iran was still a third rate power, but so was Germany in the early 1930s. Besides, will the United States, or any of the Western European countries, be any better than third-rate powers themselves in the economic and social collapse after the meteor impact and tsunami? With the destruction of virtually all Atlantic port facilities and loss of high-tech satellites, it is certain that the West will be unable to fight a large war in the Persian Gulf, even if they were willing to fight. After a cometary impact and the subsequent collapse of Western economies Iran can be expected to control the countries of the Gulf, much like Germany in the late 1930s controlled central Europe. This control will be either by outright conquest or through diplomatic alliances.

Besides military development, what other national policies is Iran pursuing? In June 1993 U.S. Secretary of State Warren Christopher actually urged Iran's Western European trade partners to begin a limited blockade on Iran (an action that they refused) with the hope of destabilizing Iran's economy. Why should he recommend such an action? Christopher presented evidence that Iran is supporting radical terrorist groups trying to overthrow the governments of Egypt, Algeria, and Tunisia. State-sponsored terrorism is nothing new to Iran. Ever since the overthrow of the Shah and the establishment of a religious fundamentalist state, Iran has both actively and passively encouraged other Islamic peoples to overthrow their own governments and also form Islamic religious states modelled after their own form of government. CIA Director R. James Woolsey has called Iran "by far the most active and dangerous sponsor of state-organized terrorism in the world."

Iran's most commonly known terrorist-sponsored groups include Hezbollah (also known as the Islamic Jihad), Hamas, and the Popular Front for the Liberation of Palestine. Hezbollah claimed responsibility for the bombing of the Israeli Embassy in Buenos Aires in March 1993. The blast killed twenty-five and wounded 250. A statement released to the press claimed the attack was part of a campaign that will not stop until "Israel is wiped out of existence." So much for the Middle East peace process! Just as Israel's treaty with Egypt during the Carter Administration did not bring any real peace to the region, treaties with Jordan, Syria, and the Palestinians will not change what has been, throughout all of recorded history, the most war-torn corner of the planet. Lasting peace in the region will require the Israelis and the Iranians to come to terms, and even the most optimistic observers see no chance of that happening.

How widespread are the Iranian-supported terrorist groups? U.S. officials believe there is an international network of Iranian-based and controlled terrorists with operatives in virtually every country in the world, including the U.S. The bombing of the World Trade Center in New York and the bombing of the U.S. Marine barracks in Beirut in the 1980s have both been linked to fundamentalist groups that derive their funding from Iran.

How can a Third World country like Iran, where the unemployment rate hovers around thirty percent, afford funding these groups? Where is Iran getting the money from? In addition to its oil exports, partly from counterfeiting operations—the CIA believes the Iranian government has been counterfeiting high-quality U.S. $100 bills, the preferred currency among international drug and weapons dealers. In the late 1980s the operation was fairly small, printing perhaps only a few hundred million dollars a year, but it is amazing how far just a few hundred million dollars will go with a terrorist group. For instance, the bombing of the World Trade Center cost no more than a few thousand dollars, yet nearly paralyzed a significant portion of the economy of one of the world's financial capitals. The CIA thinks that Iran hoped to be putting out as much as $15 billion of counterfeit money annually by the year 2000. In fact, it was primarily because of Iran's counterfeiting operation that the U.S. released a redesigned, harder-to-counterfeit $100 bill.

As a fringe benefit to helping fund its terrorist operations, Iran hopes that its counterfeiting operations will help to destabilize the

American monetary system. Iran and the United States have already entered into an undeclared economic war, with each trying to destabilize the other's economy! How long can it be before the U.S. and Iran begin a shooting war in addition to their economic war?

In addition to sponsoring its own terrorist activities, Iran has provided training and arms for the fundamentalist government of Sudan, on Egypt's southern flank, and it is likewise supporting rebels trying to overthrow the government of Algeria. However, it is in the Muslim republics of the former Soviet Union that Iran is making its greatest efforts. Iran has sent thousands of "teachers" into these countries to instruct them in their version of the Islamic faith. Now independent from the spiritually barren USSR, these people have an opportunity to finally learn about their Islamic faith and heritage. Unless another view of Islam is presented to them, they will fall under the spiritual domination of Iran's narrow view of radical fundamentalism. Yet, no other country is actively courting these newly-free republics, and Iran's teaching is being unchallenged.

The response of the United States and Western Europe to this opportunity in the newly free Muslim Asian republics is equally short-sighted. The United States' interest in this region is so low that, as part of a budget-cutting program, the CIA has ended much of its intelligence-gathering activities in the region. Even Voice of America radio programming to this region is not being increased because it is "too expensive." In short, there are no other voices being heard in these countries besides Iran's cry of Islamic fundamentalism.

What will the future hold for Iran in the days after the comet? Throughout history difficult times have resulted in the rise of extremist authoritarian rulers. For instance, the economic hardships brought on by World War I led directly to the rise of communism in Russia, Nazism in Germany, and Fascism in Italy and Spain. The time after the appearance of the comet will be no different. Anarchy will then give rise to extreme governments on both the far right and the far left throughout the world. In the Middle East, the Islamic fundamentalist form of government, initiated by Ayatollah Khomeini in Iran in 1979, will spread wildly with the apparition in the heavens and the destruction it will bring.

Just as many Christians are fascinated with Revelation and the end time, so will be the Moslems, who have their own end-time traditions.

The religious significance of the comet will be explained by the fundamentalist Islamic ayatollahs as a judgment by God on a corrupt Western society, especially since North America and Europe will take the brunt of the destruction and the Moslem world will be spared the worst of the direct effects. Moslems throughout the Middle East will be listening closely to what these leaders will say. One of the major topics of conversation is sure to be "can this be the end of the world?" What do Moslems believe will happen before the world ends? Their end-time traditions are wrapped up in the appearance of a man, a man who will be the ruler of all Islam, a man known as the Mahdi.

The term *Mahdi* translates literally as "the guided one," meaning guided by Allah (God) himself. He will be guided so directly that he will be divinely protected against all error and sin in everything he does. His every action will be believed to be God's will, he will be incapable of sinning, and it will be his duty to interpret Islam to all men. Whereas Catholic teaching is that the Pope is infallible in certain limited matters of Church doctrine, Muslims (especially the Shiite division, which is predominant in Iran) believe the Mahdi will speak with the voice of God in all matters, not just religious ones. And more, the Shiites believe he will be not only a religious leader, but a political leader of military conquest as well, uniting all of Islam under a single fundamentalist Islamic government and later subjugating the entire world.

Traditions about the Mahdi, and about his appearance and attributes, are somewhat varied throughout Islam. The Koran has little to say about him. Most of the Mahdi traditions arose in the eighth century, when Islam was still less than 100 years old. Of the two major branches of Islam, the Shiites have a strong belief in the appearance of the Mahdi just before the end of the world, and he is the cornerstone of their end-time eschatology. For them he will interpret and apply the Koran rightfully and restore God's rule over all the Earth. His appearance is so important to them that the most repeated Shiite prayer is: "May God hasten release from suffering through his (the Mahdi's) rise." For the Sunnites, on the other hand, belief in a Mahdi is a side issue, and his future appearance is not essential. Also, if he does appear, for them he will not have doctrinal infallibility, since the Sunnite mullahs do not teach blind submission to any one teacher. In fact, this difference is one of the major distinctions between the two sects. However, while the Sunnite religious authorities may not acknowledge an all-powerful Mahdi, he will certainly be able to count on the support of the Sunnite masses if he arises in a time of great trials and difficulties throughout the Islamic world, in a time commonly perceived to be the end-time.

There are many traditions about what the Mahdi will look like and what he will do. Some of them are:

1. He will have the name Muhammad, and be a descendant of the original Muhammad, founder of Islam, through his daughter Fatima.

2. The name of his father and Muhammad's father will be the same.

3. He will resemble Muhammad in disposition, but not in appearance.

4. He will have a bald forehead, and a high, hooked nose.

5. He will have a V-shaped aperture between his front teeth, and a distinctive mole (the "mark of the prophet"), which some traditions place between his shoulder blades and others on his cheek.

6. He will appear just before the end of the world, during a time of dissension and difficulties, to once again restore a fallen and secularized world to the true Islamic faith.

While there are several traditions regarding his place of origin, the earliest describe him as coming "from the East," from beyond the river Oxus, which is today known as the Amu Daryu. This river, which flows northward towards the Aral Sea, forms the border between Turkmenistan on the west and Uzbekistan on the east. Other Muslim-populated regions east of the Amu Daryu besides Uzbekistan include the countries of Kazakhstan, Kyrgyzstan, and Tajikistan, as well as large areas of southern Russia, northwestern China, and interestingly, Mongolia.

The Islamic faith reached China and Mongolia only a few decades after the death of Muhammad, and despite persecution in recent years from communism, it thrives in northwestern China, particularly in Xinjiang province, as well as in Mongolia. There is a strong possibility that the Mahdi of Islam will actually arise from the same region that Genghis Khan came from! Was Nostradamus aware of this Islamic tradition when he wrote about a Mongolian (Moslem?) invasion of France? The connection is too good to be just a coincidence. If he was not aware of this tradition, then is it possible that he could truly have seen the future? Other Islamic traditions about the Mahdi include:

1. He will promote the "true faith" and make justice triumph. He will make law replace lawlessness and chaos. This is especially

interesting, since lawlessness and chaos will be commonplace as central governments collapse in countries all over the world after the meteor impact.

2. He will find the world full of ungodliness and evil, and he will "beat" men until they return to Allah (i.e. any questioners of his policies will meet with a swift death).

3. Muslims will follow him and he will reign over a single, united Muslim kingdom. Since the number of Muslims in the world is near 1 billion, this would indeed be a very large and powerful country.

4. The "Antichrist" will appear with or shortly after him. The Islamic Antichrist tradition is very similar to the Christian tradition. Near the end of the world, Muslims believe that a "great deceiver" will arise. He will seek to lead the faithful into a "false religion." For Moslem fundamentalists any religion other than Islam is, of course, a false one. While Buddhism and Hinduism are likely to be included in a list of false religions, Christianity would likely be named the most offensive "false religion," and it is from here that the "Antichrist" of Islam may be expected. Why will they single out Christians? They probably will because of the historically close link between Christianity and Western culture, and the perceived oppression of Arab Muslim peoples by the West, not to mention the memory of the Christian-initiated Crusades during the Middle Ages.

The Koran states that many will follow the Antichrist "only because he gives them food." As has already been shown, a time is coming (with or without the meteor) when the Asian states will need increasingly more food and will be asking Western Europe for more grain. Thus, Western Civilization in general, and one of its rulers (perhaps, as one of the most visible Christian leaders, a Pope?) in particular, will become the Antichrist for all of Islam. Large-scale famine will provoke enormous political distress throughout the world, and many will believe the end-time to be either near, or actually upon them. The masses of the Muslim world will be like dry tinder awaiting the spark of a man claiming to be the Mahdi to ignite them in a holy war, a new series of Crusades, against a food-rich Christian Europe. Interestingly, this is a viable scenario for the early twenty-first century even without the appearance of the comet.

Along with the appearance of the Mahdi, Muslims believe that Jesus (whom, interestingly enough, the Muslims honor as a prophet of

God, but not as God himself) will return in the end-time as a Muslim, either with or shortly after the Mahdi. The two of them together will destroy the Antichrist, but this "Jesus" will be subservient to, even *worship*, the Mahdi! Christians will doubtless be reminded of Jesus' words from the twenty-fourth chapter of Matthew, quoted once again here: "Watch out, and do not let anyone fool you. Many men, claiming to speak for me, will come and say, "I am the Messiah!" and they will fool many people. . ." For Christians, this "resurrected Jesus" of Islam will fit many of the criteria for being their own Antichrist!

Also in the Islamic end-time, along with the appearances of the Mahdi and Jesus, will be "Gog and Magog," terms familiar to any student of the Book of Revelation, but used differently by scholars of Islam. In the twentieth chapter of Revelation is written:

> After the thousand years are over, Satan will be set loose from his prison, and he will go out to deceive the nations scattered over the whole world, that is, Gog and Magog. Satan will bring them all together for battle, as many as the grains of sand on the seashore. . . .

The passage seems to indicate that "Gog and Magog" are names (probably symbolic) of future countries. (Incidentally, note that Gog and Magog do not appear until *after* the Second Coming of Jesus and his "thousand year" reign of peace on the Earth. This battle, known as Armageddon, is believed by many to occur *before* the Second Coming, but placing it at that time ignores the context of this passage from Revelation, which states that Armageddon cannot occur until *after* the millennial rule of Jesus on the Earth!) Muslim commentators, however, interpret Gog symbolically as "flaming fire" and Magog as "surging water" rather than as countries. The fireball of the meteor and subsequent tsunami will perfectly fulfill the Islamic expectations of Gog and Magog, and will further cement in the mind of every Moslem the nearness of the end, as they anxiously await the Mahdi and the return of Jesus.

There are still more predictions about the Mahdi:

1. An army will be sent against him from Syria, but it will be completely destroyed in the desert, possibly by a great earthquake. (Another of the aftershocks of the meteor-induced quake?) When that is seen, the rulers of Iraq and Syria will come and swear their allegiance to him.

2. He will take Turkey by force and will pray at the Mosque in Istanbul, the capital of Turkey.

3. After uniting all of Islam, the Mahdi will then conquer the entire world in the name of Islam. His troops are sure to quote Muhammad himself, who predicted the conquest, and later reconquest of Spain.

4. Under the Mahdi's rule there will be unheard of prosperity and riches for the faithful. He will give his followers more gold and silver than they can possibly carry away.

5. After accomplishing all of these things, the Mahdi will rule for five, seven, or nine years (depending on the tradition), and then will come the end of the world and final judgment by Allah.

In several quatrains Nostradamus described two men, who he referred to as "The Blue Turban" and "The White Turban," who fit perfectly into the molds of the Mahdi and the Muslim-Jesus. Those quatrains will be discussed shortly. But if Islamic tradition places the origin of the Mahdi as being East of the Amu Darya, from where will the Muslim-Jesus come? Nostradamus tells us in the following quatrain:

**(24) Century 5, Quatrain 55**

Out of the Felix Arabia country,
Will be born one powerful
   in the law of Mahomet:
To vex Spain, to conquer Grenada,
And further across the sea
   at the people Ligurian.

*De la Felice Arabie contrade,*
*Natra puissant de loi Mahometique:*
*Vexer l'Espagne,*
   *conquester la Grenade,*
*Et plus par mer la gent Ligustique.*

Arabia Felix is the southernmost part of the Arabian peninsula, occupied today by Yemen and the Aden Protectorate. The man described in this quatrain will be "powerful" in the laws of Islam, which means he must be a religious leader; yet since he will "vex Spain" and "conquer Grenada," he is to be a conqueror as well. Remember that the Muslim-Jesus is also to be a warrior as well as a powerful religious leader, since he is to kill the "Antichrist" of Christianity. Two of his military campaigns are mentioned here specifically, Spain and Italy. Once again, by predicting a Muslim conquest of Spain, Nostradamus' predictions fit well with Islamic end-time prophecies!

At one time there was a Muslim kingdom in Spain, the kingdom of Grenada. The Moors, as the Muslims were known, were conquered and expelled from Spain in 1492; but remember, Muhammad himself predicted that his people, after losing it once, would retake it! "Liguria" in the last line is a reference from Latin to the Italian city of Genoa. Since the attacks will come from "across the sea" the route here is via the Mediterranean from North Africa, probably Libya and possibly Algeria as well, into both Spain and Italy. For now the man in this quatrain will be called "The White Turban," also known as "the Muslim-Jesus." And what about the Mahdi himself? Nostradamus describes him as well, in the quatrain he numbered just prior to (24):

**(25) Century 5, Quatrain 54**

| | |
|---|---|
| From beyond the Black Sea, and the great Tartary, | *Du Pont Euxine, et la grande Tartarie,* |
| A King will come who will see France, | *Un Roi sera qui viendra àvoir la Gaule,* |
| Transpiercing Alania and Armenia, | *Transpercera Alane et l'Armenie,* |
| And inside Byzantium leave his bloody rod. | *Et dedans Bisance lairra sanglante gaule.* |

In the second line "A King will come who will see France." Given the context of the quatrain, he will obviously come to "see" it as a conqueror. The first line describes his place of origin. Since Nostradamus lived in France, "beyond the Black Sea" must mean to the east of it. But that is not all, he will also be from east of "the great Tartary." Since Tartary was the name given to the entire region of Central Asia from the Caspian Sea to China, an area now occupied by the Islamic Republics of Kazakhstan, Turkmenistan, Tajikistan, Kyrgistan, and Uzbekistan, to the east of that area can only be either China or Mongolia itself.

To get to France, this "King" will first conquer "Alania and Armenia." These areas consist of the modern-day countries of Armenia, Georgia, and Azerbaijan, as well as the southwestern tip of Russia located between the Black and Caspian Seas. After moving through these countries, he will continue into northeastern Turkey and will "leave his bloody rod," again indicating war and bloodshed, in the city of Byzantium itself. Byzantium is an old name of the modern-day city of Istanbul, in ancient times known as Constantinople, the capital of the Eastern Roman Empire. Remember the Islamic expectation that the Mahdi will conquer Turkey and pray in the Mosque of Istanbul? This quatrain can only be describing the Mahdi, as the first line accurately describes his place of origin and the last an activity which will be expected of him. This is yet another quatrain in which Nostradamus' predictions correspond closely with Islamic prophecy.

Note that to get to "Alania and Armenia," the Mahdi must first pass through part of territorial Russia itself. Nostradamus implies that Russia will no longer exist as a country; he definitely indicates that they will be incapable of stopping this incursion upon Russian territory.

Why would the Mahdi want to start his war here? The Christian Armenians and Muslim Azerbaijanis have been fighting for centuries. This struggle has greatly intensified since the breakup of the Soviet Union. The newspapers contain stories on a regular basis about the fighting between these two countries. The Mahdi will no doubt march here to "assist" his Islamic brothers in their fight against the Armenians. Before his death, Ayatollah Khomeini wrote: "We consider the world's Muslims as belonging to our own country (Iran) and always consider ourselves as partners in their fate"; a philosophy which is still held by the leaders of Iran. This theme of rescuing fellow Muslims from persecution will occur again in another chapter of this book.

In the Epistle Nostradamus addressed to Henry II, King of France, there is a section describing the origin of a man who can only be the Mahdi:

> ...Then the Great Empire of the Antichrist will begin in the Atlai mountains and Xerxes will descend with great and innumerable numbers, so that the Holy Spirit, starting from the 48th degree, will make a migration, chased out by the abomination of the Antichrist: who will make war against the Royal Pope, the great Vicar of Jesus Christ, and against his Church, whose reign will be for a time, and to the end of time, and it will be preceded by an eclipse of the Sun the longest and most dismal and gloomy, since the creation of the world until the death and passion of Jesus Christ, and it will be in the month of October that the great translation will be made, and it will be such that one will think the gravity of the Earth will have lost its natural movement and it will be plunged into the abyss of perpetual darkness, in the springtime there will be omens, and afterwards extreme changes, changes of kingdoms and great earthquakes with the rise of the new Babylon, miserable daughter enlarged by the abomination of the first holocaust, which will last for only seventy-three years and seven months. . . .

Note the rambling style of this letter. In this section (as well as the whole Epistle) not one period is used! While the entire letter is very interesting, it is also extremely difficult, most of it impossible, to interpret. The interpretation above is a paraphrase rather than a strict translation; a strict rendering would render the passage nearly indecipherable. However, note the themes present. First, the rise of the "Antichrist" of Christianity from the region of the Atlai Mountains of northwest China and western Mongolia at the 48th degree of parallel. Second, this man is compared with the ancient Persian ruler/warrior Xerxes, indicating a Middle East connection. Third, the presence of a religious war, conducted by this man against the Catholic Church and the Pope. Fourth, an eclipse (the August 1999 eclipse in Europe?) that will precede the rise of the "Antichrist." Fifth, a "gloomy" time beginning in October, which represents the spreading of the dustcloud over all the Earth. Sixth, changes of government the following spring in many countries. Seventh, this passage describes aftershocks of the Great Earthquake of the meteor impact. Eighth, the rise of a new, enlarged Iran ("Babylon") due to the "holocaust" created by the meteor, and the lasting of this "new Babylon" for seventy-three-and-a-half years. All of these themes are also found in the quatrains presented in this book.

There is another quatrain in which Nostradamus describes an attribute of the Mahdi:

**(26) Century 4, Quatrain 99**

| | |
|---|---|
| The senior valiant son of the daughter of the King, | *L'aîné vaillant de la fille du Roi,* |
| Will push the back so deep the French, | *Repoussera si profond les Celtiques,* |
| At which he will put thunderbolts, how many and in such array | *Qu'il mettra foudres, combien en tel arroi* |
| Few and far, then deep into the Hesperique. | *Peu et loin, puis profond ès Hesperique.* |

Remember that the Mahdi must be of the lineage of Muhammad, through his daughter Fatima. If *King* is used loosely as a ruler, then Muhammad was indeed a king, the ruler of much of the Middle East, since the religion he instituted controlled much of the region. Also, since the Mahdi is to be descended through Muhammad's daughter, Fatima, the Mahdi will indeed be a "son of the daughter of the King." The second line describes the use of missiles against the French. Whether they are nuclear-tipped is not described, but it is not likely. An exchange of nuclear missiles would make for a war much shorter than twenty-seven years! Perhaps the missiles are long-range Scud missiles with conventional warheads. It is not inevitable that nuclear exchanges must occur in World War III. After all, during World War II, no chemical weapons were used, despite their widespread use in World War I and widespread availability to both the Allied and Axis powers. Why were they not used? Each side was afraid to be the first to launch such an attack, because of the threat of instant retaliation with the same weapons. Even at the end of the war, the Germans apparently never even considered the use of chemical agents against the advancing Allied armies. Despite fears to the contrary, World War III could easily be a conventional war.

After the attack on France noted in the first two lines of this quatrain, the Mahdi will then attack "Hesperique." This is a Latin term for "the lands of the West," and was commonly understood by any Roman to be Spain. Here is found the linkage of the Mahdi with an attack on France, and this time Spain as well.

Nostradamus has still another quatrain about the Mahdi:

### (27) Century 10, Quatrain 75

So much awaited
    he will never return,
Within Europe, In Asia appearing:
One of the league issued
    from the great Hermes,
And over all Kings of the East
    he will grow.

*Taint attend nee revenuer James,*
*Dedans Europe en Asia apparatus:*
*Un de la liège issue du grand Hermes,*
*Et suer toes Roes desk Orients crotra.*

To properly interpret the first line, one must first understand what Nostradamus had in mind. Awaited for in Europe, the Mahdi will appear in Asia instead. Awaited for by whom? By the Muslims as their long-awaited savior? Perhaps, but then he probably would have indicated the location as being in the Middle East, not "within Europe." Awaited as another conqueror, such as Hitler, Napoleon, or Mussolini? Perhaps, but given Nostradamus' previously noted descriptions of the return of another Genghis Khan, he probably meant the rise of another Genghis Khan. Those awaiting the rise of the next world tyrant, like Hitler, from Europe will be mistaken. In this quatrain Nostradamus predicts that he will "appear" from "Asia" instead.

In mythology, "Hermes" was also known as Mercury. In Greek Mythology Hermes was the messenger of the gods, the god of cunning, travelers, and commerce. In Roman Mythology he was the personal messenger and spokesman for Jupiter, who was the ruler of both the gods and men. By linking the Mahdi with "Hermes," Nostradamus is indicating that this man, the Mahdi, will claim to speak as personal messenger for God himself. "One of the league issued from the great Hermes" testifies that many have come before him, claiming to speak for God. In the political chaos present after the meteor impact, this man will subdue all of his political opponents and "over all Kings of the East he will grow," consolidating his hold on Asia.

Returning to the theme of the invasion of Turkey is the following quatrain:

**(28) Century 5, Quatrain 25**

| | |
|---|---|
| The Arab Prince Mars, | *Le Prince Arabe Mars,* |
| Sun, Venus, Leo, | *Sol, Venus, Lion,* |
| Reign of the Church | *Regne d'Église par mer succombera:* |
| by sea will succumb: | *Devers la Perse bien près d'un million,* |
| Towards the Persian | *Bisance, Egypte ver. serp. invadera.* |
| close to one million, | |
| Byzantium, Egypt the | |
| true serpent will invade. | |

The "Persian" mentioned in line three is the same person as The White Turban/Muslim-Jesus. He will invade simultaneously both Egypt and Turkey (Byzantium), with close to one million men. Not only will Turkey be fighting the forces of the Mahdi on the northeast, but the forces of the Muslim-Jesus from the east, and possibly from the Mediterranean on the south, as well.

Why does Nostradamus mention conquest of only these two countries out of all the countries in the Middle East? These two countries are perhaps the most western of all of the Muslim-populated countries, both receive enormous amounts of financial aid annually from the U.S. government, and both have secular democratic governments. Of all the Arab countries of the Middle East, these two can be expected to resist the forces of Islamic fundamentalism the longest. All of the rest will either sign treaties with the Mahdi or be overwhelmed by fundamentalist revolutions. The governments of Egypt and Turkey alone will stand against the fundamentalist forces. However, both stand in the way on the march to Europe and cannot be bypassed. If they will not join the

Mahdi and his mission peacefully, then they must be conquered.

The armed resistance by both Egypt and Turkey to the Mahdi's forces will not be as strong as might be hoped, since the Mahdi and the Muslim-Jesus will be able to count on great support from the Muslim masses in both countries. Fifth-column partisan attacks from zealous citizens in both countries will be common and will undermine Turkish and Egyptian military effectiveness. Besides, with the impact-induced cessation in aid, particularly food, most Egyptians and Turks may see no alternative but to join the Mahdi in a march on a relatively food-rich Western Europe.

It is noteworthy that in the second line of this quatrain Nostradamus once again links these events with the conquest of Italy and the Vatican; this time by a sea invasion. Once again, it is these recurring themes, found in separate quatrains, that allow other themes found in the same quatrain to be interlinked with each other and form a complete picture of Nostradamus' vision.

In the first line he provides a planetary conjunction: when the Sun and Venus are both in Leo. Since Mars was the ancient god of war, its inclusion here probably represents the warlike nature of "the Arab Prince," rather than part of the conjunction. Regardless, this is a common conjunction. Using traditional astrological constellation boundaries, the Sun enters Leo every year on July 23 and leaves on August 22. As the orbit of Venus lies inside Earth's orbit, Venus never appears to be very far away from the Sun in the sky. As a result, having both the Sun and Venus in Leo is a fairly common occurrence. It happens in the years 2000, 2001, and 2002. Additionally, If Nostradamus intended Mars as a planetary conjunction rather than as a symbol for war, that does not change the situation very much. Mars is in Leo during August of both the years 2000 and 2002. It would thus appear that in either 2000 or 2002 this invasion may occur in late July or August.

The theme of an invasion of Egypt is continued in the following quatrain:

### (29) Century 5, Quatrain 23

| | |
|---|---|
| The two contented ones will be united together, | *Les deux contents seront unis ensemble,* |
| When for the most part to Mars they will be conjoined: | *Quand la plupartà Mars seront conjoinct:* |
| The Great of Africa in terror trembles, | *Le grand d'Affrique en effrayeur tremble,* |
| DUUMVIRAT by the fleet disjoined. | *DUUMVIRAT par la classe déjoint.* |

111

The two contented ones are obviously the Mahdi and the Muslim-Jesus. They will be quite satisfied with the progress being made toward achieving a unified, all-encompassing Muslim nation at the time. Either they will be content when most of the planets are in the same constellation that Mars is in, or they will be happy when "for the most part" they are at war (since Mars was the god of war). If Nostradamus intended the first, which planets should be included? Just the ones known to his day, or should Uranus, Neptune, and Pluto be added? And just how many is "most"? If Nostradamus intended a conjunction, the possibilities are so many that it simply cannot be dated until after it occurs.

The only candidate for the title of "The Great of Africa" is Egypt, historically the only great civilization of that continent, a country with a history reaching back five thousand years. It may be trembling from an earthquake, but more than likely it will tremble from an invasion by "the two contented ones." DUUMVIRAT is an unsolved anagram, possibly a proper name for a naval commander. Who "the fleet" are and what they will be doing cannot be ascertained in this quatrain; however, "Egypt" and "the fleet" are mentioned in another quatrain:

**(30) Century 2, Quatrain 86**

| | |
|---|---|
| Shipwreck to the fleet from a wave near the Adriatic: | *Naufragà classe pèrs d'onde Hadriatique:* |
| The land and air trembles stirred up and placed onto the land: | *La terre tremble émuc sus l'air en terre mis:* |
| Egypt trembles increase of Muslims, | *Egypte tremble augment Mahometique,* |
| The Herald appointed to cry out to the east to yield. | *L'Héraut soi rendrà crier est commis.* |

Egypt has been a Moslem nation since the eighth century, so what is the point of line three? Why should Egypt "tremble" over an "increase of Muslims"? Could anything other than an Islamic fundamentalist conquest of a western-leaning secular Egyptian government be the cause?

In the last line, "The Herald" will be an ambassador, appointed to negotiate terms of surrender, and he will "yield" Egypt to the forces of "the east." These events will be associated with an earthquake, probably yet another of the many large aftershocks of the meteor strike. This one apparently will occur on or near the African-European tectonic plate border, since a tsunami ("wave") from the quake wrecks a fleet in the Adriatic Sea. Nostradamus does not say here whose fleet it will be, but since it results in the Egyptians surrendering, the fleet probably contains supplies, or even troops, from Europe. Since tsunamis have little effect in open waters, mounting up only when close to shore, this "fleet" must be in port or near shore at the time of the earthquake. This is evident from the second line, in which the water is "stirred up" and destroys the fleet by placing it "on the land."

With the surrender of Egypt, the final defeat of Turkey is all but certain. The campaign for Turkey will be picked up in the next chapter. For now, a look into the Mahdi's future:

**(31) Century 2, Quatrain 29**

| | |
|---|---|
| The Easterner will go out from his seat, | *L'Oriental sortira de son siège,* |
| Passing the mountains Apennine to see France: | *Passer les monts Apennins voir la Gaule:* |
| Transpiercing the sky, the waters and snow, | *Transpercerra le ciel, les eaux et neige,* |
| And each and every one will be struck from his rod. | *Et un chacun frappera de sa gaule.* |

The "Apennine" mountains run from north to south throughout central Italy. Implied here is the conquest of all of central Italy while the Mahdi is making his way to France. Since the Mahdi will cross the Apennines during the battle for Italy, it seems that eastern Italy must fall before the western portion does. Nostradamus makes this claim in other quatrains, as well, quatrains which will be presented in the sixth chapter of this book.

Nostradamus predicts that the invasion of France will take three distinct routes: "the sky," apparently indicating airplanes (imagine a 16th-century French physician writing about air assaults!); "the waters," easily understood as a sea invasion; and "the snow," indicating mountainous crossings (either the Alps, the Pyrenees, or both).

Note in the last line that "each and every one" will be attacked. Nostradamus is trying to communicate that this will truly be a "world" war. Since another expectation of the Mahdi is that after uniting all of Islam into a single country he will rule the entire world under Islam by the guidance of Allah, this is yet another reference to him.

There is a quatrain describing the length of the war that will come to be known as World War III:

**(32) Century 8, Quatrain 77**

| | |
|---|---|
| The Antichrist three soon completely annihilates, | *L'antechrist trois bien tôt annihilés,* |
| Twenty and seven years of blood will last his war: | *Vingt et sept ans sang durera sa guerre:* |
| The heretics dead, captives exiled, | *Les hérétiques morts, captifs exilés,* |
| Bloody corpses human water red hail on the earth. | *Sang corps humain eau rougie grêler terre.* |

Here, as in his Epistle, Nostradamus mentions the "Antichrist." In his Epistle to King Henry of France Nostradamus writes of three separate people to whom he gives the title of "Antichrist." These individuals have two main characteristics in common that apparently earn them that title. First, they wage war on France, destroying the country and killing the people, and second, they are enemies of the Christian faith as well. There has been much written by many of Nostradamus' commentators about these three individuals. Some feel that the first two have already come in the persons of Napoleon and Hitler (the first line of this quatrain could also be read as "The third Antichrist"). Perhaps, but regardless of which Antichrist he is, Nostradamus names the Mahdi among the three.

Contained in the third line is Nostradamus' prediction that the war will last for twenty-seven years! In the decimated, post-industrial society following the comet, a long, drawn-out non-nuclear war might be expected. After the conclusion of the war, a group that Nostradamus labels as "the heretics" will be dead. Nostradamus does not say whether these heretics will be Europeans who side with the Muslims (possible) or the Muslims themselves (more likely), but note the religious significance of the word *heretic*. This religious, crusade-like theme of World War III is found in many of Nostradamus' quatrains. He also cryptically mentions exile for some "captives," either European traitors or captured Muslims. Both of these themes occur in other quatrains and will be returned to in a later chapter.

The last line contains a fairly graphic description of the horrors of war. It might be better rendered as: "Bloody human corpses, the water reddened from their blood, it will be so red that it will look like it hailed blood on the earth."

Quatrains describing both the Mahdi and the Muslim-Jesus as separate individuals have been outlined. It might be enough to link them as allies, since they both invade Western Europe, but Nostradamus has two quatrains that link them together in time and space. One of those quatrains is appropriate at this juncture:

**(33) Century 9, Quatrain 73**

Into Foix will enter a King
    with a Blue Turban,
And reign for less than
    one revolution of Saturn:
King Turban white to
    Byzantium his heart banished,
Sun, Mars, Mercury near the Urn.

*Dans Fois entré Roi ceiulee Turban,*
*Et regnera moins évolu Saturne:*
*Roi Turban blanc Bizance coeur ban,*
*Sol, Mars, Mercure près la hurne.*

What links either of these with the Mahdi and the Muslim-Jesus? The Mahdi has already been mentioned as marching into France, and Foix is a city in southwestern France. Not only that, it was held by the Muslims as part of the kingdom of Grenada for nearly thirty years, an extension of their conquest of Spain. Also, the Mahdi's war will last twenty-seven years, and the "Blue Turban" will reign "for less than one revolution of Saturn," which is twenty-nine-and-one-half years. Finally, the wearing of turbans of either a Persian blue or white color is common among Muslim leaders. There can be no doubt that in this quatrain Nostradamus is writing about the Mahdi, and his associate, the Muslim-Jesus.

The last line gives a planetary configuration, "Sun, Mars, Mercury" near the constellation Aquarius ("the Urn"). While trying to date the astrological configuration of the last line is tempting, the attempt is probably useless. Why should this be so? First of all, how did Nostradamus arrive at this configuration? No one knows. Did he see into the future, see a date, then calculate forward given his knowledge of the motion of the planets? If he did, then all of his conjunctions are wrong, since knowledge of planetary motion was imprecise in the 16th-century. Any calculation Nostradamus might have made with a given planet might be inaccurate by several constellations in several hundred years. On the other hand, if while seeing into the future he recorded the actual planetary configurations, then the alignment given will be accurate. However, it should be noted that most other commentators on Nostradamus' predictions have obviously used inaccurate calculations. This can be quickly and easily verified by using any number of astronomical computer programs that have become available in the last few years. These programs quickly give incredibly accurate star and planetary positions from any point on Earth for many thousands of years in the past and into the future. Upon using several of these programs, the author of this book found *no* correlation with *any* of the predicted dates quoted by other Nostradamian commentators for his planetary alignments. Anyway, this particular conjunction must be fairly common. The Sun and Mercury are in Aquarius for one month out of the year, and Mars passes through it no more than every two-and-a-half years. Having all three together is not at all rare. Besides, they do not have to even be in Aquarius, just "near" it. This configuration may be helpful in providing verification after the fact, but can hardly be used as a predictor for the date of the event.

After the events described above have occurred, what will the political state of the Middle East be? There will be a single Muslim state dominating all of the Arab Middle East except Turkey, with which it will be at war. Surprisingly, Nostradamus has nothing to say about Israel. Was he not aware of the prediction in the Holy Scriptures of the restoration of a Jewish state? If not, then perhaps he was just a fraud, after all. Or perhaps he was silent for his own reasons. Perhaps the fate of Israel was not revealed to him. If so, there are four possible futures for Israel. First, Israel might be destroyed before the appearance of the comet. This could be easily achieved by an Iran that possesses long-range nuclear-tipped Scud missiles in the late nineties. In a surprise attack, with only a dozen or so missiles, Israel could be completely destroyed in less than an hour, long before any of the Western powers could react. And with a third of the world's oil supply at risk as it flows past a nuclear-armed Iran through the Straits of Hormuz, would the West counter-attack to punish Iran? This would be a very risky war, much more so than the Gulf War, and with Israel already destroyed the West might not risk losing its precious oil.

The second possibility is that Israel could be destroyed by the earthquake following the meteor's impact and subsequent tsunami, or in the secondary earthquake and tsunami along the African-European tectonic plate border. Third, it could be destroyed by the Muslim armies before their march on Egypt and Turkey. Before they fall, the Israelis are likely to engage in a nuclear exchange with Iran, but in a suddenly food-short world, Iran would be quite content with the loss of even ten million or more potential starvation victims for the destruction of the Jewish state. The fourth, and least likely, possibility is that Israel manages to stay neutral through World War III and Iran simply bypasses it.

What about the rest of the world? As a Frenchman, Nostradamus was interested only in Europe, particularly in France itself. North America, South America, and Australia will be cut off from the events of Europe and Asia. Russia and Sub-Saharan Africa will collapse into anarchy, while Moslem North Africa will join Iran in a unified Muslim state. China, as Iran's primary ally, will protect Iran's eastern front by going to war against the Siberian region of Russia, India, and the countries of Southeast Asia. The southeast-Asian Muslim countries of Indonesia, Pakistan, and Bangladesh may also unite with Iran in a Muslim super-state. However, even if they do not unite with Iran, their combined population of over 400 million food-short Muslims will supply the Mahdi with fresh troops throughout the long, grueling fight that will come to be known as the Third World War.

# THE BATTLE FOR
# EASTERN EUROPE

The first four chapters of this book each dealt with separate themes, different ways in which the world could be dramatically and permanently changed from what it is now. The first chapter examined natural phenomena; in particular how powerful and devastating space objects can be to the Earth. The second chapter looked at Biblical prophecy from both the Old and New Testament of a coming disaster upon humanity, and a scenario of how those prophecies could be fulfilled was presented. In the third chapter the health of the ecosystems that permit the existence of human life were examined, and they were shown not only to be weakening, but weakening at an accelerating rate. The fourth chapter considered the Islamic faith, particularly its belief in the eventual rise of a man who will unify Islam and then wage war upon the rest of the world.

It should be noted that each of these four themes is independent of the others; for instance large-scale famine could occur within the next decade or two without the rise of the Mahdi or the fulfillment of Biblical prophecy. Also, a meteor could impact the planet at any time, not just the seventh month of 1999. Each of these events does not depend on the others for its realization. Even if Nostradamus was wrong, or this author's interpretations of his predictions is in error, it is still possible that any of these four world-changing events could occur at any time.

The wise will understand that not only can sudden, unexpected, and disastrous events occur, they eventually will. For instance, seismologists now say that there is a 90% chance that the Los Angeles area will be hit by a magnitude 8.0 or larger earthquake within the next thirty years. This will destroy a large part of the city and kill perhaps as many as 50,000 people. This thirty-year time frame puts it well within the life-expectancy of most L.A. residents, yet when questioned about it, one resident replied, "I try not to think about it." In contrast, the reader is strongly encouraged at this moment to "think about it." Consider how fragile civilization is, how easily it can be disrupted. Everyone should prepare for disaster as best they are able. Whatever happened to civil defense? The end of the Cold War did not end the need for it! Have all the grown Boy Scouts forgotten their motto: "Be Prepared"? Yet it appears that most are not prepared. At a most basic level of preparedness, who has stored just a few days supply of food and water in preparation of a possible supply disruption?

Preparation for disaster should not be limited to physical needs only. After all, men and women are not just physical creatures, they are living souls as well. Even if planetary-scale disaster does not occur, within a few short decades at most a personal disaster will fall upon everyone in the form of their own death. What about preparing for that? An eternal, living soul is the only thing that is taken to the next life when this life ends. Who is prepared for their death? It could come at any time! No one knows when it will come, but that it will eventually come is a certainty. Death is something for which everyone should be prepared; sadly, most could echo the words of the Los Angeles resident who said, "I try not to think about it." Think about it! The end is coming! If not for the entire world at once, then one life at a time. What happens then? The reader is encouraged to pause here for a moment and consider their eternal destiny. . . and to prepare for it.

While the first four chapters of this book dealt with different themes, any of which could occur whether Nostradamus is right or wrong, the balance of the book assumes that Nostradamus was correct in his forecast of a comet-related meteor impacting into the Atlantic Ocean in September 1999, and that the subsequent events included in chapters two through four are correct as well. Chapter four concluded with the emergence of a new Persia, dominating the Middle East, ruled by the Mahdi and his second-in-command, the Muslim-Jesus. Towards the end of the chapter they had conquered Egypt and were in the midst of fighting in Turkey. Continuing with the battle for Turkey is the following quatrain:

**(34) Century 5, Quatrain 27**

| Through fire and arms not far away from the Black Sea, | *Par feu et armes non loin de la marnegro,* |

Through fire and arms not
    far away from the Black Sea,
He will come from Persia
    to occupy Trebizond:
Trembling in Pharos,
    Mytilene, Sun joyful,
From blood Arab
    the Adriatic covered waves.

*Par feu et armes non loin*
    *de la marnegro,*
*Viendra de Perse occuper Trebisonde:*
*Trembler Pharos, Methelin, Sol alegro,*
*De sang Arabe d'Adrie couvert onde.*

"Trebizond" (today known as Trabzon) is a Turkish port city on the Black Sea, not far from Georgia. As "Trebizond" is not especially far from the Iranian border either, the first two lines would seem to indicate the initial stages of the Mahdi's campaign against Turkey. The attack comes from Iran ("He will come from Persia"), and appears to involve a sea invasion as well as a ground campaign. Pharos is an island off the Egyptian city of Alexandria. Mytilene, also known as Lesbos, is one of the most eastern of the Greek islands, only fifteen miles from Turkey.

If "Trembling" indicates an earthquake, it will be another of the aftershocks from the impact of the comet fragment. However, in this context "Trembling" could also be understood as "fear and trembling," in which case the islands of Mytilene and Pharos are symbolic for the fear and terror occurring in the countries of Egypt and Greece during the war. Note that this quatrain links an invasion into Turkey from Iran with a simultaneous attack upon Egypt.

The word *joyful* in line three can, by using the Italian word *allegro* instead of the old French word *alegre* to translate "alegro," be translated as "brisk" instead of "joyful," and this appears to be Nostradamus' meaning here. By the use of "brisk," Nostradamus is indicating that by the time of the Persian invasion of Turkey, the huge dust and smoke clouds from the meteoric explosion and subsequent firestorm will have precipitated out of the sky, allowing the Sun to shine brightly again. The time frame for this to occur must be at least a year or two after the impact, so the events of this quatrain cannot take place sooner than the year 2001, and quite possibly later.

The last line of this quatrain is something of a puzzle. The Adriatic Sea is bounded by Italy on the west and on the east by Albania and the countries of the former Yugoslavia, all far removed from the rest of the activity mentioned. It may be that Nostradamus looks further into the future with this last line, or it may be that the Iranian Islamic forces will make an early attempt in World War III to send troops against Serbia and Croatia to assist their Muslim brothers in Bosnia. If that interpretation is correct, then the civil war in Bosnia, much like the one in Afghanistan, will not subside during the decade of the nineties, nor will the other Muslim countries of the world forget the slaughter of their Muslim brothers in Bosnia while NATO and the UN did nothing to help. Whatever Nostradamus' intent, in the naval battle described here the "Arabs" apparently will not do well as the waves of the Adriatic Sea will be "covered. . . from blood Arab."

Continuing with the battle for Turkey is the next quatrain:

**(35) Century 5, Quatrain 47**

| | |
|---|---|
| The great Arab will march far ahead, | *Le grand Arabe marchera bien avant,* |
| He will be betrayed by the Byzantinians: | *Trahi sera par les Bisantinois:* |
| The ancient Rhodes will come to meet him, | *L'antique Rodes lui viendra au-devant,* |
| And more great trouble through Austria and Pannonois. | *Et plus grand mal par austret Pannonois.* |

"The great Arab" can be either the Mahdi (also known as The Blue Turban) or the Muslim-Jesus (The White Turban), but is probably the Mahdi. The conquest of Turkey will initially proceed quickly, probably with the assistance of Turks sympathetic to the Mahdi's cause. The front-line troops, at this point in the war probably mostly Iranian, "will march far ahead" of the supply lines and reserves. This would appear to indicate a quick, successful strike deep into Turkey.

In the second line the Turks regroup and somehow isolate the advancing Iranian troops and cut them off from their supplies. Nostradamus indicates that the Mahdi's troops "will be betrayed," apparently by the Turkish pro-Iranian forces. By this time the Mahdi's intent of invading Europe will be apparent, and the Eastern Europeans will be considering plans for their most optimal defense. The decision will be made to strike before the Mahdi can regain control of Turkey, rather than waiting for an invasion of their own soil. In the last two lines, Greece ("The ancient Rhodes"), "Austria," and Hungary ("Pannonois"), probably along with other Eastern European countries such as Rumania and Bulgaria that at one time were part of the Austro-Hungarian Empire, will seize the moment and launch a counterattack ("come to meet") against the Mahdi's ("him") troops in Turkey. The last line indicates that they will achieve at least some success, causing the Mahdi "more great trouble."

In still another quatrain the battle for Turkey continues:

**(36) Century 5, Quatrain 48**

| | |
|---|---|
| After the great affliction of the sceptre, | *Après la grande affliction du sceptre,* |
| Two enemies by them will be defeated: | *Deux ennemis par eux seront défaits:* |
| Fleet of Africa to the Hungarians will appear, | *Classe d'Affrique aux Pannons viendra naître,* |
| By land and sea will take place horrible deeds. | *Par mer et terre seront horribles faits.* |

In the last chapter quatrain (25) was presented and interpreted. The last line of that quatrain stated that the Mahdi would leave his "bloody rod" inside Byzantium, which is now the modern city of Istanbul. The "rod" of that quatrain may be the same as the "sceptre" of the first line of this quatrain. If that is so, then the first line of this quatrain makes reference to events just completed; i.e. the fall of Istanbul represents "the great affliction of the sceptre." "Them" in the second line refers to the Blue and White Turbans, again known as the Mahdi and the Muslim-Jesus. After the conquest of Byzantium (Istanbul) is complete, the Iranian-led Muslim forces will have conquered all of Turkey, and will then turn their attention against "two" enemies. Of course, it is also possible that "Two enemies by them will be defeated" refers to the just-completed conquest of Egypt and Turkey.

While Hungary today is a land-locked country, in Nostradamus' time the Austro-Hungarian Empire had ports on both the Black and Adriatic Seas. Since by the time of this quatrain the conquest of Egypt will have been completed, it is the forces victorious from the Egyptian campaign that will arrive by sea ("Fleet of Africa"). Their attack will probably be against Rumania and Bulgaria on the western shores of the Black Sea, across from Turkey. The fighting will involve pitched naval as well as land battles at that time, since "horrible deeds. . . by land and sea will take place."

Note that this quatrain is numbered 5-48 in Nostradamus' numbering system, and that it sequentially follows 5-47. As previously mentioned, Nostradamus numbered his quatrains by writing them in chronological sequence on separate pieces of paper, then throwing them up into the air. He numbered them in the order in which he then picked them up off the floor. While most of the quatrains are thus numerically out of sequence, it could reasonably be expected that some of the sheets would stick together, and thus still be in chronological order. This is the case here, and this pattern will be repeated again later in this chapter.

With the battle for Turkey over and the battle for the western coast of the Black Sea raging, Nostradamus turns to the battle for Greece:

**(37) Century 3, Quatrain 3**

| | |
|---|---|
| Mars and Mercury, and the silver joined together, | *Mars et Mercure, et l'argent joint ensemble,* |
| Towards the south extreme drought: | *Vers le midi extrême siccité:* |
| Out of the bottom of Asia one will say the earth trembles, | *Au fond d'Asie on dira terre tremble,* |
| Corinth, Ephesus then in perplexity. | *Corinthe, Ephese lors en perplexité.* |

The "silver" in line one is the moon, so the first line represents an astronomical configuration. Putting possible dates on the configuration at this time is meaningless, however, as this grouping occurs at least once every year. The "south" mentioned in the second line is difficult. Does it represent southern Asia, perhaps India? Or could it possibly stand for southern Europe, perhaps Greece and/or Italy? Or, since no country is mentioned, perhaps it is even a local drought in southern France? The answer cannot be ascertained. These events are linked with another earthquake, this time in the "bottom" of Asia. This would seem to indicate Pakistan, India, or perhaps even farther east.

The last line of this quatrain is intriguing. Corinth is located in Greece on the western aspect of the Aegean Sea, while Ephesus is in Turkey on the eastern edge of the Aegean. Nostradamus appears to be using these cities as reference points in the battle between Greece and the now-conquered Turkey for control of the Greek Islands. Perhaps the two cities will be the command centers of the Greek and Islamic commanders.

Continuing with the battle for the Aegean Sea is another quatrain that mentions both Corinth and Ephesus:

**(38) Century 2, Quatrain 52**

| | |
|---|---|
| During a few nights<br>  the earth will tremble:<br>Over the springtime<br>  two efforts in succession:<br>Corinth, Ephesus in the two<br>  seas will swim:<br>War stirred up by two<br>  valiant in combat. | *Dans plusieurs nuits<br>  la terre tremblera:<br>Sur le printemps deux efforts suite:<br>Corinthe, Ephese aux deux<br>  mers nagera:<br>Guerre s'émeut par deux<br>  vaillants de luite.* |

Obviously, one of the "two seas" must be the Aegean as it is the sea located between the two cities. The other sea could be the Adriatic, but since these events will be occurring simultaneously with a campaign against Eastern Europe in Rumania and Bulgaria, the Black Sea is the more likely choice. Predicted here are two major offensives ("two efforts in succession"), but Nostradamus gives no clue as to the identity of the aggressor forces or to the results of their "efforts." The "two valiant in combat" could represent the Blue and White Turbans, or possibly the commanders of the two opposing forces, headquartered in Greece and Turkey.

There is yet another quatrain detailing a battle for control of the Greek Isles:

**(39) Century 4, Quatrain 39**

| | |
|---|---|
| The Rhodians will demand succor,<br>By the neglect of its heirs delayed.<br>The empire Arab will<br>  reveal its course,<br>By Hesperia the cause redressed. | *Les Rhodiens demanderont secours,<br>Par le neglect de ses hoirs délaissée.<br>L'empire Arabe révélera son cours,<br>Par Hesperies la cause redressée.* |

The island of Rhodes is not only one of the largest of the Greek isles, it is also the most eastern one, even closer to mainland Turkey than is the island of Mytilene. At some point during the war of the Aegean, the Rhodians will send out an urgent call for help to the Greek mainland ("demand succor"). That help will be available, but will be "delayed" due to negligence ("neglect") of the Greek commanders, and Nostradamus seems to predict that Rhodes will succumb. At that time

125

the goal of the conquest of all Europe will be admitted to by the new Persian empire ("The empire Arab") as it "reveal(s) its course."

"Hesperia," the land of the west, will forge a united diplomatic alliance against "The empire Arab." While some authors see "Hesperia" as North America, in this context the expression probably refers to Spain, France, Germany, and Britain. These countries will pledge to assist in the defense of Eastern Europe, and will begin to deploy troops. It is highly unlikely that Hesperia indicates the United States since the U.S. will not be in a position to commit troops to battle at this time in the war; its domestic problems will still be severe.

Continuing with the battle for control of the Aegean sea is the following quatrain:

**(40) Century 5, Quatrain 95**

| | |
|---|---|
| Nautical oar will invite the darkness, | *Nautique rame invitera les ombres,* |
| The great Empire will it then provoke: | *Du grand Empire lors viendra conciter:* |
| The sea Aegean from wood jammed | *La mer Aegée des lignes les encombres* |
| Hindering the waves Tyrrhenian fleet. | *Empêchant l'onde tirrenne defflottez.* |

The expression "Nautical oar" in the first line is almost incomprehensible. All that can be said for now is that it appears to represent a person or people. Under the cover of "darkness" an attack by this person (or people) will be launched against Turkey. Evidently this will come during a lull in the fighting, and it will provoke another attack from the Mahdi's legions ("the great Empire"). If the placement of this quatrain is appropriate at this juncture, then the target of that counterattack will probably be Greece.

The Tyrrhenian Sea is located in the triangle between Sardinia, an Italian possession in the Mediterranean Sea located just west of southern Italy, Sicily, and Italy, so the "Tyrrhenian fleet" is probably of Italian origin. This quatrain appears to represent Italy's entrance into the war. However, the wreckage of ships in the Aegean from the fighting between the navies based in Greece and Turkey will leave enough debris to make "The sea Aegean from wood jammed" and "hinder" the Italian ("Tyrrhenian") fleet from operating as it wishes.

Perhaps the number of quatrains Nostradamus wrote about the fighting in the Aegean Sea indicates that this portion of World War III will take several years to complete, because there is still another quatrain about the battle for the Aegean:

(41) Century 2, Quatrain 3

For the fire of the sun on the sea
Out of Negrepont the fish
   half-cooked:
The inhabitants will come
   to cut them
When in Rhodes and Genoa
   will fail the biscuit.

*Pour la chaleur solaire sus la mer*
*De Negrepont les poissons demi cuits:*
*Les habitants les viendront entamer*
*Quand Rhod et Gennes*
   *leur faudra le biscuit.*

"Negrepont" is the Greek island of Euboea, the largest of the Greek islands and as close to Greece as Rhodes and Mytilene are to Turkey. "For the fire of the sun" is an interesting wording. If "the fire of the Sun" means sunlight, then a physical impossibility is present as the Sun's rays simply cannot get hot enough for "fish" to be "half-cooked. . . on the sea." But what creates the fire in the Sun? It is the power of the atom, released through the process of fusion, the very same process found in exploding hydrogen bombs. Here appears to be the first, and possibly only, use of nuclear weapons specifically predicted by Nostradamus during World War III.

Note that the nuclear weapon, or weapons, will not be used in a land attack. The entire world will be well familiar with the power of tsunamis by this time, and this represents an attempt by the Islamic armies to trigger a tsunami against the Greek coastal defenses and fleet. Since one of the main purposes of World War III will be to take over land for food production, it will be counterproductive to irradiate the farmland. Apparently, the Mahdi will not be as concerned about the sea. Perhaps he will gamble that the Allies will not want to raise the nuclear stakes with a retaliatory strike at a land-based target, or perhaps he will convince the Allies that the purpose of the explosion will be to obtain food, and the tsunami will be an unintended side-effect.

How can a nuclear explosion help feed a hungry populace? The concussion from the explosion will result in the death of many fish throughout the Aegean, and the hungry of "Rhodes and Genoa," obviously along with the Islamic forces in Turkey and the captured Greek Isles, will eat them. Implicit in this quatrain is a widespread food shortage in the Mediterranean region, since eating irradiated fish is only something the desperately hungry will do. "Genoa" may refer to the Italian city of Genoa, since it is possible that fish may be carried there by the Mediterranean currents, but it more likely refers to the Italian sailors from the previously noted "Tyrrhenian fleet," which may have Genoa as its home port. Apparently they will be in a sheltered location and avoid the worst effects of the tsunami.

The scene shifts slightly after the tsunami wipes out the coastal defenses, for the next quatrain details events within the Greek mainland:

(42) **Century 5, Quatrain 90**

| | |
|---|---|
| Into the Cyclades, in Perinthus and Larissa, | *Dans les cyclades,* <br> *en perinthe et larisse,* |
| Within Sparta and the whole Peloponnesus: | *Dedans Sparte tout le Peloponnesse:* |
| Very great famine, plague through false dust, | *Si grande famine, peste par* <br> *faux connisse,* |
| Nine months will last and all of the peninsula. | *Neuf mois tiendra et tout le chersonèse.* |

Larissa, still known by that name, is a major city of east central Greece; Sparta is located in the southern part of the Peloponesian peninsula; Perinthus indicates ancient Thrace which is now part of far-western Turkey, near the Greek border; but in this quatrain it is the third line that provides the key. Again the continual theme of "Very great famine" is found, placing it in the years after the comet. "False dust" is an expression difficult to understand, but since it results in a "plague" of some sort it appears to be some type of biologic or chemical weapon. The question here is whether the Mahdi will deliberately attack Greece with biological weapons, or whether an accidental release of Allied weapons will occur. The plague and famine will last for nine months and involve all of Greece, which is part of the Balkan "peninsula," as well as the Greek islands ("Cyclades"). If biological agents are used, then the plague, not surprisingly, will spread beyond the original targeted area and infect Turkey ("Perinthus") as well.

Note that quatrains (41) and (42) appear to involve very modern technology, with the use of nuclear and biological/chemical weapons. Those quatrains had no possible fulfillment until the latter half of the twentieth century. Apparently those weapons will be found unsuitable for use, probably because of unpredictable fallout patterns and resultant deaths among the attacker's units, because Nostradamus has no other quatrains about the deliberate use of nuclear or biological weapons during World War III after the Mahdi's conquest of Greece has been completed.

Continuing with events in Greece is the following quatrain:

### (43) Century 5, Quatrain 91

| | |
|---|---|
| At the great agreement | *Au grand marché qu'on* |
|    which will be that of liars, | *dit des mensongers,* |
| Of the whole TORRENT | *Du tout TORRENT* |
|    and countryside of Athens: | *et champ Athenien:* |
| They will be surprised | *Seront surpris par les chevaux légers,* |
|    by means of the light horses, | *Par Albanois Mars, Leo,* |
| Through Albania Mars, Leo, | *Saturne un versien.* |
|    Saturn a pouring out. | |

The chronological order of this quatrain (Century 5, Quatrain 91) and the previous one (Century 5, Quatrain 90) is apparently another instance in which the sheets of paper stuck together as Nostradamus threw them into the air, resulting in a correct sequential numbering. In the first line some sort of cease-fire or peace treaty ("the great agreement") will take place, but both sides will know that the other is lying ("which will be that of liars"). It will simply be a time to rest the troops, rearm them, and bring up reinforcements.

Who or what "TORRENT" might be is unknown at this time, but it would appear to indicate a place of some sort. The third and first half of the fourth lines indicate a surprise Muslim attack from a light cavalry unit ("surprised by means of the light horses") from "Albania," which will penetrate all the way to Athens. It is unclear if the Muslims will have secured Albania by a sea invasion themselves, or if the Albanians will ally themselves with the Mahdi, since 70% of the Albanian population is Muslim.

The last half of the last line appears to be another conjunction. "Poured out" is generally regarded as being symbolic for the constellation Aquarius, the water bearer. If this interpretation is correct, then the time when all of this will happen will be when Mars is in Leo and Saturn is in Aquarius. But remember, planetary motions during the 16th century were not perfectly understood, and a great deal of error crept in for prediction 400 years into the future! This configuration occurred last in 1993, and will not occur again until the year 2025. Is it possible for Greece to hold out for over twenty years while the rest of Europe is being overrun? Probably not, it is more likely that all of Nostradamus' configurations are inaccurate. Of course it is also possible that the author of this book is the one who is inaccurate! In that case, the reader is again encouraged to consider this book as an entertaining work of science fiction, a "what if. . ." dream. Other possibilities include setting this quatrain with a different war in the far future, and placing it near the end of WW III during the liberation of Greece, instead of early in the war.

Also of note in this quatrain is Nostradamus' last word: "versien." Nostradamus needed a word to rhyme with the word "Athenien" in the second verse. Apparently unable to discover a meaningful rhyme, he changed the spelling of the word "verseau" to "versien" to get his rhyme. While Nostradamus had many talents and skills, he was never famous as a great poet!

Returning to the theme of a plague in Greece is the following:

**(44) Century 9, Quatrain 91**

| | |
|---|---|
| The horrible plague Perinthus and Nicopolis, | *L'horrible peste Perynté et Nicopolle,* |
| The Peninsula will it fall upon and Macedonia: | *Le Chersonèse tiendra et Marceloyne:* |
| The Thessalonians will be devastated and the Amphipolians, | *La Thessalie vastera l'Amphipolle,* |
| A malice unknown, and refused by Anthony. | *Mal inconnu, et le refus d'Anthoine.* |

The events of this quatrain are remarkably similar to those of quatrain (42). Nostradamus evidently thought this theme was well worth repeating. Once again a "horrible plague," or perhaps the same plague as the one in quatrain (42), is mentioned for the entire Grecian peninsula. He describes this "plague" as being a "malice," indicating here that it will be an intentional attack and not an accident. The fact that it will be "unknown" would seem to indicate that this will be a new type of disease. It is possible, however, that Nostradamus also meant that this will be a use of biological weapons that will be "unknown" in war before this time.

It is not known at this time who the "Anthony" of the last line will be. He would appear to be a Greek military or civilian leader, who will refuse to use biological weapons in return. As noted before, after the campaign for Greece there seems to be no deliberate use of these types of weapons during World War III. Nostradamus then mentions specific cities: Nicopolis, which is the present-day Adriatic port city of Preveza; Perinthus, already described as being in far-northwestern Turkey; Amphipholis, near the present-day city of Salonika in Macedonia; and Thessaly, which is located on the Aegean Sea in northeastern Greece. In the second line the region of "Macedonia" is also mentioned. Note that ancient Macedonia is divided up between modern Greece and Bulgaria, so it is likely that the "plague" will spread northward into the Balkans, and may carry eastward into Turkey and other lands controlled by the Mahdi as well.

And a final note about the battle for Greece:

**(45) Presage 129 Novembre.**

| | |
|---|---|
| The enemy afraid to fall back into Thrace, | *L'ennemi tant à craindre retirer en Thracie,* |
| Leaving cries, howling, and pillage desolated: | *Laissant cris, hurlements, et pille désolée:* |
| To leave noise on land and sea, religion murdered, | *Laisser bruit mer et terre, religion mutrie,* |
| Jovial ones routed, every sect afflicted. | *Joviaux mis en route, toute secte affoulée.* |

At some point during the battle for Greece the Islamic forces, fearing a counterattack, will retreat by land and sea into western Turkey ("Thrace"). They will leave behind them "cries, howling, and pillage(d)" towns in which all the inhabitants will either flee or die, since the towns will be "desolated." The second and third lines indicate the two main goals of the raid; the "pillaging" (possibly a food raid?), and the execution of Christians ("religion murdered"). "Jovial" ones is something of a mystery. If Nostradamus' intention here was the ancient Roman god Jove, also known as Jupiter and the Greek god Zeus, then this may be an obtuse reference to Muslims, since both were pagans in his mind. If so, then the Mahdi's troops will be caught during their retreat and defeated ("Jovial ones routed").

Moving northwards from Greece is a quatrain about Macedonia:

**(46) Century 2, Quatrain 96**

Torch fiery to the evening sky
    will be seen
Near of the end and
    principal of the Rhone:
Famine, steel: tardy
    the succor provided,
The Persian turns
    invading Macedonia.

*Flambeau ardent au ciel soir sera vu*
*Près de la fin et principe du Rosne:*
*Famine, glaive: tard le secours pourvu,*
*La Perse tourne envahir Macedoine.*

Some type of celestial event described as a "Torch fiery" will grace "the evening sky" of eastern France. It will be visible from both the mouth ("Near of the end") of the Rhone river where it empties into the Mediterranean as well as the origin ("principal") of the river further northwards. This "fiery torch" is likely to be a fragment of debris kicked into orbit by the meteor's impact, which will re-enter the upper atmosphere and burn up while still high in the night sky. The visibility of the meteor at both the origin and mouth of the Rhone indicates that the path taken by the fragment as it re-enters the atmosphere will be along a north-south axis.

At the time that this meteor appears there will be "famine" and war ("steel" being symbolic for swords) in Greece, and the Iranian-led armies ("The Persian") will "turn" northward "invading Macedonia," on the Greek-Serbian border. For this to occur the "Persian" conquest of Greece must be considerable by then. Nostradamus also notes that help ("succor") to defend the remnants of Greece will arrive "tardy" from the countries of Western Europe.

Shifting northeast from Greece is the following:

**(47) Century 3, Quatrain 58**

Near the Rhine from
    mountains Noric
Will be born one great
    of people too tardy arrived,
Who will defend Sarmatia
    and Pannonia,
One will not know of him
    what will have become.

*Auprès du Rhin des*
    *montagnes Noriques*
*Naîtra un grand de gens*
    *trop tard venu,*
*Qui défendra Saurome*
    *et Pannoniques,*
*Qu'on ne saura qu'il sera devenu.*

A German or Austrian (the "Noric" kingdom in Nostradamus' time) commander will move his troops into the western republics of the former Soviet Union ("Sarmatia") and Hungary ("Pannonia"). Nostradamus accuses this commander of arriving "too tardy" on the eastern front, so perhaps the "tardy" reference in quatrain (46) pertains to him as well. This "Noric" commander will become a missing-in-action casualty, and perhaps his entire army along with him. In the confusion of the next world war, it may be possible for entire armies to be encircled and destroyed in the (soon to be) desolated vastness of Byelarus and Ukraine without any knowledge of their end being brought back to the West.

Continuing with the Eastern Europe theme, the Moslems continue their advance into Hungary:

### (48) Century 10, Quatrain 61

| | |
|---|---|
| Betta, Vienna, Emorte, Sopron, | *Betta, Vienne, Emorte, Sacarbance,* |
| Will want to deliver to the Barbarians Pannonia: | *Voudront livrer aux Barbares Pannone:* |
| By pike and fire enormous violence, | *Par pique et feu enorme violence,* |
| The conspirators found out by a matron. | *Les conjurés découverts par matrone.* |

"Betta," or Baetica, was once a Roman province, today it is part of southern Spain. Emorte is also in southern Spain. "Vienna" is the capital of Austria. "Sopron" is in western Hungary, very near the border with Austria. How can these diverse areas be related? It would appear that Nostradamus is linking the frontline of the war in Austria and Hungary with events occurring simultaneously in southern Spain, giving a picture of where the frontlines might be in two different areas at the same time. While the campaign for Spain will not be discussed until the next chapter it seems quite likely, with 200 million Islamic soldiers to draw upon, that the Mahdi will attack on all fronts simultaneously.

Some unnamed "conspirators," probably Hungarian, will plot to surrender Hungary to the "Barbarians." Nostradamus calls these "Barbarians" Muslims in other quatrains, so they would appear to be the Mahdi's troops. A comparison of the Blue Turban/Mahdi with Genghis Khan is appropriate at this juncture. When Genghis first surrounded a city he demanded its surrender. If it surrendered he spared the occupants (most of them, anyway), and enrolled them in the front lines of his army. If they refused to surrender he executed each and every one of them when the city finally fell, and then razed the city. That slaughter and burning of the city is symbolized here by the "enormous violence" and "by fire and pike." In the face of enormous pressures from the East, and insufficient reinforcements and supplies from the West, surrender and life will be an option seriously considered throughout Eastern Europe. The "conspirators" will be discovered, and publicly discredited, by a "matron," an older woman. Their future at the hands of their countrymen might not be a pleasant one.

Continuing with the attack upon Eastern Europe is another quatrain involving Hungary:

**(49) Century 10, Quatrain 62**

| | |
|---|---|
| Close to Sorbin for the assault of Hungary, | *Près de Sorbin pour assaillir Ongrie,* |
| The herald of Brudes will come to inform them: | *L'héraut de Brudes les viendra avertir:* |
| Chief of Byzantium, Solin of Slavonia, | *Chef Bizantin, Sallon de Sclauonie,* |
| To the law of the Arabs he will convert them. | *A loi d'Arabes les viendra convertir.* |

This is yet another instance in which Nostradamus numbered two quatrains in what was their original chronological order. In the Middle Ages "Sorbin," also known as the Sorbian March, was found south of the Elbe river below the city of Wittenberg, and it extended as far as Bohemia. Wittenberg, a German city, is located south of Berlin, approximately eighty miles from the Polish border, so the "Arabs" will have succeeded at this time in carrying out a great sweeping move to the north through Poland and the eastern part of Germany. After completing that, they will turn south, through the remnants of Slovakia and the Czech Republic, in order to isolate Hungary.

The "Herald" from the city of "Brudes" (also known as Buda, or Bude, it was once the capital of Turkish Hungary) will come to discuss the terms of surrender. Ancient "Slavonia" was bounded by the Drave, Danube, Theiss, and Save Rivers. This area is now part of Croatia, Slovenia, and southern Austria. "Solin" is a now-abandoned city near the present-day Croatian city of Dubrovnik. While the conquest of the former Yugoslavia has not even been discussed yet, in this quatrain it has already been finished.

Under attack from the north, east, and south, and in danger of having their supply lines cut from the west, Hungary will be in dire straits. Apparently they will surrender to the Islamic hordes as a leader headquartered in Croatia, called the "Chief of Byzantium" (the White Turban/Muslim Jesus, perhaps?) will come and convert the Hungarians to Islamic religious and civilian law ("the law of the Arabs"). Perhaps those who sought to surrender to the Mahdi will survive, even prosper, after all. In the tradition of Genghis Khan, the Hungarians will then be forced to march against Western Europe. . . at gun point.

Moving westward, the next quatrain details an attack upon the former Czechoslovakia:

### (50) Century 9, Quatrain 94

Weak galleys will be
  united together,
Enemies false the most strong
  on the rampart:
Weak assaulted Bratislava trembles,
Lubeck and Meissen will
  take the barbarian part.

*Faibles galères seront unies ensemble,*
*Ennemis faux le plus fort en rempart:*
*Faibles assailies Vratislaue tremble,*
*Lubecq et Mysne tiendront*
  *barbare part.*

In the third line Nostradamus predicts that "Bratislava," a port on the Danube River and the current capital of Slovakia, will be attacked. The first line is obscure, but appears to indicate that river boats ("Weak galleys") from two different armies will be used ("united together"). "Lubeck" is a city on the Baltic Sea, "Meissen" a city on the Elbe River, near the German-Czech border. They are several hundred miles apart, so how can they be connected with the events taking place in "Bratislava"? The key is in the second line. "False enemies" are enemies who should be allies instead. Here the citizens of areas recently conquered by the Mahdi, "Lubeck" and "Meissen," will be forced to assist ("take the barbarian part") in the attack against the capital of Slovakia.

Why will the citizens of Eastern Europe join the Mahdi, perhaps even willingly, in attacking the West? One of the reasons may be due to the strategy that the Allies will be forced to adopt at the time. Drawing upon the Muslim masses of all of Asia, the forces of the Mahdi will outnumber the troops of the West by a comfortable margin, perhaps in some battles by a ratio of more than ten-to-one.

While the West will possess superior weaponry early in the war, the high-maintenance and expense of producing replacements will erode the West's firepower advantage after just a few years of combat. Also, events like the one that transpired in Bosnia during the spring of 1994 are enlightening. During a one-plane raid upon a Serbian position, the first two bombs that were dropped failed to explode, the third failed to release from the aircraft, and the fourth was off target, destroying only two Serbian tents. The cost of those four bombs was $12 million, the payoff two tents! During World War III the Muslims will gladly trade two tents for $12 million dollars' worth of armaments. Nor does this $12 million figure include the wear on the aircraft, or the potential loss of a plane with a production cost in the hundreds of millions of dollars from a Stinger-type anti-aircraft missile costing only in the hundreds of thousands of dollars. Yes, the Islamic armies will accept even tremendous casualties during the early years of the war in order to erode the superior weaponry of the West. After all, the root cause of World War III will be a fight over resources, especially food, and the Mahdi will be having trouble feeding his troops anyway. Half a division destroyed in battle will be worth more than a full-strength half-fed division.

Besides the cost of producing hi-tech weaponry, the tremendous damage caused by the earthquake and tsunami to the industrial capabilities of the U.S. and Western Europe make it doubtful that the West will be capable of replacing, at any cost, the F-16s, attack helicopters, and main battle tanks lost due to combat or mechanical failure in the early years of the war. The Western leaders, when they will become aware of the Mahdi's strategy of trading millions of his soldiers' lives just to wear out the West's weapons, will be forced to use those weapons sparingly. As a result they will not be able to afford being drawn into an all-out battle in Eastern Europe. Even if they gain a great tactical victory, their material losses will be irreplaceable, while the Mahdi will have a continual supply of tens of millions of new Asian Islamic troops and easily replaced relatively low-technology weapons to draw upon.

Given the West's difficulty in producing and replacing advanced weapons and their numerical inferiority, what will be their strategy? Remember that quatrain (47) described an entire Western European army simply disappearing into the vast plains of Eastern Europe while trying to stand and fight. That is not something the West will be able to afford, so a new strategy will be adopted. Simply put, the West will have to trade land for time. They will fortify themselves behind superior defensive positions and use field artillery and small-arms fire in order to kill as many Muslims as possible. When the Muslims, through the sheer strength of their numbers, break through the front or flank a position, the West will withdraw to their next prepared position. Counterattacks will be local and limited. The West will not even attempt a major offensive until they are sure that they can crush the forces of Islam and drive the Mahdi from Europe permanently. It is likely that some of the Eastern European rulers will know that the West will be unable to protect them from the Mahdi, and that the West will make no effort to even try a permanent defensive stand. Instead of allowing the West to destroy their countries by fighting the Muslims every step of the way back to the Atlantic Ocean, some countries will instead opt to peacefully join the Mahdi. It will be their hope that doing this will spare their lands and civilian population the terrors of war. How successful this strategy will be remains to be seen.

Quatrain (49) indicated that the Balkans would be conquered. Leaving Central Europe and turning to the former Yugoslavia is the following quatrain:

**(51) Century 2, Quatrain 32**

| | |
|---|---|
| Milk, blood of frogs prepared in Dalmatia. | *Lait, sang grenouilles escoudre en Dalmatie.* |
| Conflict given, plague close by from Balenne: | *Conflit donné, peste près de Balenne: Cri sera grand par toute Esclavonie,* |
| Cry will be great through all of Slavonia, | *Lors naîtra monstre près et dedans Ravenne.* |
| Then born a monster close by and within Ravenna. | |

Here is the conquest of the former Yugoslavia. In an attempt to maintain regional continuity the quatrains have been presented slightly out of a strict chronological sequence. The events here must occur slightly before the conquest of Hungary.

The geography in this quatrain is dispersed. "Dalmatia" is today part of Croatia, "Balenne" is a small village close to the Italian city of Capua, and "Ravenna" is in northern Italy, very near the Adriatic Sea. Thus, while the former Yugoslavia is being conquered, Italy will be falling as well. The complete Italian campaign will be discussed in the next chapter. The "milk" and "frog blood" of the first line is obscure, perhaps "frog" is an indirect reference to the slaughter of French troops participating in the defense of Croatia, since "frog" has long been a nickname for the French. What type of "monster" Nostradamus had in mind for Ravenna is unknowable at this time.

And another quatrain about the former Yugoslavia:

**(52) Century 2, Quatrain 84**

| | |
|---|---|
| Among Campania, Siena, Florence, Tuscany, | *Entre Campaignie, Sienne, Flora, Tuscie,* |
| Six months nine days not rain one drop: | *Six mois neuf jours ne pleuvra une goutte:* |
| The strange language into land Dalmation | *L'ètrange langue en terre Dalmatie* |
| It will run over, devastating the whole land. | *Courira sus, vastant la terre toute.* |

All of the places mentioned in the first line are on the western Italian coast, west of the Apennine Mountains, from near Pisa in the north (roughly 150 miles south of Genoa) to about fifty miles south of Naples in the South. Since Nostradamus' time there has not been a drought of six-month duration in Italy, so this quatrain cannot possibly be fulfilled as of yet. World War III will probably be at least several years old by the time the "strange language" of a foreign army can overrun Dalmatia, so it is evident that the climactic disturbances caused by the meteor explosion will be felt for many years after its impact into the Atlantic.

One of the great difficulties in fighting WW III will be supplying the armies. Given the drought, the Italians at this time will have great difficulty even keeping their troops fed, let alone in any type of fighting condition. The "strange language" being spoken in Croatia will most probably be Arabic, the language of the Koran, known by Muslims worldwide. In the last line the conquest of the former Yugoslavia is again predicted ("devastating the whole land"), apparently by those speaking the Arab tongue.

The land of Dalmatia appears in yet another quatrain:

**(53) Century 9, Quatrain 60**

Conflict Barbarian in the
  Headdress black,
Blood shed, will tremble
  the Dalmations:
Great Ishmael will place
  his promontory,
Frogs tremble assistance Lusitania.

*Conflit Barbare en la Cornette noire,*
*Sang épandu, trembler la Dalmatie:*
*Grand Ismael mettra*
  *son promontoire,*
*Ranes trembler secours Lusitanie.*

In quatrain (51) "frog blood" was shed in Dalmatia, apparently indicating the death of French troops sent to help in the defense of Eastern Europe. Here is another quatrain in which "frogs" appear in Croatia. "Lusitania" is another name for the country of Portugal, its linking with and aiding "frogs" in the last lines indicates that the French will be fighting in Dalmatia at that time. In this quatrain Nostradamus shows them as being in trouble, and it will be the Portuguese who will come to their aid.

This quatrain contains one of the few references to Portugal found in any of Nostradamus' quatrains that appears to be relevant to World War III. Portugal, a small country, will sustain tremendous damage from the tsunami, but apparently enough Portuguese will survive the disaster, or have fled before the impact, to man an army. They will relieve an embattled French force in Croatia, under attack from a Muslim ("Barbarian") general wearing a black turban ("Headdress black"). This "Barbarian" general will establish his theater army headquarters ("promontory") in Croatia in order to coordinate the attacks into Austria and across the Adriatic into Italy.

Leaving southeastern Europe, Nostradamus has a fascinating quatrain about events that will occur in Poland during World War III:

**(54) Century 5, Quatrain 73**

Persecuted will be God
  and the Church,
And the holy Temples
  will be exploited,
The infant the mother put
  naked in shirt,
Will Arabs and Poles be allies.

*Persécutée sera de Dieu l'Eglise,*
*Et les saints Temples seront expoliez,*
*L'enfant la mère mettra*
  *nue en chemise,*
*Seront Arabes aux Pollons ralliés.*

This quatrain contains one of the common themes of WW III, that of religious persecution. Specifically, the destruction of the Catholic Church in Poland is predicted here. "The infant" and "mother" of the third line are probably the infant Jesus and his mother, Mary. This is either a symbolic reference to Christianity being thrown out (is it possible that Poland might really abandon the Catholic faith?), or perhaps a physical event involving two statues at a Polish cathedral. The last line is truly amazing. Nostradamus predicts that Poland will actually side with the Mahdi! Before dismissing this as impossible, consider recent history. Did anyone foresee the rapid deterioration of Soviet-controlled Eastern Europe? The stresses upon all nations will be far greater in the first decade of the next century and governments and public opinions will change with incredible speed. But how could devoutly Catholic Poland actually abandon the Christian faith and submit to Islamic domination? Once again, the answer is found in how Genghis Khan quickly rose to dominate most of Asia and Eastern Europe. He allowed his subjects who surrendered peacefully a great deal of independence in their internal affairs, and this will be one of the major concerns facing the Poles. Also, note that Poland is essentially a flat plain with no natural boundaries. There are no mountains or rivers providing any significant hindrances to invading forces. This is one of the reasons Poland has been overrun for centuries by armies from Europe and Russia. In the face of overwhelming numerical forces from the masses of Asia and little assistance from the West (all of the other quatrains regarding Eastern Europe during WW III show Western military aid as being either too late or inadequate), Poland will surrender and join with the Mahdi. There is something ironic here. Imagine, after being overrun by Germany in WW I and WW II, the Poles will actually have the chance to help overrun Germany in WW III! This alliance will create a gaping hole in the northern flank of the Allies, and will lead directly to the encirclement, and fall, of Hungary, Slovakia, the Czech Republic, and eastern Austria, described earlier in the chapter.

# THE COLLAPSE OF
# WESTERN EUROPE

After the conquest of Eastern Europe by the Mahdi, what will happen next? Will he be satisfied with dominating the eastern half of the continent, with controlling as much of Europe as Genghis Khan ruled? Sadly, Nostradamus predicts the continuation of the Muslim advance into Western Europe as well. This chapter details attacks on Italy, Germany, Spain, England, Switzerland, Netherlands ,and Belgium. France, due to the volume of quatrains specifically related to it, will be discussed in the next chapter. That Nostradamus saw the continuation of the Islamic advance into Western Europe and France is clear from the following quatrain:

**(55) Century 6, Quatrain 80**

From Fez the realm will reach
   to those of Europe,
Their city on fire, and
   blade to cut:
The great one of Asia land
   and sea a great troop,
So that blues, Persians,
   cross to the death pursued.

*De Fez le regne parviendra*
   *à ceux d'Europe,*
*Feu leur cité, et lame tranchera:*
*Le grand d'Asie terre et mer à*
   *grande troupe,*
*Que bleus, pers, croix à mort*
   *dechassera.*

The Moorish Kingdom of "Fez," which ended several hundred years ago, was located in North Africa. Since its capital city is now part of Morocco, perhaps Nostradamus is referring to that country in this quatrain. As Morocco was also the jumping-off point for the Muslim invasions that captured Spain centuries ago, using the name "Fez" here appears to be an obscure reference to Muhammad's prediction of the two conquests of Spain that his followers would carry out. North Africa is also home to what the United States has referred to as a "renegade" government in Libya, and a developing Islamic-fundamentalist movement in Algeria, which may eventually topple the government there. After the fall of Egypt, all of the countries of Muslim North Africa can be expected to quickly align themselves with the Mahdi and actively fight in World War III. Attacks from North Africa will be made across the Mediterranean at targets in Italy and Spain.

The first two lines of this quatrain indicate Nostradamus' belief that troops from North Africa ("from Fez") will invade Europe ("will reach to those of Europe"), burning down a city ("their city on fire") that he does not name. During this great war, many cities are likely to be burned to the ground, so which city Nostradamus had in mind cannot be ascertained here. "The great one of Asia" is the Blue Turban, mentioned here as "blues." He and his followers ("Persians") will invade by "land" (from Eastern Europe) "and sea" (from North Africa). The last line describes the troops of the Blue Turban/Mahdi chasing down the European troops if they retreat ("cross to the death pursued"). Note again the religious nature of World War III as the Muslims will fight against the "cross," an obvious reference to Christians.

Another quatrain, while not specifically mentioning the nationality of the attackers, fits well into the theme of a broad attack on Western Europe:

### (56) Century 5, Quatrain 94

| | |
|---|---|
| He will translate into greater Germany, | *Translatera en la grande Germanie,* |
| Brabant and Flanders, Ghent, Bruges, and Boulogne: | *Brabant et Flandres, Gand, Bruges, et Bologne:* |
| The truce feigned, the great Duke of Armenia | *La trêve feinte, le grand Duc d'Armenie* |
| Will assail Vienna and Cologne. | *Assaillira Vienne et la Cologne.* |

This particular quatrain makes more sense by reading the last two lines first. The Mahdi will be "the great Duke of Armenia." Why is this so? Well, since the Mahdi was described in quatrain (31) as being "The Easterner" who "will go out from his seat," and since in quatrain (25) he is described as "Transpiercing Alania and Armenia," it is apparent that he will move his base of operations to that region. It also makes good military sense because he will then be able to use Armenia as his base of operations for the invasion of Turkey. After the conquest of Turkey he will deny further intentions of war ("the truce feigned") while gathering his forces for an invasion of Eastern Europe.

The first line of this quatrain indicates that the Mahdi will "translate," or transfer, his command center from Armenia into Germany as his new theater of operations moves farther to the west. While the precise location of his headquarters is not mentioned in this quatrain, quatrain (58) names Mainz as the city. From there the conquest will be carried into Belgium and the Netherlands ("Brabant and Flanders, Ghent, Bruges") reaching all the way to the Atlantic Ocean, and even into northern France ("Boulogne").

There is another quatrain detailing essentially the same theme:

**(57) Century 3, Quatrain 53**

| | |
|---|---|
| When the greatest will carry off the prize | *Quand le plus grand emportera le prix* |
| Of Nuremberg, of Augsburg, and those of Basel | *De Nuremberg, d'Ausbourg, et ceux de Basle* |
| Through Cologne the chief Frankfort retaken | *Par Agrippine chef Frankfort repris* |
| They will cross through Flanders right into Gaul. | *Traverseront par Flamant jusqu'en Gale.* |

"The greatest" is the Mahdi, carrying off through conquest the "prize" of the southern German cities of "Nuremberg" and "Augsburg," as well as the Swiss city "of Basel," which is located on the Swiss border with France and Germany. The German cities of "Cologne" and "Frankfort" are both on the Rhine River, a natural defensive border, with Cologne being to the north and west of Frankfort. Apparently the Mahdi's troops will make a breakthrough at Cologne which, along with attacks from Nuremberg, Augsburg, and Basel, will result in Frankfort being encircled and "retaken" by the Islamic hordes, indicating that control of this city will change hands at least several times during the war.

143

After the great victory at Frankfort, the Islamic armies will sweep through the tsunami-devastated low countries of the Netherlands and Belgium (much of whose land is currently below sea level and likely to be permanently reclaimed by the sea after the earthquake and tsunami), on their way into northern France.

There is one other quatrain about events in Germany that helps to correlate events in Germany with those occurring in the rest of Europe at that time:

**(58) Century 5, Quatrain 43**

| | |
|---|---|
| The great ruin of the sacred things not distant, | *La grande ruine des sacrés ne s'éloigne,* |
| Provence, Naples, Sicily, Sees and Pons: | *Prouence, Naples, Sicille, Seez et Ponce:* |
| Into Germany, at the Rhine and at Cologne, | *En Germanie, au Rhin et la Cologne,* |
| Vexed to death by all those of Mainz. | *Vexés à mort par tous ceux de Magonce.* |

The geography here is quite varied: "Provence" is in southeastern France, "Naples" in southern Italy, the Mediterranean island of "Sicily," "Sees" in French Normandy, "Pons" just north of Bordeaux in France, the "Rhine" River in Germany, and the German city of "Cologne," located on the Rhine River. "Mainz" is near Frankfort, to the south and east of Cologne.

The "great ruin of the sacred things" places this quatrain during World War III, since it provides a link with the religious aspect of the next world war. The source of problems afflicting the areas listed in the second and third lines is the city of "Mainz." Strategically situated in central Germany, about midway along what will be the Allies eastern front, the Mahdi will move his theater headquarters there. From Mainz he will oversee campaigns against the rest of western Germany, Sicily, southern Italy, and various parts of France. This quatrain appears to indicate that along with the capitulation of Poland, the entire eastern front will collapse relatively early in the war since the "ruin" will be "not distant," meaning not too long into the war. Undoubtedly, the Mahdi's losses to get to Germany will be quite heavy, and the war may stall into a period of semi-peace for a few years while the combatants rest and new troops are trained.

How can Germany, a superpower in its own right, collapse to a third-world army like Iran while Sicily will still be free? While the answer is not entirely clear, there are several factors to consider. First, the nuclear winter after the comet is likely to do horrific damage to the entire German infrastructure, as well as the people. Deaths from the nuclear winter may be very high in Germany, perhaps much greater than on the Mediterranean-warmed island of Sicily. Second, located more in the heart of Europe and much farther from the warming effects of the seas than Italy or France, food production is likely to suffer greatly from late frosts in the years after the comet, and widespread famine is likely. Third, as a result of World War II, Germany's military is now primarily defensive in nature and is not as strong as might be hoped for in the event of an attack from Asia. Fourth, as has already been shown in the first chapter, Nostradamus predicts that the bulk of the Mahdi's forces will march across Europe, just as Genghis Khan did. After the collapse of Eastern Europe, Germany alone will face the bulk of the Asian hordes, which will be reinforced by the Poles and other Eastern European allies of the Mahdi. Fifth, while Nostradamus has many quatrains involving French troops in Greece, Italy, and Spain, he has little to say about French troops in Germany. It would thus appear that the Germans will be on their own to hold the eastern front while the French assist in holding the southern front with the other Mediterranean countries.

This chapter began with a quatrain describing an attack upon Europe from North Africa. There are other quatrains detailing attacks from North Africa into the underbelly of Europe. Here is one of them:

### (59) Century 2, Quatrain 30

| | |
|---|---|
| One who the gods of Hannibal infernal | *Un qui les dieux d'Annibal infernaux* |
| Will revive, terror of humanity | *Fera renaître, effrayeur des humains* |
| Never more horror nor more worse days, | *Onc plus d'horreur ne plus pire jounaux,* |
| Which will come through Babel to the Romans. | *Qu'avint viendra par Babel aux Romains.* |

"Hannibal" was the most famous general of the North African city-state of Carthage. He led an army over the Alps and attacked Rome during the Punic wars, over 2,000 years ago. Later, Carthage was completely destroyed by the Romans and the city and fields were salted to poison them. Today, what was once the verdant, beautiful city of Carthage is now in the middle of a desert. Nostradamus indicates that the "gods" will revive another "Hannibal" from North Africa, another general who will invade Italy. "Babel" in the last line refers to another ancient state, Babylon, which ruled what is today part of Iran and Iraq. This quatrain implies that the "Babylonians," along with the North African general "Hannibal," will attack Rome at the same time. Note that only a unified Muslim invasion of Italy could possibly bring together armies from both North Africa ("Hannibal") and Iran ("Babel").

There is another quatrain in which a reference is made to the Punic wars:

### (60) Century 2, Quatrain 81

| | |
|---|---|
| By fire from the sky the city almost burned: | *Par feu du ciel la cité presque aduste:* |
| The Urn menaces yet again Deucalion: | *L'Urne menace encore Deucalion:* |
| Vexed Sardinia by the Punic foist, | *Vexée Sardaigne par la Punique fuste,* |
| After which Libra will leave her Phaeton. | *Après que Libra lairra son Phaeton.* |

"Fire from the sky" appears to be an aerial bombardment of some sort, something impossible before the use of airplanes in combat during World War I. The "Urn" of the second line is the constellation Aquarius, and "Deucalion" was a figure from ancient Greek mythology equivalent to the Biblical Noah. In the third line, the Mediterranean island of "Sardinia" will be attacked by a "Punic," i.e. North African, "foist." A "foist" was a low, long, fast ship, propelled by sails or a single oar bank. The World War II equivalent of a foist would be a Patrol-Torpedo (PT) boat; today's choice would be some sort of fast attack ship. "Phaeton" was another figure from classical Greek mythology. He was allowed to drive the chariot of Apollo, the Sun god, for one day across the skies. However, he was unable to control the chariot properly, and Zeus finally struck him down with a thunderbolt when he feared that Phaeton would set the whole Earth on fire by driving the Sun too close to it.

What do all of the items above have to do with World War III? While the variety of events contained in this quatrain are somewhat difficult to link together cohesively, an interpretation is possible. During a raid from North Africa against Sardinia, an Allied city (somewhere) will also be under an aerial bombardment. The occurrence of these two events will be linked with the constellations of Libra and Aquarius, and with the classical Greek figures of a man who built an ark for a flood and another who was destroyed for bringing the Sun too close to the Earth. An obscure astrological conjunction, perhaps with Sun leaving Libra while a menacing planet (Saturn?) will be in Aquarius, is Nostradamus' intention.

There are still other quatrains with a "Punic" theme. Several will be addressed later, but one more is appropriate here:

**(61) Century 1, Quatrain 9**

| | |
|---|---|
| From the Orient will come the heart Punic | *De l'Orient viendra le coeur Punique* |
| To vex Adria and the heirs of Romulus, | *Fâcher Hadrie et les hoires Romulides,* |
| Accompanied by the fleet Libyan, | *Accompagné de la classe Libyque,* |
| Trembling Malta and neighboring isles vacant. | *Trembler Melites et proches îles vides.* |

The first line links the invaders from the "Orient," i.e. The Blue Turban, with those from North Africa ("heart Punic"). As an Islamic tradition is the only possible link between the two, and since an invasion of Europe is again predicted, the link with World War III is clear.

"Adria" is a small town near Venice in northern Italy, not far from Croatia, but it is also possible that Nostradamus intended the entire Adriatic Sea here. "Romulus" was a man from Roman mythology. Tradition has it that he was one of the founders of, and gave his name to, the city of Rome. Thus, the first two lines show armies from the south and the east attacking Venice and Rome, supported by ships from Libya. Meanwhile, the peoples of the smaller islands near "Malta," located in the eastern Mediterranean near Spain, will have been evacuated to Malta itself, where they will be "trembling" in fear (or perhaps yet another aftershock earthquake?) awaiting their turn to be attacked, too.

Sardinia and Malta are, of course, not the only Mediterranean islands. Nostradamus also describes an attack on Sicily:

**(62) Century 8, Quatrain 84**

Paterno will hear from Sicily cries,
All the preparations from
    the Gulf of Trieste,
Which will be heard as far
    as the Trinacrie,
On account of so many of sails
    fled, fled the horrible plague.

*Paterne ouïra de la Sicile cri,*
*Tous les aprests du gouffre de Trieste,*
*Qui s'entendra jusqu'à la Trinacrie,*
*De tant de voiles fui,*
    *fui l'horrible peste.*

"Paterno" is the name of a city in Sicily, and also the name of another town just to the north of Rome. If the former is intended the first line makes no sense, since it would read "A Sicilian town hears a cry from Sicily." However, if the latter Paterno is intended, then its nearness to Rome might render the first line as: "Rome, the Italian capital, hears a cry for help from Sicily." This will directly lead to "preparations" for a relief force "from the Gulf of Trieste." The city of Trieste is the most eastern point of northern Italy, only miles from Croatia. News about the coming aid will be heard in "Trinacrie," which is an old name for the island of Sicily. The last line indicates a great fleet of ships ("so many sails"), apparently from the Iranian Navy, and the presence of some sort of "horrible plague." Implied in the last line is the evacuation of the Sicilian population into Italy, people who will become refugees because of the war and the "plague."

This quatrain also allows for some correlation with events in Eastern Europe. For instance, if the armies of Islam are already in Croatia, then it is doubtful a relief fleet would be organized from the city of Trieste. Thus, it is likely that the campaign for Sicily will take place at about the same time that battles are occurring farther east, perhaps in Greece and Hungary. This thought is reinforced in the following quatrain:

**(63) Century 9, Quatrain 28**

Sails allied from the
    port of Marseilles,
Into Venice port to march
    to the Pannonians:
Set out from the gulf and
    bay of Illyria,
Devastation to Sicily, Ligurians
    shots from cannons.

*Voile Symacle port Massiliolique,*
*Dans Venise port marcher*
    *aux Pannons:*
*Partir du gouffre et sinus Illirique,*
*Vast à Socille, Ligurs*
    *coups de canons.*

An Allied fleet ("sails allied"), in all likelihood primarily French given their point of departure, will leave "from the port of Marseilles" and sail south around Italy and "into Venice." Their mission will be to provide troops for the ongoing battle of Hungary ("to the Pannonians"). Then Nostradamus again describes a fleet leaving from the Adriatic (the "gulf and bay of Illyria"), apparently with the destination of Sicily. It appears that the Mahdi will be aware of the Allied troops and fleet in Marseilles, and will hold off on the invasion of Sicily until those troops will have been committed to the battle for Hungary. As discussed in the previous quatrain, this "fleet" will then pick up Italian forces from Trieste, less than sixty-five miles to the east of Venice, and return to Sicily with them. Along with the fleet originally from Marseilles, which will then be carrying the troops from Trieste to Sicily, a bombardment of some sort ("shots from cannon") will be provided by a Genoan unit (the "Ligurians") against the Islamic forces. Nostradamus does not specify if this will be naval or ground-based artillery. However, all of these efforts would seem to be in vain. That the Allies will eventually lose Sicily is seen in the following quatrain:

**(64) Century 7, Quatrain 6**

| | |
|---|---|
| Naples, Palermo, and all Sicily, | *Naples, Palerme, et toute la Sicille,* |
| Through barbarian hand will it be uninhabited: | *Par main Barbare sera inhabitée:* |
| Corsica, Salerno and the Isle of Sardinia, | *Corsique, Salerne et de Sardeigne l'isle,* |
| Famine, plague, war, end of evil far away. | *Faim, peste, guerre, fin de maux intentée.* |

"Naples" is on the Italian west coast, roughly two-thirds of the way down the peninsula. "Palermo" is one of the major cities on "Sicily." Again, note Nostradamus' prediction that Sicily will be "uninhabited," i.e. evacuated (or murdered!), by "barbarian" hands. But Sicily will not be the only uninhabited part of Italy. The first two lines indicate that Naples, and by implication all of southern Italy, will be abandoned before the advancing Muslim armies. After consolidating their Sicilian base, the Muslims will continue into Naples, whether by land or sea Nostradamus does not say. "Salerno," less than fifty miles east of Naples, will be lost as well, as will the islands of "Corsica" and "Sardinia." It appears that at this time the Mahdi's navy will be master of the Mediterranean. In the last line, "Famine, plague, war" must all take place for a long time yet, since the "end of evil" (the end of the war) will still be "far away."

A note to the reader at this juncture: remember Nostradamus predicts that World War III will last for twenty-seven years! The events of these few quatrains relating to Sicily may span several years, and there will undoubtedly be many more battles and events than what Nostradamus describes. These quatrains provide only snippets of information relating to particular events at certain times.

The battle continues northward in Italy:

**(65) Century 10, Quatrain 60**

| | |
|---|---|
| I weep Nice, Monaco, Pisa, Genoa, Savona, Siena, Capua, Modena, Malta: | *Je pleure Nisse, Mannego, Pize, Gennes, Sauone, Sienne, Capue, Modene, Malte:* |
| The above blood and sword for gift, | *Le dessus sang et glaive par étrennes,* |
| Fire, trembling earth, water, unfortunate reluctance. | *Feu, trembler terre, eau, malheureuse nolte.* |

"Nice, Monaco. . . Genoa," and "Savona" are all coastal cities, and "Pisa" is just a few miles inland. "Modena" is in central northern Italy, "Capua" and "Siena" are farther south, to the west of the Apennine Mountains, with "Capua" just to the north of Naples. "Malta" is an independent island-country in the Mediterranean. What is the purpose in listing these places? It is possible that Nostradamus mentions these as a sort of roll-call of the great battles of World War III. It is also possible that he is again describing the front lines of the battlefield at a particular time during the war. In that case, Italy east of the Apennines will fall before the area west of the mountains, and the front will be on a zig-zag line shaped like a backwards "z" running from the Mediterranean near Naples directly eastward to the Apennines, then northeast to near Bologna, then east again to the Adriatic. At the same time that the Italians and the forces of Islam will be fighting on this front coastal raids will be occurring throughout western Italy and southern France, and the island of Malta will be invaded.

Nostradamus has a warning for the French troops fighting in Italy at this time:

**(66) Century 3, Quatrain 43**

People from around the Tarn,
    Lot, and Garonne
Take care the mountains Apen-
    nines when passing:
Your tomb near Rome,
    and Ancona,
The black bristle beard
    will a trophy erect.

*Gens d'alentours de Tarn, Loth,*
    *et Garonne*
*Gardez les monts Apennines passer:*
*Votre tombeau près de Rome,*
    *et d'Anconne,*
*Le noir poil crêpe fera trophée dresser.*

The "Tarn" and "Lot" are both rivers of southwestern France, tributaries of the "Garonne," which flows through Bordeaux on its way
to the Atlantic. French units originating from those areas will be
assisting the Italians in western Italy, and will cross the "Apennines"
and pass into eastern Italy in an attempt to stem the Muslim
onslaught in the eastern half of Italy. "Ancona" is a port city on the
Adriatic, and while almost directly north of Rome, it is still well to
the east and a little to the south of Modena. Apparently the French
will suffer serious losses in a battle for Ancona, and the rest will per-
ish in the battle for Rome. The "black bristle beard" of the last line
appears to be the Muslim commander. He will "erect" a monument
("trophy") of his victory over the Allies at Ancona and/or Rome. This
"black bristle beard" will be heard from again.

Quatrain (65) mentioned simultaneous attacks on both Malta and
Genoa. There is another quatrain which continues that theme:

**(67) Century 4, Quatrain 68**

In the place very near not distant
    from Venus,
The two greatest of Asia and Africa,
From Rhine and Hister of which
    they will have been said
    to have come,
Cries, tears at Malta and
    part of Liguria.

*En lieu bien proche non*
    *éloigné de Venus,*
*Les deux plus grands de l'Asie*
    *et d'Affrique,*
*Du Ryn et Hister qu'on*
    *dira sont venus,*
*Cris, pleurs à Malte et côté Ligustique.*

The context demands that "Venus" be a place, not the planet. It
could represent Venice, Venosa, Verona, Vicenza, Portus Veneris, or
any of several other similarly named Italian cities. Several of these are
in northeastern Italy, and it seems likely that one of those northeastern Italian cities, probably Venice, is the intended site. While some

151

Nostradamian scholars see "Hister" as an anagram for "Hitler" and place this quatrain during World War II, this is not likely. In Nostradamus' time the lower part of the Danube River was called the Hister, and since the "Rhine and Hister" are mentioned together, "Hister" most likely refers to the river Danube, not Hitler. "Liguria" is an old name for the city of Genoa.

Synthesizing all the above information shows that this quatrain describes a linking-up of the Mahdi's forces from Asia, who will have travelled across the European continent, with those from North Africa, who will have fought their way up the Italian peninsula. This meeting of the armies will occur in northeast Italy, possibly near Venice. The Asian forces will consist of troops pulled out of the German campaign at the Rhine River, as well as fresh troops coming from the Danube River region in Eastern Europe. At this same time Malta and Genoa will again both be in "tears" from sea attacks.

There is yet one more quatrain detailing coastal raids into Italy:

**(68) Century 2, Quatrain 4**

| | |
|---|---|
| From Monaco to as far as near Sicily | *Depuis Monech jusqu'auprès de Sicille* |
| The whole beach homes desolated: | *Toute la plage demeurera désolée:* |
| There will not remain suburb, city nor village, | *Il n'y aura faubourg, cité ni velle,* |
| Which by Barbarians suppose pillaged and robbed. | *Que par Barbares pillée soit et volée.* |

This quatrain is fairly obvious and self-explanatory. The entire western Italian coast will be subject to raiding parties from Muslim "Barbarians," and as a result the entire coast will be abandoned by the civilian population. Obviously, Nostradamus foresees the Islamic forces as having complete control of the Mediterranean at this time. Note that he uses the word "suburbs" in the third line, which were fairly small and insignificant in his own day, but are important home sites in the latter part of the twentieth century throughout all of western civilization.

This quatrain brings up an interesting question, namely, how do the Muslims gain control of the Mediterranean Sea? Will not the modern Allied navy, which includes aircraft carriers, frigates, guided-missile cruisers, etc. be more than a match for any navy the Mahdi and his Iranian naval commanders might put to sea? In the early years of the war, yes, but several years into the war the high-maintenance needs of modern warships may render them unusable, as the infrastructure necessary to support those ships will collapse. At a minimum, several of the weapons and communications functions of each ship are likely to be lost. Besides, the U.S., French, and British navies were designed to encounter the Soviet navy in the mid-ocean; even the Mediterranean is not large enough for these fleets to maneuver adequately.

In contrast, the naval strategy that the Mahdi will adopt will likely be a low-tech, high-volume shipbuilding plan, with emphasis on near-shore capabilities. Specifically, the Muslims will probably build tens of thousands of twenty to forty-foot long craft with either fiberglass or composite hulls. These lightweight ships will be propelled either by sail or oar. Without engines this type of ship will be invisible to heat-seeking missiles, without any metal they will be difficult for radar-guided missiles to hit: they will essentially be "stealth" ships, but at a much lower cost than the Allies' "stealth" fighters and bombers. In order to destroy these ships, Allied aircraft will need to make visual contact on low-level runs, using either laser-guided or gravity bombs. However, this will expose the Allied aircraft to return fire from hand-held Stinger-type missiles. With a crew on each ship of perhaps only ten sailors, the Muslims will be quite satisfied with the loss of dozens of these ships in exchange for a single Allied jet, a jet which will be irreplaceable when lost. Additionally, if the Iranian naval commander conducts his operations during cloudy or foggy weather, then even low-level visual attacks will be impossible.

Another type of vessel likely to be used by the Iranian navy will be a slightly enhanced ocean-going version of a jet-ski, launched in mid-sea from a mother ship. Light, fast, highly maneuverable, and relatively inexpensive, the Mahdi's navy may field tens of thousands of these vessels during World War III. The offensive weapons of these jet-skis and small rowed/sail ships will be a single Chinese-type Silkworm missile, just one of which is capable of completely destroying an aircraft carrier. And since the Silkworm has a range of many hundreds of miles, the Iranian navy will not even have to venture close to the Allied fleet; they will be firing at targets still over the horizon! While these missiles will not be in abundant supply for the Muslims, perhaps on only every tenth or twentieth ship, the Allies will not know which ships will carry the missiles and will be obligated to try to sink every single small boat that comes within hundreds of miles of the fleet. Iranian losses in these battles, while large, will be unimportant to them. What is the loss of even a thousand of these ships if just one manages to land a critical hit on an aircraft carrier? Within a decade at most these small ships could sink much of the Allied fleet in the Mediterranean, driving the rest into the Atlantic.

Will the Allies be able to counter with a similar shipbuilding strategy? No, because with the massive advantage in men that the Mahdi will possess during World War III, the Allies will no more be able to risk trading ships and men in the Mediterranean than they will be able to risk equal losses of soldiers on the eastern front. Within a decade at most, the Mahdi will be complete master of the Mediterranean. At that time these small ships will no longer carry Silkworm anti-ship missiles, but Scud-type missiles with conventional warheads. These missiles will be fired against the Mediterranean port cities of Italy, France, and Spain, from a distance far enough at sea that the Allies will not be able to return fire. Since North Korea, a likely ally of the Mahdi during World War III, has been estimated to have accumulated tens of thousands of Scuds over the past few decades, this will not be a weapon the Muslims will run out of during the war.

Turning to the events happening just after those described in quatrain (65) is the following:

### (69) Century 5, Quatrain 22

| | |
|---|---|
| Before Rome's great one will give up his soul, | *Avant qu'à Rome grand aie rendu l'âme,* |
| Terror great to the army foreign: | *Effrayeur grande à l'armée étrangère:* |
| By squadrons the ambush near Parma, | *Par escadrons l'embûche près de Parme,* |
| Then the two red ones together will celebrate. | *Puis les deux rouges ensemble feront chère.* |

"Before" the fall of Rome and before the death of a Pope ("Rome's great one"), the Muslims ("the army foreign") will suffer a great defeat, described as an "ambush" near the city of "Parma," which is located just northwest of Modena. This will cause two cardinals, called "the two red ones," because of their red hats, to "celebrate" the victory. The context seems to indicate that either the Cardinals will conceive the attack, or actually be responsible for command of the local Allied forces. With the collapse of civil authority it is quite possible that religious authorities will step into the power vacuum and once again govern affairs of state as they did centuries ago.

Continuing, the Moslem forces finally reach Rome:

**(70) Century 5, Quatrain 46**

| | |
|---|---|
| By hats red quarrels and new schisms | *Par chapeaux rouges querelles et nouveaux schismes* |
| When the elected one will be the Sabine: | *Quand on aura élu le Sabinois:* |
| People will produce against him great sophisms, | *On produira contre lui grands sophismes,* |
| And will Rome be harmed by Albania. | *Et sera Rome lésée par Albanois.* |

The "Sabine" is an area just to the northeast of Rome. An Italian Pope ("the elected one") from this area will be chosen. His reign will be marked by "quarrels" amongst the cardinals of the Church ("hats red"), and by "schisms" and heresies. Many will tell "great" lies ("sophisms") about him, and it will be during his reign that "Rome" itself will be attacked ("harmed") by troops originating from "Albania." Apparently, Italy will be attacked not only from the African coast, Sicily, and Eastern Europe, but across the Adriatic from Albania as well. The shortest distance across the entire Adriatic Sea is from Albania to southeastern Italy, a little over fifty miles, so it should not come as a surprise that the Moslems will pick Albania as their staging area for an Italian second (or even third?) front. The "Albanian" troops will probably then work their way northwards up the Italian peninsula east of the Apennine Mountains until, as described in quatrain (65), they reach at least as far north as Bologna, giving the front its backwards "z" shape. At that time, being well to the north of Rome, they will pierce through the Apennines and encircle central Italy, cutting Rome off from reinforcement by land (and the Iranian navy will control the seas). The "harm" that Rome will suffer "by Albania" is detailed in many other quatrains in this chapter.

In quatrain (6) the death of a Pope was related to the disappearance of the comet, and here in quatrain (70) is a second reference to a Pope. In fact, predictions about the Papacy are fairly common in Nostradamus' writings; there are more than fifty quatrains with some reference to either a Pope or to Rome (Vatican City). There are several which may be relevant to the next decade or two. Here is one of them:

**(71) Century 5, Quatrain 92**

| | |
|---|---|
| After the seat has been held seventeen years, | *Après le siége tenu dix-sept ans,* |
| Five will change in the same term: | *Cinq changeront en tel révolu terme:* |
| Then one will be elected at the same time, | *Puis sera l'un élu de même temps,* |
| Who to the Romans will not too much conform. | *Qui des Romains ne sera trop conforme.* |

Seventeen years is a long reign for a Pope. There have been a few who have had longer reigns over the 400 years since Nostradamus wrote this quatrain, but none of exactly "seventeen years," so this quatrain is unfulfilled to date. At the time of the final editing of this book, John Paul II is in his seventeenth year, so if it applies to John Paul II, Nostradamus predicts that he will die before October of 1996. Afterwards, there will be five Popes in a seventeen year period. If the sixth Pope, the one who "will not too much conform" to the wishes of the other Italian Cardinals, is the same Pope as the one mentioned in quatrain (70), the one who will provoke "quarrels" and "new schisms" within the Church, then this allows for a rough dating of when World War III will reach Rome; somewhere around the year 2012 or 2013. Since the comet is to come in 1999, and at least one or two years will pass afterwards before World War III is initiated, the battle for Rome may occur no more than eleven or twelve years into the war. Of course, all these dates are predicated on Pope John Paul II being the first Pope referred to in this quatrain, hardly a certainty! Back to the battle for Rome:

**(72) Century 2, Quatrain 93**

| | |
|---|---|
| Very near the Tiber will press the Libyans: | *Bien près du Tymbre presse la Libytine:* |
| A little before great inundation: | *Un peu devant grande inondation:* |
| The chief of the ship imprisoned, thrown into the bilge: | *Le chef du nef pris, mis à la sentine:* |
| Castle, palace in conflagration. | *Château, palais en conflagration.* |

The "Tiber" river flows from North to South through central Italy, eventually winding through Rome before turning west and flowing into the Mediterranean. The troops from North Africa, here designated specifically as "Libyans," will conduct some sort of offensive, their effort carrying them to "very near the Tiber." Shortly afterwards a "great inundation" of troops will arrive and cross the Tiber, leaving Rome surrounded. "The chief of the ship" of the third line is understood by the vast majority of Nostradamus' commentators as being a Pope, who is the "chief" of the Catholic church ("ship"). Either unable or unwilling to escape, he will be imprisoned in one of the invading ships ("thrown into the bilge"). Perhaps he will be unwilling to leave because he will be the leader of what remains of the civilian government of west central Italy at the time. Regardless, Nostradamus indicates that Vatican City ("Castle, palace"), and possibly all of Rome, will be burned to the ground.

Continuing with the Muslim attack upon Rome:

### (73) Century 5, Quatrain 62

On the rocks blood one
    will see rain,
Sun East, Saturn West:
Close to Orgon war, at Rome
    great evil seen,
Ships sunk to the bottom,
    and taken the Trident.

*Sur les rochers sang on verra pleuvoir,*
*Sol Orient, Saturne Occidental:*
*Près d'Orgon guerre, à Rome*
    *grand mal voir,*
*Nefs parfondrées, et pris le Tridental.*

During a naval invasion of the coastline near Rome so many will die that their "blood" will be like "rain. . . On the rocks." The second line gives a conjunction: a rising "Sun" in the "East" and "Saturn" setting in the "West." Trying to date the conjunction, however, is pointless since it occurs for several months every year. The most that can be said is that the attack will come at dawn, since the "Sun" will be in the "East."

"Orgon" is a town in southern France. Is it possible that the Muslims will already be that far into France at the time Rome falls? Probably not—it is more likely that Nostradamus intends that a unit of French soldiers from Orgon will somehow be important in this battle. Not only will the invaders suffer high casualties, they will also lose much of their naval force as well ("ships sunk to the bottom").

Neptune, the god of the sea, was classically pictured as carrying a "Trident," a symbol of his rulership of the seas. Perhaps "and taken the Trident" means that the invading forces will lose control of the seas, or perhaps this is another reference to the Pope, who possesses the staff ("trident") of St. Peter. Unfortunately, Nostradamus does not say if the invaders are Muslim or if this represents an Allied counter-attack. Nevertheless, it appears that the attackers will not do well.

There is still another quatrain about events near Rome:

**(74) Century 5, Quatrain 63**

From the vain enterprise credit
    and undue complaint,
Boats wandering through Italy,
    cold, hunger, waves
Not far from the Tiber of blood
    the land tainted,
And upon humanity will be
    diverse plagues.

*De vaine emprinse l'honneur*
    *indue plainte,*
*Galiotes errants par latins,*
    *froids, faim, vagues*
*Non loin du Tymbre de sang*
    *la terre teinte,*
*Et sur humains seront diverses plagues.*

Yet another instance in which Nostradamus left two quatrains in their original order! Since Nostradamus does not specify a nationality, it can be assumed that those conducting the "vain enterprise" and doing the complaining will be the French forces in Italy. In the second line the "Boats" are described as "wandering" through Italy, so apparently their missions will not be well coordinated. Once again, note the shedding of "blood" near the Tiber, this time associated with the recurrent theme of "diverse plagues." It would appear that the Tiber River will serve as a natural boundary against the advancing Muslim troops and several large battles will be fought there.

Quatrain (72) stated that eventually the Islamic armies will take Rome. This is also shown in the next quatrain:

**(75) Century 4, Quatrain 98**

The Albanians will pass
    within Rome,
By means of Langres the
    multitude muffled up.
Marquis and Duke
    no pardon to men,
Fire, blood, smallpox
    no water to fail the crops.

*Les Albanois passeront dedans Rome,*
*Moyennant Langres demipler affublés,*
*Marquis et Duc ne*
    *pardonnent à homme,*
*Feu, sang, morbiles point d'eau*
    *faillir les blés.*

In quatrain (70) the "Albanians" were predicted to "harm" Rome; here is shown how they will do it. The "Albanians" will "pass within" the city, actually invading it. "Langres" is a city in northeastern France, what the troops from Langres are doing is not clear, and the third line is equally murky. Perhaps a French unit from Langres will be trapped inside of Rome during its fall. In the last line, in addition to the burning of Rome (is it possible that the Mahdi will fiddle while it burns?), and the common World War III themes of bloodshed and crop failure, is the mention of an outbreak of "smallpox."

Smallpox is a unique disease in that it is not carried by an animal host—only human beings are capable of contracting, and spreading, the disease. Historically, it has also been a very virulent affliction, since over the past few thousand years smallpox has killed more people than any other disease. However, vaccinations, along with a major effort by world health authorities, made smallpox, in 1977, the first disease to ever be completely eradicated by mankind. Or was it eradicated? The virus still lives on, frozen in 600 test tubes at the Centers for Disease Control in Atlanta and at Russia's Institute for Viral Preparations in Moscow. The virus was originally scheduled to be destroyed at the end of 1993, and once again in 1995, but protests by researchers, who are still hoping to study the virus and learn from it how to treat other diseases more effectively, have delayed the execution date indefinitely. However, security at the Moscow site is notoriously lax; a television report showed that the facility has only two guards, and they are unarmed! Given the anarchy likely to be present in the early years of the next century, is it possible that the virus will escape and start infecting the world again? Nostradamus predicts another smallpox epidemic! Complicating the situation is the fact that world health authorities stopped vaccinating for smallpox in the 1980s. An entire generation is now growing up without immunity to the greatest killer in history, a killer that is not yet quite dead. Should it be released again, either accidentally or intentionally by terrorists, millions will die and many more will be maimed before it can be brought under control again.

A final quatrain for now about the Papacy in Rome:

**(76) Century 8, Quatrain 99**

| | |
|---|---|
| By the power of three Kings temporal, | *Par la puissance des trois Rois temporels,* |
| Into a different place will be put the holy Seat: | *En autre lieu sera mis le saint Siège:* |
| Where the substance of the spirit corporal, | *Où la substrance de l'esprit corporel,* |
| Will be restored and received for the right and true seat. | *Sera remise et reçus pour vrai siège.* |

After the conquest of Rome and the Vatican, the "holy Seat" of the Pope will be moved to another location (obviously with a new Pope since Nostradamus predicts that one will die with the fall of Rome), and the Holy Spirit will accept it as the new physical ("corporal") location ("the right and true seat") of the Church. In the next chapter, quatrains are presented that show the new location as being in France. While Nostradamus has thus far indicated two armies responsible for the conquest of Rome, the "Albanians" and the "Libyans," here he indicates that a third force will be involved ("By the power of three Kings temporal"). However, he gives no clue as to who the third army is or where it might come from. Perhaps it is the force that has finished the conquest of Croatia and is coming down the Italian peninsula from the north, or perhaps marine units landing on the beaches from the west.

And here is one last quatrain, which may or may not be relevant in this setting, about the Papacy:

**(77) Century 5, Quatrain 49**

| | |
|---|---|
| Not from Spain, but from ancient France | *Nul de l'Espagne, mais de l'antique France* |
| Will he be elected for the trembling ship, | *Ne sera élu pour la tremblante nacelle,* |
| To the enemy will be made promise, | *À l'ennemi sera faite fiancé,* |
| Who during his reign will cause a cruel plague. | *Qui dans son règne fera peste cruelle.* |

With the exception of John Paul II, all of the Popes since 1522 have been Italian. According to the first line of this quatrain there will come a time when there will be two leading candidates for the Papacy, one "from Spain" and the other "from ancient France." Nostradamus predicts that the French candidate will win. How likely is this, given a politically intact Italy? This can only occur in a world in immense turmoil, with particular distress in Italy. That distress could be World War III, with combat on Italian soil itself. In that case "the trembling ship" could be the Church, trembling because of the war, plagues, famines, and environmental deterioration present in the early years of the next century. The themes of an "enemy" and a "plague," along with a destroyed Italy, probably place this quatrain sometime during World War III. Of course, it is also possible that it applies to some time in the future after the war is over.

A final quatrain about the death of a Pope:

**(78) Century 2, Quatrain 97**

| | |
|---|---|
| Roman Pontiff guard yourself from approach | *Romain Pontife garde de t'approcher* |
| Of the city which two rivers water, | *De la cité que deux fleuves arrose,* |
| Your blood will come to spill near there, | *Ton sang viendra auprès de là cracher,* |
| You and yours when flowers the rose. | *Toi et les tiens quand fleurira la rose.* |

Many commentators of Nostradamus' writings have noted Nostradamus' prediction of the moving of the Papacy from Rome to a "city" between "two rivers" based on this quatrain and on quatrain (79). As has already been shown, Nostradamus believed that Rome and Vatican City will some day be destroyed. This quatrain predicts the violent death of a Pope ("Roman Pontiff. . . Your blood will come to spill near there"), as well as an unnumbered group of travelers with him ("You and yours"), in a "city" that lies between "two rivers." This will occur at a time in the spring when the local roses are beginning to bloom ("when flowers the rose"). One of the "two rivers" may be identified in the next quatrain:

**(79) Century 7, Quatrain 22**

| | |
|---|---|
| The citizens of Mesopotamia | *Les citoyens de Mesopotamie* |
| Irate against their friends of Tarragona: | *Irez encontre amis de Tarraconne:* |
| Games, rites, banquets, all of the people put to sleep, | *Jeux, rites, banquets, toute gent endormie,* |
| Vicar to the Rhone, captured city, those of Ausonia. | *Vicaire au Rosne, pris cité, ceux d'Ausone.* |

The Pope ("Vicar" of the Catholic Church) will move "to the Rhone" river. One of the major cities on the Rhone is Avignon, lying between the Rhone and Durance Rivers. Avignon, as described in the discussion of quatrain (7), was the home of the Papacy during a time of turmoil in Italy between the years 1309 and 1378. Here, the move to Avignon is associated with a "captured city," probably Rome, and the fall of all of southern Italy ("Ausonia").

"Mesopotamia" was the ancient kingdom of the Middle East that preceded the Persian Empire, but Nostradamus does not appear to use the term to refer to that area in any of the quatrains in which it appears. Instead, he appears to intend the Greek meaning of the word "Mesopotamia," which translates as "between the two rivers." This definition fit the ancient Mesopotamians well enough: they lived between the Tigris and the Euphrates Rivers. If the setting is France, this quatrain could apply to Avignon. It could also apply to Paris as this city lies at the conjunction of the Marne and the Seine, or any number of other cities. "Tarragona" is a port of northeastern Spain, just west of Barcelona on the Mediterranean. The "citizens of" French "Mesopotamia" will be "irate" with their Spanish friends "of Tarragona," who will be involved in "Games, rites, banquets" and "put to sleep" at a time during the war when their help is urgently needed. The lack of assistance from "Tarragona" (their fleet perhaps?) will result in the fall of all of Rome, along with all of southern Italy, and is associated with the Papacy moving to a new city, probably Avignon.

After the fall of Rome, the Italian campaign continues farther north:

**(80) Century 7, Quatrain 30**

| | |
|---|---|
| The sack approaches, fire great blood shed, | *Le sac s'approche, feu grand sang épandu,* |
| Po, great rivers, to the clowns the enterprise: | *Po, grands fleuves, aux bouviers l'entreprise:* |
| Of Genoa, Nice, after long wait, | *De Gennes, Nice, après long attendu,* |
| Fossano, Turin, at Savigliano the capture. | *Foussan, Turin, à Sauillan la prise.* |

The "Po" is one of the greatest rivers of Italy, running through northern Italy from west to east, emptying into the Adriatic south of Venice. What the other "great rivers' are is not clear. Perhaps Nostradamus intends the tributaries of the Po, perhaps events occurring at other rivers in Europe. Who the "clowns" will be is not clear, either. The word *bouviers* can also be translated as "cow-herders," but this does not help with the meaning at all. "Nice," in France, and "Genoa," in Italy, are both major Mediterranean ports and are located within 150 miles of each other. "Fossano," "Turin," and "Savigliano" are in a line less than fifty miles long running from north to south in northwestern Italy.

How are all these locations related? The Po River will serve as a natural defensive boundary to the advancing Muslim troops from the south. The line from Turin to Fossano will be a continuation of that defensive line, giving a sideways "L" shape to the front at that time. At the same time the coastline from Nice to Genoa will be under attack from the sea, so the "sack" described in the first line is for one of those two cities. Between Nice and Genoa, and slightly inland, lies the city of Fossano. Continuing north from Fossano is Savigliano, and still farther to the north Turin. Someone, or some army, will be captured at Savigliano, halfway between Turin and Fossano, but whether the forces of Islam are doing the capturing or being captured is not clear.

Assuming that the Mahdi is able to set up another front in Italy on a north-south line extending north from Nice, and is also able to take Genoa, then Milan will be in danger of being cut off from the other Allied units. In that case Milan's only line of supply will be a tortuous route through the Alps, a very difficult supply line to say the least, into the Swiss cities around Lake Geneva and then westward into France.

Another battle is described along the same front:

**(81) Century 4, Quatrain 90**

| | |
|---|---|
| The two armies at the wall not able to join, | *Les deux copies aux murs ne pourront joindre,* |
| During that instant will tremble Milan, Ticinum: | *Dans cet instant trembler Milan, Ticin:* |
| Hunger, thirst, they will doubt so strongly | *Faim, soif, doutance si fort les viendra poindre* |
| Neither meat, bread, nor any single mouthful of food. | *Chair, pain, ni vivres n'auront un seul boucin.* |

"Ticinum" is an old Latin name for the city of Pavia. Both Pavia and "Milan" are just north of the Po River in north central Italy. Either two Islamic armies will attempt to link up to encircle the cities and fail, or two Allied forces will fail while attempting to relieve the encircled

163

cities. In view of the previous quatrain, the latter scenario is more likely. Regardless of which is true, the events of this time will be associated with a famine and lack of potable water in the two cities, both recurrent Nostradamian themes of World War III. The "tremble" could either be another aftershock of the great meteor-induced earthquake, or the inhabitants of the region might be trembling from fear.

The next quatrain provides an overview of the general collapse of society in Italy and Spain during the invasion of those countries:

**(82) Century 3, Quatrain 68**

| | |
|---|---|
| People without chief of Spain, of Italy | *Peuple sans chef d'Espagne, d'Italie* |
| Dead, overthrown within the peninsula: | *Morts, profligés dedans le Chersonèse:* |
| Their dictator deceived through loose folly, | *Leur dict trahi par légère folie,* |
| The blood will swim everywhere in the crossing. | *Le sang nager partout à la traverse.* |

The first two lines could refer to separate events occurring in Spain and Italy simultaneously while both governments are crumbling, the troops of both in one or the other's country during some part of the war, or both armies during the campaign of the Greek peninsula. As Nostradamus does not specify in which "peninsula" the deaths will occur, it could be Spain, Italy, or even Greece. The interpretation favored here, for no particular reason, is that the quatrain refers to events simultaneously occurring in both Spain and Italy. In that case, the entire organizational structure of both civilian and military affairs will be in a state of collapse in both countries as the Islamic armies move northward. Death will be commonplace and the armies will be "overthrown." Their "dictator" (note the change! Democracy does not work in crisis situations!) will more likely be the equivalent of a tribal chief of old, rather than the leader of an entire cohesive nation. This "dictator" will be a fool, suckered into launching an offensive, either across a river or by coastal invasion ("the crossing"). If applicable to this particular point in time, it may represent a counterattack across the Po. The Muslims will be well prepared, and the attack will result in such large losses that Allied "blood" will cover the water "everywhere" during the crossing, before the troops can even establish a beachhead on the opposite bank.

164

At this juncture Nostradamus provides another look at what will be going on in other parts of Europe during the campaign of northern Italy:

**(83) Century 3, Quatrain 75**

| | |
|---|---|
| Pau, Verona, Vicenza, Saragossa, | *Pau, Verone, Vicence, Sarragousse,* |
| From far off swords territories from blood wet: | *De glaives loin terroirs de sang humides:* |
| Plague so great will come with the great shell, | *Peste si grande viendra à la grande gousse,* |
| Close at hand help, and very far off the remedy. | *Proche secours, et bien loin les remèdes.* |

"Swords" implies soldiers, that they will come "from far off" makes them the Asian troops of the Mahdi, not those of another European power, and "territories from blood wet" reinforces the idea of war on a large scale. The fact that the Mahdi will have enrolled significant numbers of Asian (Pakistani? Indonesian? Malaysian?) Muslims in his army indicates that whatever wars will be taking place in southeast Asia will be over by this time, and the Mahdi will be concentrating his forces in an all-out assault upon Europe.

"Pau," in southwestern France and "Saragossa," in northeastern Spain, are both near the French-Spanish border and apparently represent the Islamic advance points into those countries at the time of this quatrain. At the same time that fighting will occur at the Spanish-French border the campaign in Italy will have reached "Verona" and "Vicenza." Both cities are north of the Po river and to the north of Bologna.

The meaning of the "Plague" that comes from the "great shell" is open to debate. It probably just represents the devastation caused by a massive artillery bombardment, but battlefield-sized tactical nuclear weapons are a possibility. Also possible is that the "help" and "remedy" of the last line may again indicate the use of chemical and/or biological weapons, the "help" being gas masks and protective clothing and the "remedy" being medicines used against the toxins. A final possibility is that the "help" is just that, physical reinforcements of fresh troops, but the "remedy" of the war, a final peaceful settlement, will still be "very far off."

And, finally, the collapse of the Allied forces in Italy:

**(84) Century 2, Quatrain 72**

| | |
|---|---|
| Army Celtic in Italy vexed | *Armée Celtique en Italie vexée* |
| From every part conflict | *De toutes parts conflit* |
|    and great ruin: |    *et grande perte:* |
| Romans fled, O Gaul repulsed! | *Romains fuis, ô Gaule repoussée!* |
| Close to Ticino, Rubicon | *Près du Thesin, Rubicon* |
|    battle uncertain. |    *pugne incerte.* |

French troops will be having great difficulties in Italy at this time. The second line indicates a collapse of the entire front, with resultant "great ruin." The Italian troops ("Romans") will panic and abandon their positions, and the French will be defeated near the "Ticino" river. The Ticino, a tributary of the Po, flows from north to south and joins the Po between Turin and Milan. After the collapse of the front, the Islamic forces will continue to advance westward unchecked until an indecisive battle will be fought at the "Rubicon," a small stream on the French-Italian border. The fight will then continue into Switzerland and western Italy, leaving Milan surrounded on the east, south, and west by Muslims, with the Alps to the north. How long will the city be besieged? A very long time according to the next quatrain:

**(85) Century 7, Quatrain 15**

| | |
|---|---|
| Before the city of the | *Devant cité de l'Insubre contrée,* |
|    Insubrian countryside, | *Sept ans sera le siège devant mis:* |
| Seven years will the siege | *Le très grand Roi y fera son entrée,* |
|    be in front of it: | *Cité puis libre hors des ennemis.* |
| The very great King will enter it, | |
| City then liberated out | |
|    from its enemies. | |

Milan is the center of the "Insubrian" region. It will be under "siege" for "Seven years!" For the city to survive that long at least some aid must get through, so while the city will be cut off from France, perhaps some supply will be available over the Alps through Switzerland. After seven years it will be "liberated out from its enemies" by a "very great King," which introduces a new topic altogether, that of the restoration of a king to rule France. As already discussed, democracies do not do well in times of crisis. By design they are slow, methodical forms of government, designed to be slowly changing so that one bad ruler cannot ruin a country. However, in times of crisis, quick-acting, authoritarian leadership is needed. Nostradamus predicts that France, with a long history of royalty, will return to a kingship form of government. By the time that Milan will be liberated, seven years after being surrounded, the French military leader (who will also rule the civilian population through martial law) will have been declared king. More about the individual that France will proclaim as King in a later chapter.

In the following quatrain the scene shifts to events occurring in Switzerland:

**(86) Century 6, Quatrain 81**

| | |
|---|---|
| Weeping, cries and complaints, howling, terror, | *Pleurs, cris et plaintes, hurlements, effrayeur,* |
| Heart inhuman, cruel black and cold: | *Coeur inhumain, cruel noir et transi:* |
| Lake of the Isles, from Geneva the chiefs, | *Leman les Iles, de Gennes les majeurs,* |
| Blood will pour out, wheat famine to none mercy. | *Sang épancher, frofaim à nul merci.* |

"Weeping, cries and complaints, howling, terror" paint as graphic a picture of World War III as one line of a poem can possibly present. The second line is a reference to a Muslim commander, perhaps the Mahdi himself, with a "Heart inhuman, cruel black and cold." What might earn him such a title? Certainly not the treatment of his own loyal followers. No, this descriptive title will be earned for his butchery of civilians and captured Allied soldiers. During World War III, with "famine" a frequent occurrence, a captured soldier that must be guarded and fed will be a greater liability than if he were still on the opposite side of the battlefield. Prisoners of war will be treated harshly, when not slaughtered outright at the time of their capture.

"Lake of the Isles" is unclear as a single place. Edgar Leoni, in his excellent and highly recommended book *Nostradamus and His Prophecies* (which is currently out of print) interprets the third line as intending Lake of Geneva, located in Switzerland, the islands of the western Mediterranean (Malta, Corsica, and Sardinia), and the western Italian city of Genoa. If he is correct, then the Mahdi will still be

167

trying to capture some of the Mediterranean islands after conquering almost all of Italy, and at the same time the armies of Islam will be at the outskirts of Genoa and into at least part of Switzerland.

Can the Mahdi conquer all of Switzerland, a country into which no foreign army has even attempted to enter over the past few hundred years, a country that is essentially a mountainous fortress? Perhaps he will be able to subdue the Swiss people, but not likely. Aside from Geneva, Nostradamus has nothing to say about a Muslim conquest of the Swiss, so perhaps they, along with the Milanese, will manage to fend off the Mahdi. If, however, the Mahdi does conquer much of Switzerland, there will be two main reasons. First, Switzerland, being a mountainous country noted for its winter sports, is likely to have some very long winters while the rest of the world suffers through the comet-induced nuclear winter. The weather alone might cause many hundreds of thousands of deaths, severely weakening the populace before World War III even begins. Second, the last line of this quatrain describes yet another famine, and even troops in well-defended mountainous positions cannot fight well if they are starving to death.

There is another quatrain about the conquest of Geneva:

**(87) Century 9, Quatrain 44**

Migrate, migrate from Geneva
  every single one,
Saturn from gold into iron
  itself changed,
Those against RAYPOZ
  exterminated every one,
Before the advent the sky
  signs will show.

*Migrez, migrez de Genève trestous,*
*Saturne d'or en fer se changera,*
*Le contre RAYPOZ exterminera tous,*
*Avant l'avent le ciel signes fera.*

Nostradamus advises those of Geneva, in far western Switzerland on the French border, to flee when some sort of "signs" the "sky. . . will show." This could either represent another comet or a large chunk of meteoric debris re-entering and burning up in the sky. "RAYPOZ" appears to be an anagram for the name of the Muslim conqueror of Geneva. If that is so, then it appears that "RAYPOZ" will completely raze the city and massacre its inhabitants. The second line of this quatrain is unclear. Perhaps Nostradamus intended nothing more than that the "golden" civilization of the latter twentieth century will be changed into one more like that of the "iron" ages by the tides of time, as "Saturn" was celebrated as the god of time.

During the presentation of the Italian campaign several quatrains also mentioned events occurring simultaneously in Spain. Here are other quatrains that deal with Islamic attacks from North Africa into Spain:

**(88) Century 3, Quatrain 20**

| | |
|---|---|
| By the country of the great river Guadalquivir | *Par les contrées du grand fleuve Bethique* |
| Far into Iberia to the kingdom of Grenada | *Loin d'Ibere au Royaume de Grenade* |
| Crosses repulsed by the people Mahometan | *Croix repoussées par gens Mahometiques* |
| One of Cordoba will betray the country. | *Un de Cordube trahira la contrade.* |

Once again, whether Nostradamus knew it or not, this quatrain perfectly matches Muhammad's prediction that his followers would recapture Spain ("Iberia") after capturing and losing it once. The Moorish Kingdom of "Grenada" was defeated in 1492, and the Muslims have not had a presence in Spain since that time. The "Guadalquivir" River flows from east to west in southern Spain before emptying into the Atlantic Ocean. The city of "Grenada" is also in southern Spain, only fifty miles from the Mediterranean.

This quatrain appears to present the initial Muslim WW III entry into Spain, across the Mediterranean near the Rock of Gibraltar. The religious nature of World War III is emphasized again as Moslems are described as driving back Christian ("crosses") forces. The city of "Cordoba" is in south central Spain, on the north bank of the Guadalquivir. A leader of the city will capitulate to the Muslims without a fight, and in keeping with the tradition of Genghis Khan, the city will probably be spared and its inhabitants enrolled in the front lines of the Mahdi's armies as they march northward. Seemingly, though, the Muslims are unable to hold Cordoba as the following quatrain attests:

**(89) Century 8, Quatrain 51**

| | |
|---|---|
| The Byzantine will make an oblation, | *Le Bisantin faisant oblation,* |
| After having Cordoba to himself again: | *Après avoir Cordube à soi reprise:* |
| His road long rest vines lopped, | *Son chemin long repos pamplation,* |
| Sea passing prey through the Straits of Gibraltar captured. | *Mer passant proie par la Colongna prise.* |

169

"The Byzantine" is an Islamic VIP, perhaps even the Mahdi himself, who during the conquest of Turkey prayed at the mosque in Byzantium (now Istanbul). Or perhaps the White Turban will make Istanbul his home, earning him the title "The Byzantine." Whoever he is, his conquest of "Cordoba. . . again" will cause him to offer a sacrifice of some sort to Allah. His road will be "long" and then he will "rest." "Vines lopped" appears to refer to plundering and pillaging of Spanish controlled farmland. At this time someone of importance will be captured by the Iranian navy at sea as he (or they?) tries to pass through the Straits of Gibraltar. Who might this person be? There is no way to be sure what Nostradamus had in mind with the last line of this quatrain.

Continuing with the campaign through Spain, the next quatrain deals with both land and sea battles:

**(90) Century 3, Quatrain 64**

| | |
|---|---|
| The chief of Persia will fill up great Olchades, | *Le chef de Perse remplira grande Olchades,* |
| Fleet triremes against people Mahomet | *Classe trirème contre gens Mahometiques* |
| From Parthia, and Media: and pillage the Cyclades: | *De Parthe, et Mede: et piller les Cyclades:* |
| Rest long time at the great port Ionian. | *Repos longtemps au grand port Ionique.* |

"Olchades" is an old Latin term for the inhabitants of southeastern Spain around the port city of Cartagena. "The chief of Persia," probably The White Turban, will mass troops there ("fill up great Olchades"), probably via troop transports from North Africa. At the same time that the White Turban is massing troops in Spain, an Allied fleet of "triremes" will fight a sea battle "against" the Iranian fleet ("people Mahomet"), presumably in an attempt to prevent the transfer of troops into Spain.

In the discussion on quatrain (60), "foists," single-oared, low, fast boats, were considered to be Nostradamus' explanation of a modern PT boat. If the comparison holds, then "triremes," which were ocean-going ships with three levels of oars, will equate with modern destroyers or cruisers. Of course, after the disastrous effects of the tsunami and the toll of years of war on Allied shipping and port facilities, the Allies may be completely without those kind of ships! In addition, the collapse of industry may make such ships, with their high maintenance needs, unusable just a few years into the next century. If this is so then it is possible that Nostradamus actually means that the Allies, too, will equip their navy with a fleet of high-volume, low-tech metal or fiberglass-hulled rowed ships!

"Parthia and Media" were provinces of the ancient country of Persia, obviously a reference to modern Iran. The "Cyclades" Islands are a series of small islands located between Greece and Crete. It seems unlikely, but possible, that the forces of Islam will be well into Spain while still fighting the Greeks. Perhaps, as the U.S. did with many of the Japanese-held Pacific islands during World War II, the Cyclades will be simply bypassed early in the war by the Iranians and taken later, at a more convenient time. Or, as during any war, battle fronts fluctuate over time, perhaps the Cyclades will be reconquered by Italian or French-based forces, and taken yet again at the time of this quatrain by the Muslims. The most likely explanation, though, is that for some reason, perhaps a revolt, the Iranians will punish the Cyclades by pillaging their cities and towns.

The last line would appear to indicate that the Muslims will be the victors in the sea battle mentioned in the second line, as they put in for a "rest for a long time" (repair of damaged ships?) at a port on the Ionian Sea. As the Ionian Sea is located between Sicily and Greece, any coastal city of western Greece, southeastern Italy or eastern Sicily could be "the great port Ionian."

Continuing with the invasion of Spain, the campaign moves farther north:

**(91) Century 6, Quatrain 88**

One great realm will be
  left desolated,
Near the Ebro will be
  formed an assembly:
Mountains Pyrenees
  render consolation,
Then during May will
  the land tremble.

*Un regne grand demourra désolé,*
*Auprès de l'Hebro se feront assemblées:*
*Monts Pyrénées le rendront consolée,*
*Lorsque dans Mai seront*
  *terre tremblées.*

The "great realm" "left desolated" will be Spain, over half conquered at this time. The "Ebro" river is in northern Spain and flows from northwest to southeast, emptying into the Mediterranean. Since

Madrid is located south of the Ebro, within the area already in Islamic hands, the seat of government will move northward to a city near the Ebro, perhaps Sarragosa. The Spaniards will still be able to retreat to a place of safety and rest ("consolation") near the "Mountains Pyrenees," which they will still control. Yet another major earthquake will occur ("the land tremble"), this time during the month of "May."

Continuing even farther northward:

**(92) Century 3, Quatrain 62**

| | |
|---|---|
| Near of Douro by sea Tyrrene closed, | *Proche del duero par mer Tyrrene close,* |
| He will come to pierce the great mountains Pyrenees. | *Viendra percer les grands monts Pyrénées.* |
| The hand more short and his opening covered, | *La main plus courte et sa perce glose,* |
| To Carcassonne he will lead his men. | *A Carcassonne conduira ses menées.* |

The "Douro" River originates in northern Spain near the city of Burgos, less than seventy-five miles from the Bay of Biscay (the "sea Tyrrene closed"). Beginning there a Muslim general will conduct feints and brief raids ("The hand more short") hinting at an offensive in one location, while massing hidden troops at another ("his opening covered"). This surprise offensive will succeed and eventually carry through the Pyrenees mountains and into France to the city of "Carcassonne," which is slightly less than fifty miles from Spain and only a few miles from the Mediterranean.

And a final, summarizing quatrain about the fall of Spain:

**(93) Century 1, Quatrain 73**

| | |
|---|---|
| France at the five sides through neglect assailed, | *France à cinq parts par neglect assaillie,* |
| Tunis, Algiers stirred up by Persians: | *Tunis, Argiels émus par Persiens:* |
| Leon, Seville, Barcelona having failed, | *Leon, Seville, Barcelone faillie,* |
| There will be no fleet for the Venetians. | *N'aura la classe par les Venitiens.* |

The cities of line three are located throughout Spain: "Leon" in the northwest, "Seville" in the southwest, and "Barcelona" in the far northeast. By choosing these three cities from the far corners of Spain, Nostradamus is hinting that all of Spain will fall to the legions of Islam. The forces that will conquer Spain will come from "Tunis," the capital of Tunisia, and "Algiers," the capital of Algeria. Besides being Islamic cities of Arab North Africa, both Tunis and Algiers are major Mediterranean ports as well, and will probably be the home-ports of Iran's western Mediterranean fleet. Note that both "Tunis" and "Algiers" will be "stirred up" by Islamic fundamentalists originating from Iran ("by the Persians"). In all the years since Nostradamus died, only now are the political realities of the world such that this quatrain is even becoming possible.

Nostradamus places the conclusion of the conquest of Spain at the same time as a battle in Venice and the lack of an Allied Mediterranean fleet. The end result is that "France" will have to fight on five fronts simultaneously ("at the five sides. . . assailed"). Those fronts are: the Italian-Swiss (along the eastern French border with Italy and Switzerland), the German-Belgian (along the northern French border), the Mediterranean coast, the Spanish border, and the Atlantic coast (by coastal attacks from bases in northern Spain and Belgium).

Interestingly enough, while Nostradamus has much to say about the Islamic conquest of Spain, Portugal, its companion on the Iberian peninsula, is not even mentioned. The reason for that omission is that after the tsunami, Portugal, being the closest part of Europe to the impact site, will likely be wiped off the face of the earth. While much of the land will still be there, everything on it will be completely destroyed by the earthquake, tsunami, and firestorm. The Portuguese people sensible enough to flee into Spain will survive, but the country itself will not, and during World War III it will still be a desolate wasteland not even worth conquering.

England, described in the first chapter as literally being "half-drowned" from the tsunami, will not be much better off. While individual Britons are portrayed prominently later in the war, as a country Great Britain will also be completely destroyed. Nostradamus has only one quatrain relevant to them in this setting:

**(94) Century 3, Quatrain 78**

| The chief of Scotland, | *Le chef d'Escosse, avec six* |
| with six of Germany | *d'Allemagne* |
| Through the men of the sea | *Pars gens de mer Orientaux captif:* |
| Oriental captured: | *Traverseront le Calpre et Espagne,* |
| They will traverse the Cape | *Présent en Perse au nouveau* |
| and Spain, | *Roi craintif.* |
| Present in Persia to | |
| the new King feared. | |

As already described, England, including London, will be destroyed by the tsunami and the King of England will move the seat of government to the Scottish Highlands, an area well above sea level and untouched by the tsunami, thus becoming "The chief of Scotland." This "chief," along with "six of Germany," will be captured by Iranian (Pakistani? Indonesian?) sailors ("men of the sea Oriental"). Perhaps these seven Europeans will be the "passing prey through the straits of Gibraltar captured" referred to in quatrain (89). "They will traverse the Cape" (of Gibraltar) and pass to the south of "Spain," travel east across the Mediterranean, and be given to the "new King feared" of "Persia," most likely the White Turban, but possibly the Mahdi himself, as a "Present."

With the failure of Germany, Belgium, the Netherlands, Italy, and Spain, the destruction of Portugal and England by the tsunami, the nuclear winter induced devastation of Scandinavia, and the continued preoccupation of the United States with internal affairs, all that will stand between the Mahdi and complete mastery of all of Europe is France. The following chapter details the battles on French soil during World War III.

# THE BATTLE
# FOR FRANCE

As noted in quatrain (93), Nostradamus predicts that France will be attacked simultaneously from five sides. Of the five, he has little to say specifically about attacks on the Atlantic front. Attacks there will most likely consist of raiding forays onto the French Atlantic coast; the more massive attacks are likely to occur on the other four fronts. Since attacks on the Atlantic front will be based from either Spain or Belgium, they are included in with the sections for the Spanish and northern fronts. For the sake of clarity, the action on the other four fronts will be outlined for each front separately from beginning to end throughout the course of the war. Beginning with the southwestern front, the battle continues from Spain over the border into France with a quatrain summarizing action on the whole front:

**(95) Century 9, Quatrain 63**

Complaints and tears,
 cries and great howls,
Near Narbonne at Bayonne
 and in Foix:
Oh what horrible calamities
 and changes,
Before which Mars revolves
 a few times.

*Plaintes et pleurs, cris et
 grands hurlements,*
*Près de Narbon à Bayonne
 et en Foix:*
*O quels horribles calamités
 changements,*
*Avant que Mars révolu
 quelques fois.*

Two of the cities under attack in this quatrain are "Narbonne," only a few miles from the Mediterranean Sea, and "Bayonne," only a few miles from the Atlantic Ocean. Both of these are very near the Spanish border. The third city is "Foix," located between them. "Foix" was already mentioned in quatrain (33) as one of the specific cities that The Blue Turban will come to conquer. By linking Foix and The Blue Turban with Narbonne and Bayonne, a picture of the entire front emerges, from the Atlantic Ocean to the Mediterranean Sea.

The last line contains a prediction for how long the war will last on this front. A complete orbit of Mars takes 687 days, nearly two years. If a "few" means two, then the fighting on this front will last for less than four years. However, the word "few" is fairly loosely defined and could imply three, perhaps even four, orbits of Mars. In those cases the fighting on the Spanish front might last for six, possibly even eight, years.

Quatrain (92) described the initial entry of the Muslim forces from Spain into France. Here is the likely continuation of that quatrain:

**(96) Century 1, Quatrain 5**

Chased away without making long combat,
Through the pays they will be more strongly struck:
Village and city will have a more great debate:
Carcassonne and Narbonne will have hearts tested.

Chassés seront sans faire long combat,
Par le pays seront plus fort grevés:
Bourg et cité auront plus grand débat:
Carcassonne, Narbonne auront coeurs éprouvés.

As previously explained, after crushing the Spanish forces the attacking Muslim armies will feint along the western portion of the French-Spanish border, then launch a surprise, massive attack over the eastern half of the border. The initial attack will apparently surprise the French and will sweep away all French troops, encountering only minor resistance since the Allies will be "Chased away without making long combat." "Pays" was a French term for a unit of government, similar to a township or county in the U.S. There will be "great debate" throughout the region's villages and cities about how this could be allowed to happen and how to best deal with it.

As predicted in both this quatrain and quatrain (92), the advance will carry to Carcassonne, less than 60 miles from the Spanish border. In this quatrain Nostradamus also predicts that the Muslims will carry to Narbonne, less than 40 miles directly to the east of Carcassonne, as well. What the forces of Islam will find in Narbonne is predicted in the following quatrain:

**(97) Century 9, Quatrain 64**

| | |
|---|---|
| The Macedonian will pass mountains Pyrenees, | *L'AEmathion passer monts Pyrénées,* |
| In March Narbonne will not offer resistance: | *En Mars Narbon ne fera résistance:* |
| By land and sea will be so great intrigue, | *Par mer et terre fera si grande menée,* |
| Capetian not having land secure for residence. | *Cap. n'ayant terre sûre pour demeurance.* |

"The Macedonian" will be an Islamic general, either a Macedonian native or the conqueror of Macedonia. Operating from a base in Spain he will "pass mountains Pyrenees" and capture the city of "Narbonne. . . In March." The French "will not offer resistance" to the attack. Perhaps the French will deem Narbonne indefensible and abandon it, or perhaps the city will already be destroyed by either artillery or previous attacks and the French will see no point in defending it.

The last two lines shift the scene slightly. "Capetian" in the last line is a reference to the Pope, here searching for a new residence in France. This helps to place the quatrain as occurring after the sack of Rome, but before the Pope will receive a grant of land within France. Spain, then, must be completely in Muslim hands at about the same time as the Allied pocket around Rome collapses. However, this quatrain provides no help identifying the front in northern Italy or southeastern France. The third line of this quatrain could mean many things, but appears to refer to military intelligence activities and attempts to deceive the enemy as to where forces are concentrated.

One final quatrain about the battle for Narbonne; probably dating to just before the sack of Rome:

**(98) Century 4, Quatrain 94**

| | |
|---|---|
| Two great brothers will be chased from Spain, | *Deux grands frères seront chassés d'Espagne,* |
| The elder vanquished under the mountains Pyrenees: | *L'aîné vaincu sous les monts Pyrenees:* |
| Red will turn the sea, Rhone, bloody Lake Geneva from Germany, | *Rougir mer, Rosne, sang Leman d'Alemagne,* |
| Narbonne, Beziers, from Agde contaminated. | *Narbon, Blyterre, d'Agath contaminées.* |

The "Two great brothers" either refers to two army groups retreating from Spain, or personally to the leaders of those armies. The "elder" one will be unable to escape into France and will be slaughtered ("vanquished") against the foothills of the "Pyrenees." While this will be occurring, a bloody sea battle ("Red will turn the sea") will take place at an unspecified location (perhaps the battle for Rome already described?), and an attack on the eastern front "from Germany" will "bloody. . . Geneva," Switzerland. Still another attack will be taking place at the "Rhone" River.

"Narbonne," as already described, is a port city near the Spanish border. So is the city of "Agde," roughly twenty-five miles to the east of Narbonne. Between them, and slightly inland, is the city of "Beziers." Besides being completely driven out of Spain at this time, the Allies will also be defending Geneva, part of the eastern front, and the mouth of the Rhone River on the Mediterranean front as well.

The last line appears to indicate an infectious plague ("contaminated") of some sort, originating from "Agde." The following quatrain provides more information about the source of the plague:

**(99) Century 8, Quatrain 21**

| | |
|---|---|
| At the port of Agde three foists will enter, | *Au port de Agde trois fustes entreront,* |
| Carrying the infection, not faith but pestilence: | *Portant l'infect, non foi et perstilence:* |
| Passing the bridge a thousand thousands carried away, | *Passant le pont mil milles embleront,* |
| And the bridge broken at the third resistance. | *Et le pont rompre à tierce résistance.* |

"Three" ships ("foists") will enter "Agde," the passengers and crews infected with a plague ("infection") of some sort. The text implies that they will be clergy members, but instead of bringing just their "faith," they will carry "pestilence" with them as well. From where will they originate? Given the nature of the Italian campaign, they will most likely be refugees from a pocket of Italians surrounded in Rome.

Integrating the information here with that of the last few quatrains shows that the Allied pocket around Rome will hold out until the Muslims are in Switzerland and at the Rhone River. Perhaps it will be a plague of some sort that will finally weaken the defenders of Rome and allow the Muslims to capture it. Since the religious aspect of World War III will guarantee execution for clergy members, they will be evacuated whenever possible.

The "pestilence" that the priests will be unwitting carriers of will kill ("carry away") one million people ("a "thousand thousands") in southwestern France. This is an extremely high death toll from a plague, and many of Nostradamus' commentators have regarded it as an exaggeration. However, given the large increase in world population during the twentieth-century, along with this site as an apparent refugee center from Italy (and probably Spain as well), and furthermore the living conditions likely to be present in a post-industrial World War III world, a death toll of one million from an epidemic is very possible. The disease, as mentioned in the prior quatrain, will spread into Narbonne and Beziers.

The high death toll, over a million killed, will seriously weaken the defenses on the Spanish front, where the armies of Islam will, at some point, cross a bridge ("bridge broken") on their third attack upon it ("at the third resistance"). While there are many bridges in this part of the world, Nostradamus has a quatrain that may describe the bridge he has in mind. On the Atlantic side of the Spanish-French border is set the following:

**(100) Century 8, Quatrain 86**

| | |
|---|---|
| Through Erani Tolosa and Villafrance, | *Par Arnani Tholoser Ville Franque,* |
| Band infinite through the mountain Sierra de San Adrian: | *Bande infinie par le mont Adrian:* |
| Passing the river, Combat by bridge the plank | *Passe rivière, Hutin par pont la planque* |
| Bayonne entered with every one Bichoro crying. | *Bayonne entrer tous Bichoro criant.* |

The three towns ("Erani, Tolosa and Villafrance") and the mountain ("Sierra de San Adrian") of the first two lines are all situated on the Spanish side of the border. An "infinite" army will pass "San Adrian" and make a successful river crossing, probably over the Bidasoa, which flows from south to north near the French border. They will "bridge" the river on a "plank," implying the type of bridge that an engineering unit might quickly lay down. The advance will carry over the border and into the city of "Bayonne," an Atlantic port city only fifteen miles from Spain. "Bichoro" is difficult to translate. In centuries past it was the war cry of the Protestant Huguenot from this region during their wars with the Catholics, so perhaps Nostradamus is hinting at the religious nature of the war again.

Another quatrain, this time rather general, about southwestern France:

**(101) Century 5, Quatrain 98**

| | |
|---|---|
| At the fourth-eighth degree climacteric, | *À quarante-huit degré climatérique,* |
| At the finish of Cancer so great dryness: | *À fin de Cancer si grande sécheresse:* |
| Fish in sea, river, lake cooked hectic, | *Poisson en mer, fleuve, lac cuit hectique,* |
| Bearn, Bigorre through fire in the sky in distress. | *Bearn, Bigorre par feu ciel en détresse.* |

The first line appears to be a reference to the 48th degree of north latitude, which passes near the French cities of Langres, Orleans, Le Mans, and Rennes. As will be seen later in this chapter, the Islamic forces coming from the north will penetrate this far into France, so perhaps Nostradamus is giving a rough description of where the northern front will be at this time. This is linked with a drought ("so great dryness"), and both are to occur "at the finish of Cancer," roughly middle to late July.

While a drought severe enough to kill fish in both rivers and lakes is understandable, it is hard to conceive how they might die in the sea from the heat. Perhaps environmental changes will produce a large fish kill in a sea that will then wash ashore. These events are also linked with "fire in the sky," apparently a nighttime artillery bombardment at "Bearn" and "Bigorre." Both were counties of southwestern France, with Bigorre nestling against the Pyrenees halfway between the Atlantic and the Mediterranean.

That Bearn and Bigorre will eventually fall and the Muslims will continue deeper into France is shown in the following quatrain:

(102) Century 1, Quatrain 46

| | |
|---|---|
| Everything near by from Auch, from Lectoure and Mirande | *Tout auprès d'Aux, de Lectore et Mirande* |
| Great fire from the sky in three nights will fall: | *Grand feu du ciel en trois nuits tombera:* |
| Reason it will occur will be stupendous and marvelous: | *Cause aviendra bien stupende et mirande:* |
| Very little after the earth will tremble. | *Bien peu après la terre tremblera.* |

"Auch" is directly west of Toulouse and south of Agen, "Lectoure" is to the north of Auch, "Mirande" to the southwest of it. Perhaps the "three nights" of "great fire from the sky" will be a meteor storm, similar to those described in the first chapter, but they only last a few hours at most, certainly not for three nights. Some sort of nighttime aerial bombardment is much more likely as the cause of the "fire." The reason for the sky show is not given; however, since Nostradamus describes it as "stupendous and marvelous," it would appear to be a counterattack upon the Muslims. Shortly afterwards ("Very little after") yet another earthquake will occur ("the earth will tremble").

There is another quatrain that mentions Auch and Mirande:

(103) Century 8, Quatrain 2

| | |
|---|---|
| Condom and Auch and around Mirande, | *Condon et Aux et autour de Mirande,* |
| I see from the sky fire which will them surround: | *Je vois du ciel feu qui les environne:* |
| Sun Mars conjoined to the Lion, then at Marmande | *Sol Mars conjoint au Lion, puis Marmande* |
| Thunderbolts, great hail, wall tumbles into the Garonne. | *Foudre, grande grêle, mur tombe dans Garonne.* |

The city of "Condom" is just west of Lectoure, less than forty miles from "Auch." Again note the theme of "from the sky fire." Since "Marmande" is a city on the "Garonne" River sixty miles north of "Condom," the four cities mentioned in this and the prior quatrain form a rough north to south line over a forty-mile distance. The Muslims will be on the western aspect of this line and the French-led Allied troops on the east. The conjunction of the third line places the battle during late July or August, since that is when the Sun is in Leo. Mars is in Leo with the Sun fairly often. In the next century this conjunction will occur in 2004, 2006, 2008, 2019, 2021, and 2023 just to name a few years.

The "sky fire" theme again implies either an artillery barrage or a bombing raid. A "wall," probably some sort of defensive works, will tumble into the "Garonne" (at Marmande?) during the offensive. In the next quatrain, Nostradamus continues the front northwestward along the Garonne from Marmande:

**(104) Century 12, Quatrain 65**

He will keep the fort through
    fury compelled,
Every heart to tremble. Langon
    arrival terrible:
The blow of foot thousands
    itself returns,
Gironde. Garonne, never rage
    more horrible.

*À tenir fort par fureur contraindra,*
*Tout coeur trembler. Langon*
    *avent terrible:*
*Le coup de pied mille pieds se rendra,*
*Guirond. Guaron, ne furent*
    *plus horribles.*

An Allied "fort" will hold ("will keep") solely because of the furious charisma ("through fury compelled") of its commander ("He"), with "every heart" trembling over the outcome of the battle. Why will there be such fear over holding this "fort"? Because the "Garonne" River is the last natural defensive boundary in southwestern France. Failure here will likely mean a gaping hole in the Allied lines, passage across the Garonne, and the collapse of the final line of defense in southwestern France. At this line the French will commit all of their reserves; there will be nothing to counter a Muslim breach in the lines. The attack upon "Langon," located on the Garonne halfway between Marmande and Bordeaux, about twenty-five miles from each, will be especially terrible. What will start with a "blow of the foot" (Nostradamus uses the illustration here of a simple kick), perhaps an engagement of only a few platoons, will turn into a major battle. In the last line, the front is described as being along the Gironde river and its estuary, the "Gironde."

Nostradamus provides a summarizing quatrain of the Islamic advance to this point:

**(105) Century 4, Quatrain 79**

| | |
|---|---|
| Blood Royal flee, Monheurt, | *Sang Royal fuis, Monhurt,* |
|     Le-Mas-d'Agenais, Aiguillon, |     *Mas, Esguillon,* |
| It will be filled up by them | *Remplis seront de Bourdelois* |
|     of Bordelais and Landes, |     *les Landes,* |
| Navarre, Bigorre points and spurs, | *Navarre, Bygorre pointes et aiguillons,* |
| Profoundness of hunger | *Profonds de faim vorer de Liège glands.* |
|     to devour cork oak acorns. | |

In the first line is another teasing reference to French royal blood, here advised to flee three towns. "Monheurt" and "Aiguillon" are west of Agen, and "Le-Mas-d'Agenais" is to the northwest, yet another city on the Garonne River. "Bordelais" is the peninsula west of Bordeaux, and "Landes" is the department (a French unit of government, similar to a state in the U.S.) to the south of it. "Navarre" and "Bigorre" are south of Landes. The "points" refer to the spears, bayonets, etc. of the foot soldier, and the "spurs" to mounted troops, both indicating that events of these areas are associated with a war. The famine so often to be seen in World War III is found yet again in the last line.

This appears to be the farthest extent of the Islamic advance into southwestern France. The greatest penetration of the Islamic armies will be on a front running from the western bank of the Gironde where it empties into the Atlantic Ocean, southwest through Bordeaux and along the south bank of the Garonne until reaching Agen, then turning south to Auch before turning to the east again, where it will be picked up as part of the southern, or Mediterranean, front. Before progressing further, though, Nostradamus has a group of interesting quatrains about the British in southwestern France:

**(106) Century 5, Quatrain 34**

| | |
|---|---|
| From deepest of the English West | *Du plus profond de l'Occident Anglois* |
| Where is the head of | *Où est le chef de l'sle Britannique* |
|     the isle of Britain | *Entrera classe dans Gyronde par Blois,* |
| Will enter a fleet will into | *Par vin et sel, feux cachés* |
|     the Gironde for Blois, |     *aux barriques.* |
| Through wine and salt, | |
|     fires cached in the barrels. | |

The first line is something of a mystery. Does the "English West," mean England, the western part of England, or perhaps even Canada, with its former ties to the British Commonwealth? Since it is clarified in the second line as being the seat of government of Britain, and the seat has been previously defined as moving to Scotland, it would appear that Nostradamus means that the capital will move to western Scotland. Regardless of where they come from, the British will send "a fleet" into the "Gironde" estuary "for Blois." Many commentators feel that "Blois," several hundred miles away and not even a seaport, is a misprint for "Blaye," which is on the Gironde, just north of Bordeaux. While this is possible, it is more likely that Blois will be the capital of France at this time (the fall of Paris will be addressed later) and that the British will be sending troops into the battle for the southwest at the request of the French military government.

The "fire" of the last line is easily understood as explosives or weapons of some sort, but the "wine and salt" are unclear. Perhaps they are metaphors for something else. Unfortunately, Nostradamus provides no clue about when the British arrive, whether early or late in the campaign for the southwest.

The following is yet another instance of quatrains that are sequenced in their original, proper order:

**107) Century 5, Quatrain 35**

Through city free of the great sea of the Moon,
Which entryway still in its stomach the stone,
English fleet will come beneath the drizzle
A branch seized, the great opens war.

*Par cité franche de la grande mer Seline,*
*Qui porte encore à l'estomac la pierre,*
*Angloise classe viendra sous la bruine*
*Un rameau prendre, du grand ouverte guerre.*

The Bay of Biscay is shaped like a crescent moon, making it "the great sea of the Moon." The city of La Rochelle has a long history as a free city, and the French word for rock is "rocher," so the first two lines appear to refer to the city of La Rochelle. La Rochelle is an Atlantic port roughly 100 miles north of Bordeaux. At this city the English fleet will come in under cover of fog and mist ("beneath the drizzle"). The "branch" is probably symbolic for a spear or gunstock; in short, it is symbolic for weapons. They will be "seized" and the "great" commander of the French (or British? Possibly both together?) will open a new campaign. It is also possible that the British fleet will consist of troop ships, the troops of which will then move south to the front along the Garonne River from their disembarkment point in La Rochelle. Support for that idea is found in the following quatrain:

**(108) Century 9, Quatrain 38**

| | |
|---|---|
| The entry of Blaye through La Rochelle and the English, | *L'entrée de Blaye par Rochelle et l'Anglois,* |
| Will pass beyond the great Aemathien: | *Passera outre le grand Aemathien:* |
| Not far from Agen will await the Gaul, | *Non loin d'Agen attendra le Gaulois,* |
| Succor from Narbonne disappointed through conversation. | *Secours Narbonne déçu par entretien.* |

It is this quatrain, showing the English and the French fighting on the same side against a commander shown in other quatrains to be Muslim, which allows the linkage with the other quatrains showing English troops fighting in southwestern Europe during what will be known as World War III. In the first line, "English" troops, entering France "through La Rochelle," will organize themselves in the city of "Blaye," then continue south ("pass beyond") the troops of the Macedonian (Aemathia) commander, having punched a hole in the Islamic front lines. While this will be occurring, a French commander will wait near Agen for reinforcements from Narbonne in order to strike from the east and encircle an entire Muslim army group. Nostradamus does not write exactly why the "Succor from Narbonne" will not be forthcoming ("disappointed"), but possibly the reinforcements at Narbonne will be verbally ordered by army headquarters to stay put ("a conversation"), or perhaps even sent elsewhere. The French commander will be quite disappointed when they will not arrive, ruing the loss of a great opportunity.

That the English will permanently stay in southwestern France is shown in the ensuing quatrain:

**(109) Century 9, Quatrain 6**

By Guienne an infinity of English
Will occupy by the name
    of Anglaquitaine:
From Languedoc Lapalme
    Bordelais,
Which they will name
    after Barboxitaine.

*Par la Guienne infinité d'Anglois*
*Occuperont par nom*
    *d'Anglaquitaine:*
*Du Languedoc Ispalme Bourdelois,*
*Qu'ils nommeront après Barboxitaine.*

"Bordelais" is the peninsula just west of Bordeaux, "Guienne" an old province of southwestern France, and "Languedoc" the province to the east of Guienne, extending all the way to the Rhone River. "Lapalme" is a small city near Narbonne. An "infinity" of English, apparently still unable to cope with the devastation wrought by the tsunami in their home country, will permanently occupy southwestern France. Their territory will run from the Spanish border on the southwest to Bordeaux on the north and east all the way to the Rhone River. They will be given this territory in exchange for helping defeat the Mahdi's troops here. This will benefit the French by allowing them to concentrate their forces on the eastern and northern fronts, where the fighting will be fiercer. The English will change the name of their land, calling it "Barboxitaine." While interpretations of this enigmatic word vary, the best interpretation is roughly "the Beard's west." Apparently the leader of the English forces will have a beard. His name is mentioned in another quatrain as well:

**(110) Century 5, Quatrain 59**

To the chief of the English
    at Nimes too long a stay,
Towards Spain to
    the aid Redbeard:
Many will die through
    war opened that day,
When in Artois will fall
    a bearded star.

*Au chef Anglois à Nimes trop séjour,*
*Devers l'Espagne au secours Aenobarbe:*
*Plusieurs mourront par Mars*
    *ouvert ce jour,*
*Quand en Artois faillir étoile en barbe.*

Apparently the English will be given control of the western portion of the Mediterranean front at some point during the war, as Nimes is only a few miles to the west of Avignon. Also, as will be shown later, Avignon will mark the deepest penetration of the

Muslims on the eastern front. In this quatrain Nostradamus shows that the English commander ("the chief of the English") will be caught out of position, holding a position at "Nimes" after a battle, while his troops are urgently needed in another fight on the Spanish front. The crisis will be saved by the intervention of another English commander, "Aenobarbe," literally translated as "Redbeard" from the Latin. The campaign started on "that day" will result in "many" deaths.

All of these events will occur when a "bearded star" will fall in Artois, which is well to the north of this area, close to the Belgium border. This "bearded star" will not be another comet, but a large chunk of debris blown into Earth orbit by the original meteoric explosion. Its "beard" will be the glowing tail it will leave while re-entering the atmosphere. With billions of fragments, some quite large, blasted into space and falling back to Earth gradually over a period of many years, this event will by no means be rare.

The last few quatrains mention that the English will settle the southern coast of France as far as the Rhone River. Moving geographically from the Spanish to the Mediterranean front, and in all likelihood to a time several years earlier than quatrain (110), the battle for the Mediterranean coastal cities is continued. During the invasion of Italy, raids into these cities were noted in several quatrains. Starting from the eastern edge of France, near the Italian border:

(111) **Century 3, Quatrain 10**

| | |
|---|---|
| From blood and hunger more great calamity | *De sang et faim plus grande calamité,* |
| Seven times it will appear at the marine beach | *Sept fois s'apprête à la marine plage:* |
| Monaco from hunger, place captured, captivity, | *Monech de faim, lieu pris, captivité,* |
| The great led in a yellow iron cage. | *Le grand mené croc ferrée cage.* |

"Monaco," less than ninety miles west of Genoa, will be attacked "seven times" by sea ("the marine beach"). The defenders of Monaco will repulse the first six attacks before falling on the seventh. Nostradamus does not specify over what period of time those attacks will occur—the time span could cover several weeks or several years. Once again the nearly continual theme of "hunger" is found, and again it is associated with war ("blood"). The third line would appear to indicate that the reason for the fall of Monaco will be at least partially due to hunger-weakened defenders.

After the fall of Monaco the people will be enslaved ("place captured, captivity"), probably because of their resistance, and their leaders ("the great") will be "led" away "in a yellow iron cage," perhaps as a display to the victorious Muslim troops. Of course, while Nostradamus notes that the populace will be enslaved, if the Mahdi is anything like Genghis Khan, there will be many executed for their resistance. If the rest will be spared, it will be only because the Mahdi will have need for slave labor at the time.

Nice, less than fifteen miles to the west of Monaco, will take notice of the fate of the people of Monaco. The following quatrain describes what their response will be:

**(112) Century 7, Quatrain 19**

| | |
|---|---|
| The fort of Nice<br>    will not see combat: | *Le fort Nicene ne sera combattu:* |
| Vanquished will it be<br>    through shining metal. | *Vaincu sera par rutilant métal.* |
| Its case will a long time<br>    be debated, | *Son fait sera un long temps débattu,* |
| To the citizens strange frightful. | *Aux citadins étrange épouvantal.* |

"Nice" will not be defeated through "combat," but through a mysterious "shining metal." The events surrounding the fall of "The fort of Nice" will "a long time be debated." "The citizens" of some city, either Nice or another one nearby, will regard the event as very "strange" and with some fear as well, "strange" because it will be so unusual, "frightful" because they will fall into the hands of the new Genghis Khan.

What are the possibilities for "shining metal"? The most obvious is money, but it is hard to see a French city surrendering to the Mahdi for silver and gold during World War III. More likely the city will surrender without a shot being fired when the citizens see the sun gleaming on a large array of artillery, helmets, firearms, and possibly even a few tanks arrayed against them. The city fathers will surrender the city to avoid massacre and enslavement of the inhabitants, à la Genghis Khan. The wisdom of this act will be debated for generations, as Nice has mountains located to both the north and southwest, with a large plain between. Control of Nice for the Islamic armies will mean access to a plain that will allow greater maneuverability than in the mountains. For the French, the fall of Nice will mean that the next great physical boundary to the Mahdi's advance will be the Rhone River, 125 miles to the west. Yet how could Nice surrender so easily, without a fight? Perhaps the next quatrain will clarify the situation somewhat:

**(113) Century 3, Quatrain 82**

| | |
|---|---|
| Frejus, Antibes, villages all around Nice, | *Freins, Antibol, villes autour de Nice,* |
| They will be devastated heavily by sea and by land: | *Seront vastées fort par mer et par terre:* |
| The locusts land and sea wind propitious, | *Les sauterelles terres et mer vent propice,* |
| Captured, dead, trussed, pillaged without law of war. | *Pris, morts, troussés, pillés sans loi de guerre.* |

"Frejus" and "Antibes" are both coastal towns on a little peninsula just to the west of Nice. Not only will the Islamic hordes be coming from Monaco to the east, they will have established a beachhead at Frejus and Antibes as well. The whole coastline will be under attack, and the Muslims will attempt to encircle Nice and cut off relief and reinforcements. The "locusts" of the third line refers to either the number of Muslim soldiers being as numerous and uncountable as a swarm of locusts, or perhaps the "wind propitious" will actually bring in a locust swarm from North Africa. The end result is that the defenders of these coastal towns will be either "Captured" and "trussed" or "dead."

Pillaging of the conquered areas will be so common throughout the war that it hardly deserves special mention here, but "without law of war," is a fascinating expression. Is it possible that Nostradamus actually foresaw the Geneva Convention after World War I, with its code of ethics for the treatment of prisoners? If so, things will not go well for those who are captured. As previously mentioned, POWs will be harshly treated when not quickly executed during World War III. Surrounded, with an ultimatum to surrender to live, or fight and be slaughtered after defeat, the leaders of Nice will choose life. Even though it will open all of southeastern France to the Mahdi, that is why Nostradamus predicts they will surrender without a fight. Of course, the "what if" question will be whether they could possibly hold out until relieved; after all, Milan will be doing it at this time.

Continuing westward along the Mediterranean coast, Nostradamus has nothing to report until reaching Marseilles, ninety miles to the west of Nice. The events of this next quatrain will probably occur prior to the quatrain just discussed:

(114) **Century 1, Quatrain 18**

Through the discord
  negligence of the Gauls
Will a passage to the
  Mahomettans be opened:
Of blood soaked
  the land and sea Siena,
The port Phoenician of sails
  and ships covered.

*Par la discorde négligence Gauloise*
*Sera passage à Mahomet ouvert:*
*De sang trempé la terre et mer Senoise,*
*Le port Phocen de voiles et nefs couvert.*

The "port Phoenician" is Marseilles, settled originally by the ancient Phoenicians. The breakdowns of the post-comet world will not be in technology only; here "discord" and "negligence" by the French military authorities about where and how to fight indicate a breakdown in the command structure that will cause "a passage" to be "opened. . . to the Mahomettans" (Muslims). As a result, these Asian hordes will see the opportunity to take Marseilles. This will occur while the Islamic conquest of Italy will have reached Siena. The events of this time probably will occur several years before the fall of Nice and Monaco, as the Muslims will not have progressed into northern Italy yet. Will they hold it? Apparently they will not, as the next quatrain attests:

(115) **Century 3, Quatrain 79**

The command fatal everlasting
  through the chain
Will come to turn by
  order consistent:
Of the port Marseilles will be
  broken the chain:
The city captured, the enemy
  while and while.

*L'ordre fatal sempiternel par chaîne*
*Viendra tourner par ordre conséquent:*
*Du port Phocen sera rompue la chaîne:*
*La cité prise, l'ennemi quand et quand.*

The first two lines of the quatrain are obscure enough to be incomprehensible. The "chain" of the third line refers to the boom chains of

Marseilles. These chains were still in use until very recently, spread across a harbor to protect it from attacking ships and submarines. In the relatively low-technology days of World War III, Nostradamus predicts a return of their use. The booms of Marseilles will be broken by the invading Iranian navy, allowing them to directly invade the harbor, and this will result in "The city captured." The Muslim armies themselves, however, will be captured in turn while they are taking the city (the expression "while and while" does not translate well directly into English). But this is not the only time Marseilles will fall:

**(116) Century 10, Quatrain 88**

| | |
|---|---|
| Foot and horse at the second watch, | *Pieds et Cheval à la seconde veille,* |
| They will enter and devastate all by the sea: | *Feront entrée vastient tout par la mer:* |
| Inside the port of Marseilles he will enter, | *Dedans le poil entrera de Marseille,* |
| Tears, cries, and blood, not once ever times so bitter. | *Pleurs, cris, et sang, onc nul temps si amer.* |

This invasion is more likely to occur after the fall of Nice rather than before it. Why should this be so? Because, during the "second watch," presumably of the night, an attack of foot soldiers and mounted troops (armored vehicles?) will be coordinated with another sea invasion, and the Mahdi must already have control of areas to the east to be able to conduct this attack. The Muslim commander ("he") "will enter" the city that he has conquered and, the "Tears, cries, and blood" indicate that yet one more time, things will not go well for the defenders. It would appear that few of the defenders will be spared execution here.

There is a quatrain describing the leader of the Muslim navy and the origin of the fleet that will subdue the western Mediterranean:

**(117) Century 3, Quatrain 90**

| | |
|---|---|
| The great Satyr and Tiger of Hyrcania, | *Le grand Satyre et Tigre de Hyrcanie,* |
| Gift presented to those of the Ocean: | *Don presenté à ceux de l'Océan:* |
| A chief of fleet will leave from Carmania, | *Un chef de classe ira de Carmanie,* |
| Who will seize land at the Tyrrhenian Phocaean. | *Qui prendra terre au Tyrren Phocean.* |

"Hyrcania" was the southeastern shore of the Caspian Sea, today part of Iran. An Iranian called "The great Satyr and Tiger of Hyrcania" will present a "gift" of some sort to the Mahdi's Navy. Possibly this area of Iran will provide the sailors for the fleet, and the Caspian Sea, completely enclosed by land under Iranian control by that time, will serve as their training ground, much as the Great Lakes did for the U.S. Navy during World War II. Or perhaps northern Iran will be the manufacturing site for the deck armaments of the fleet.

"Carmania" is the land area that lies at the mouth of the Persian Gulf, which will also be under Muslim control for many years by the time of this quatrain. The "Tyrrhenian" Sea lies on the west coast of southern Italy, and Nostradamus always seems to refer to Marseilles when discussing a "Phocaean" seaport.

In summary, an Iranian fleet assembled together in the Persian Gulf, possibly armed, manned, or trained from northern Iran, will sail through the Suez Canal and into the Mediterranean. They will dominate the west coast of Italy and launch a successful invasion of Marseilles. In the second chapter of this book it was noted that the Book of Revelation predicts that 200 million Muslim troops will fight during World War III. Many, perhaps most, of those soldiers will come from east of Iran—from Pakistan, northern India, Indonesia, etc.—so the marines transported on these ships that will seize Marseilles will probably come from farther east than Iran. Many, perhaps most, of the Muslim soldiers in southern France will be from Pakistan, Bangladesh, Indonesia, and perhaps even China.

An interesting side note here is that in Nostradamus' time the Suez Canal had not even been contemplated. A fleet from Carmania would have had to sail around the horn of Africa to reach the Mediterranean, a feat difficult to envision. Thus, it would appear that Nostradamus foresaw the completion of the Suez Canal as well!

Continuing westward along the Mediterranean coast from Marseilles, only fifteen miles further is the city of Bouc:

(118) Century 1, Quatrain 28

| | |
|---|---|
| The tower of Bouc will fear the foist Barbarian, | *La tour de Boucq craindra fuste Barbare,* |
| A time, long time after the boat western: | *Un temps, long temps après barque hesperique:* |
| Cattle, people, belongings, both will cause great waste, | *Bétail, gens, meubles, tous deux feront grand tare,* |
| Taurus and Libra, what mortal pike! | *Taurus et Libra, quelle mortelle pique!* |

The "tower" of the city of Port-de-'Bouc" probably represents their defensive works. They, too, will be invaded by low, fast, Persian "foists." At a much later date ("long time") they will be re-invaded by Allied forces ("the boat western"). As a result of both invasions there will be tremendous destruction ("both will cause great waste") of personal property ("belongings") and animals ("Cattle") of the region, as well as tremendous loss of life ("people"). The "pike" was one of the weapons of foot soldiers in days of old. "Taurus and Libra" could refer to the timing of the two invasions (April 20 to May 20 for Taurus, September 23 to October 23 for Libra), or perhaps Nostradamus is referring to astrological signs associated with the two invaders. If so, then "Taurus" is possibly a force of Turkish origin, as the Ottoman Empire was supposedly influenced by the Bull. "Libra," mentioned in other quatrains as a western power of World War III, will be examined later.

The following quatrain, while containing nothing specifically linking it with Bouc, appears to be yet another example of quatrains still in their original order:

(119) **Century 1, Quatrain 29**

When the fish
   terrestrial and aquatic
Through strong wave
   to the beach will be put,
Its form strange soft and horrible,
Through sea to the walls
   very quickly the enemies.

*Quand le poisson terrestre et aquatique*
*Par forte vague au gravier sera mis,*
*Sa forme étrange suave et horrifique,*
*Par mer aux murs bien tôt les ennemis.*

The only type of "fish" capable of being both "terrestrial and aquatic" is a seagoing landing craft with wheels, a relatively low-tech ship that has been in use since World War II. The attack will occur during a time of heavy seas ("strong wave") such that it will appear that the wave itself will put the landing craft ashore. Nostradamus describes the form of the ship as "strange" and "horrible," easy enough to understand, but "soft" is somewhat baffling. Perhaps, with the expectation of losing many of them, the Mahdi will opt for the cheapest and fastest manufacturing methods for these ships. In that case their hulls will consist of a waterproof canvas or similar material stretched over a wood frame. They will not be seaworthy for long, but when half or more of them may be destroyed within a few minutes after hitting the water for the first time as they separate from their mother ships, this may not be much of a concern. In the last line the invaders "very quickly" reach the defensive walls of the city after hitting the "beach."

The "tower of Bouc" described above in quatrain (118) appears in another quatrain as well:

(120) **Century 1, Quatrain 71**

| | |
|---|---|
| The tower marine three times captured and renewed | *La tour marine trois fois prise et reprise* |
| Through Spain, Barbarians, and Genoa: | *Par Espagnols, Barbares, Ligurins: Marseille et Aix, Arles* |
| Marseilles and Aix, Arles through those of Pisa, | *par ceux de Pise,* |
| Devastation, fire, iron, pillage of Avignon from Turin. | *Vast, feu, fer, pillé Avignon des Thurins.* |

On three occasions, once "Through (from) Spain," once from the sea via the "Barbarian" (Barbary) coast of North Africa, and once from Italy ("Genoa"), the "tower marine" of Bouc will be "captured," and three times it will be liberated ("renewed") by the Allied forces. As Bouc will be at roughly the midpoint of the Mediterranean front, the land-based attacks from both Muslim-controlled Spain and Italy are understandable.

While the battle for "Marseilles" has already been discussed, here the Muslims have moved inland to Aix-en-Provence, fifteen miles directly north of Marseilles. This will be associated with a land-based attack from northern Italy upon "Arles," a city twenty miles northwest of Bouc on the Rhone River, by the same forces that conquered Pisa ("through those of Pisa"). "Avignon," another twenty miles upriver from Arles and the likely new home of the Pope, will be "pillaged" by the Muslim army that will have defeated the Allied forces at "Turin."

At this point, the Mediterranean front blends into the eastern front. One final quatrain defining the farthest Islamic advance along this front, still another quatrain that Nostradamus left in its original order:

(121) **Century 1, Quatrain 72**

| | |
|---|---|
| Of the whole Marseilles the inhabitants will change, | *Du tout Marseille des habitants changée,* |
| Run and pursuit as far as near Lyon. | *Course et poursuite jusqu'auprès de Lyon.* |
| Narbonne, Toulouse through Bourdeaux outraged: | *Narbonne, Tholouse par Bourdeaux outragée:* |
| Killed captives nearly one million. | *Tués captifs presque d'un million.* |

"Marseilles" will be abandoned by the French, and the fact that "the inhabitants will change" seems to indicate Muslim civilian settlement of the city. Since one of the Mahdi's goals during World War III will be to procure productive farmland in order to feed his starving Asian masses, relocation of civilian populations into conquered European cities may be a routine event. It will be easier to move the people to the food than to continually bring the food to the masses of Asia. The French refugees from Marseilles will stream north, and with the collapse of the front they will be chased ("Run and pursuit") until nearly reaching the city of Lyon, also on the Rhone River, but over 150 miles to the north!

Returning to events on the Spanish front, Narbonne and Toulouse will both be under attack, and both will be outraged that the commander from Bourdeaux will not release reinforcements to them. The casualty count for the offensive will be almost one million, a count that was impossible to achieve in any war until this century!

The eastern extent of the Muslim advance on the Spanish front was left at Auch. Quatrain (121) shows that the front will extend directly eastward from Auch to Toulouse and then to near Narbonne. It seems that the French will control the Mediterranean coast from near Narbonne to roughly the Rhone River, at which time it becomes the eastern front.

In quatrain (120) an Italian-based attack upon Avignon was foretold. Continuing with the battle for Avignon the scene now becomes the eastern front. Starting from Avignon and moving north along the front, in geographic order but in probable chronologic disorder, the war continues:

**(122) Century 3, Quatrain 99**

| | |
|---|---|
| At the fields grassy of Alleins and of Vernegues | *Aux champs herbeux d'Alein et du Varneigne* |
| Of mountains Luberon near the Durance, | *Du mont Lebron proche de la Durance,* |
| Camps of both sides conflict will it be so very bitter, | *Camps de deux parts conflit sera si aigre,* |
| Mesopotamia will fail in France. | *Mesopotamie défaillira en la France.* |

Slightly to the east of Avignon and just north of Marseilles is the setting for this battle. "Alleins" and "Vernegues" are small cities about halfway between Avignon and Marseilles, both south of the "Durance" River. The "Luberon" mountains are just to the north of the river. A very sharp fight ("so very bitter"), with high casualties on both sides, will occur there. For the most part the fighting appears to take place in the "fields grassy" between the Luberon Mountains. and the Durance River, with breakthrough points by the Muslims into French-controlled Alleins and Vernegues. The end result will be the failure of "Mesopotamia," the land between the two rivers. As the Durance flows into the Rhone in Avignon, it appears that Avignon is the "Mesopotamia" referred to in this quatrain, and that it will fall to the forces of the Mahdi. Apparently the Pope will have to move yet again. It is likely that his presence in Avignon will make it a key target in an Islamic Holy War. Afterwards the Mahdi's armies will likely be spent in this part of France, for there are no predictions in any of Nostradamus' quatrains about their progressing further west than the Rhone in southern France.

Continuing north along the Rhone from Avignon, roughly 120 miles, is the city of Lyon. Nostradamus has several quatrains about the battle for this city, the first three of which Nostradamus left in their original sequential order:

**(123) Century 9, Quatrain 68**

| | |
|---|---|
| From Montelimar will the noble be obscured, | *Du mont Aymar sera noble obscurcie,* |
| The evil will come at the junction of the Saone and Rhone: | *Le mal viendra au joint de Saone et Rosne:* |
| Within woods cached soldiers day of Lucy, | *Dans bois cachés soldats jour de Lucie,* |
| Which never was there so horrible a throne. | *Qui ne fut onc si horrible trône.* |

"Montelimar" is a city eighty miles south of Lyon. Both Montelimar and Lyon are on the Rhone River. Either the "noble"(man) from there will be "obscured" (killed?) during fighting in Lyon, or a separate clash will occur there while Lyon is under attack. The city in the second line is, of course, Lyon, as the "Saone and Rhone" rivers join within that city. The feast "day of (Saint) Lucy" is December 13, and thus the events at this time will occur in early winter. Nostradamus foretells some significance in this campaign for a group of soldiers in a forest ("within woods cached soldiers"), evidently laying an ambush. While he does not give the nationality of these soldiers, since the French will be retreating and defending, they are the likely candidates to be in the woods. The last line restates the horrors of war.

Continuing with the next quatrain about events in Lyon is the following:

**(124) Century 9, Quatrain 69**

| | |
|---|---|
| On the mountain of Sain-Bel and L'Arbresle | *Sur le mont de Bailly et la Bresle* |
| Will be cached of Grenoble the trusted ones: | *Seront cachés de Grenoble les fiers:* |
| Beyond Lyon, Vienne on them so much great hail, | *Outre Lyon, Vien eux si grande grêle,* |
| Locust on earth not in remnant one third. | *Langoult en terre n'en restera un tiers.* |

"Sain-Bel" and "L'Arbresle" are a few miles apart, on a mountain about twelve miles to the northwest of "Lyon." "Grenoble," fifty-five miles to the southeast of Lyon, probably will have fallen by this time since it will be behind the front lines. Indeed, the Mahdi's troops will probably pass through Grenoble on their way to Lyon. The elite ("trusted ones") French forces that defended Grenoble will have retreated and taken up positions on high ground ("cached") to the northwest of Lyon. The "great hail" represents an artillery cross-fire barrage, falling upon the massed Muslim forces outside Lyon from the high ground and from "Vienne," located slightly to the south. "Locusts" have been described in a previous quatrain as being Muslim troops, and the use of that term here seems appropriate as well. This artillery barrage will be so effective that it will kill or wound two-thirds of the Muslim force as there will be "not in remnant one third." What will the Muslim response be? While mountainous terrain may make the artillery on Sain-Bel and L'Arbresle unreachable, Vienne will be susceptible. After new troops arrive, a fierce offensive will be launched at Vienne:

**(125) Century 9, Quatrain 70**

| | |
|---|---|
| Weapons sharp inside the torches cached, | *Harnois tranchants dans les flambeaux cachés,* |
| Within Lyon, the day of the Sacrament, | *Dedans Lyon, le jour du Sacrement,* |
| Those of Vienne will be all hacked to pieces, | *Ceux de Vienne seront trestous hachés,* |
| By the cantons Latins Macon does not lie. | *Par les cantons Latins Mascon ne ment.* |

The first line is obscure. The "day of the Sacrament" is specifically the feast of Corpus Christi, but in a general sense it could be any Sunday since the sacrament of Holy Communion is distributed at all Sunday Masses. "Vienne" will fall, literally "hacked to pieces," a strong suggestion of hand-to-hand combat. The ones doing the "hacking" will have come from the "canton Latin," which is southeast Switzerland. "Macon" is on the Saone River, thirty miles to the north of Lyon. Why they "do not lie" is a mystery, but the implication is that the frontline in the battle for Lyon will range from at least Macon, thirty miles to the north of Lyon, to Vienne, fifteen miles to the south.

Nostradamus has another quatrain describing the fall of Vienne:

**(126) Century 12, Quatrain 24**

| | |
|---|---|
| The great succor coming from Guienne, | *Le grand secours venu de la Guyenne,* |
| It will be arrested completely near Poitiers: | *S'arrêtera tout auprès de Poitiers:* |
| Lyon surrendered through Montluel and Vienne, | *Lyon rendu par Mont Luel et Vienne,* |
| And plundered everywhere people of trades. | *Et saccagés partout gens de métiers.* |

"Guienne," as previously noted, was the large province of southwestern France on the Spanish border. An army from here will be called to assist in the defense of "Lyon" on the eastern front, but will be diverted instead to "Poitiers" on the northern front, roughly 125 miles north of Bordeaux. Obviously, either the campaign on the Spanish front will still be in Spain, or else the French and English will have pushed the Islamic forces back into Spain at this juncture. Regardless, without reinforcements Lyon will fall. The fall is attributed to defeats at "Montluel," a few miles to the northeast of Lyon, and at "Vienne," just to the south. These failures will result in a pincer movement with Lyon being squeezed on three sides. In the last line, civilians ("people of trades," or tradesmen) apparently will not evacuate the city in time and will also suffer greatly.

Nostradamus has one final quatrain about the battle of Lyon in which he provides a casualty count:

**(127) Century 8, Quatrain 34**

After victory of Lion over Lion,
Upon the mountain
  of Jura Slaughter,
Destruction and brown ones
  seven million,
Lyon, Vlme to Mausoleum
  death and tomb.

*Après victoire du Lion au Lion,*
*Sus la montagne de Ivra Secatombe,*
*Delues et brodes septième million,*
*Lyon, Vlme à Mansol mort et tombe.*

Two commanding generals, both referred to as "Lions," probably for their bravery, will meet and one will be victorious. The "Jura" mountains are to the northeast of "Lyon," north of Geneva. After the victory there will be "Slaughter, Destruction" upon the mountains of Jura. The "seven million. . . brown ones" are obviously either Arab or Asian troops, "brown" due to their darker complexions than the French. The French must be the victors as the battle continues northeastward from Lyon, where they will "slaughter. . . seven million" of these Muslim soldiers. Throughout all history, there has never been a casualty count from one battle even close to seven million. It can only be possible during World War III. A French soldier, apparently the victorious Lion, whose name will be an anagram of "Vlme," will be mortally wounded in the battle and will be taken to Lyon where he will die and then be buried at a mausoleum. An alternate location is the city of St.-Paul-de-Mausolee, near Avignon.

In summary, an engagement in far eastern France, near the German border, will result in a crushing defeat for the Mahdi, and the loss of seven million of his troops. It will also result in the death of the French "Lion." It is unclear if these events will occur before the sack of Lyon, or afterwards, while the French are pushing the Mahdi back towards Germany.

The next quatrain may help describe how the French manage to kill seven million of the Mahdi's troops:

**(128) Century 7, Quatrain 7**

Over the combat of
  the great horses light,
People will cry out the great
  crescent destroyed:
To kill by night mountains,
  garb of shepherds,
Abysses red into the ditch deep.

*Sur le combat des grands*
  *chevaux légers,*
*On criera le grand croissant confond:*
*De nuit tuer monts, habits de bergers,*
*Abîmes rouges dans le fossé profond.*

The first line indicates that the French troops will be a light cavalry unit ("horses light"), infiltrating the Jura "mountains." In the third line Nostradamus indicates that they will disguise themselves as "shepherds." Rather than directly engaging in combat, their mission will include the destruction of bridges, laying of mine fields, and rear-guard attacks from the mountains once the offensive begins. When in place, they will serve to slow retreat to the east and reinforcement from the Muslim reserve forces in the plains to the east and north of Lyon. This will enable an attack from Lyon to completely crush the enemy, while the "shepherds" savage the rear echelon units. Nostradamus describes this surprise attack as a night offensive ("to kill by night"), with so much "red" blood spilled that it will flow "deep" into the "ditch" (at the base of the mountains that the "shepherds" will be on?). This may represent the eventual, and final, collapse of the Islamic forces in this area, but there are still other quatrains that tell of fighting on the eastern front. Continuing northward from Lyon is the following quatrain:

**(129) Century 11, Quatrain 97**

| | |
|---|---|
| Through Villefranche, Macon in disarray, Inside the bundles of wood will be soldiers cached: Change of times in spring for the King, By means of Chalon and Moulins all hacked up. | *Par ville franche, Mascon en désarroi, Dans les fagots seront soldats cachés: Changer de temps en prime pour le Roi, Par de Chalon et Moulins tous hachés.* |

As previously mentioned, "Macon" is about thirty miles to the north of Lyon, on the Saone River. "Villefranche" is about halfway between Macon and Lyon. A breach in the center of the Allied lines at Villefranche ("through Villefranche") will create defensive problems to the north in Macon ("Macon in disarray"). The second line of the quatrain does not specify whose soldiers will be lying in ambush in the woods, but since the attackers will be the Mahdi's Asian hordes, it will likely be the French waiting in ambush.

The "King" of the third line is unnamed, but will probably be French since a favorable "Change of times" is implied. What will the "Change" be? It will be an Allied victory, and it is described in the last line. "Chalon" is about fifty miles directly north of Macon, "Moulins" about seventy miles to the west of Chalon. It is possible that at the time of this quatrain the northern front will have penetrated on the eastern corner to only thirty miles north of Lyon. If this interpretation is correct, then a spring offensive between Chalon and Moulin will result in the Mahdi's forces being cut to pieces, literally "all hacked up." Remember that in quatrain (125) "those of Vienne" were "all hacked to pieces," too. Perhaps technology will deteriorate to a point where Napoleonic-war type battles will be fought. In those battles massive lines of troops either fired at each other en masse at close range or charged each other and joined in hand-to-hand combat, with the aim of "hacking" up the enemy.

Another interpretation of the quatrain is that troops from Chalon and Moulin will hide ("cached") in a forest ("Inside the bundles of wood"), turning what may start as a Muslim breakthrough at Villefranche into a crushing defeat for the Mahdi.

Continuing with the eastern front, the scene shifts northward, to the city of Langres, over 100 miles directly to the north of Macon:

**(130) Century 2, Quatrain 50**

| | |
|---|---|
| When those of Hainaut, of Ghent and of Brussels | *Quand ceux d'Hainault, de Gand et de Bruxelles* |
| Will see at Langres the siege laid down: | *Veront à Langres le siège devant mis:* |
| Behind their flanks will be wars cruel, | *Derrière leurs flancs seront guerres cruelles,* |
| The wound ancient will be worse than the enemies. | *La plaie antique fera pis qu'ennemis.* |

"Ghent" and "Brussels" are major cities in the Low countries to the north of France; "Hainaut" was an old province of the Netherlands. After their own lands will have fallen, the soldiers from these areas will retreat into France and be given the task of defending "Langres." Nostradamus describes the attack here as a "siege" rather than an all-out frontal offensive, thus something similar to the trench warfare of World War I may occur here. While apparently capable of holding Langres, the defenders will be made aware of furious battles "Behind their flanks," probably from a Muslim force descending from the north. What might "The ancient wound" be? How could it be "worse" than something "the enemies" could do? Nostradamus probably intends treason and cowardice. While capable of holding their position, the defenders will fear being cut off and surrounded and will abandon Langres, probably fleeing to the southwest.

Far to the north of Lyon, roughly 175 miles, and about 150 miles east of Paris is the city of Nancy, in far northeastern France. The battle here, if it involves troops coming from the east, will likely precede the battle for Lyon. If the Mahdi is coming from the north, then the timing is less certain, but probably also preceding the events of Lyon:

(131) Century 10, Quatrain 7

| | |
|---|---|
| The great conflict which is being prepared at Nancy, | *Le grand conflit qu'on apprête à Nancy,* |
| The Macedonian will say all I subdue: | *L'Aemathien dira tout je soumets:* |
| The Isle Britain through wine, salt in concern, | *L'Isle Britanne par vin, sel en souci,* |
| Between two Philips a long time will not hold Metz. | *Hem. mi. deux Phi. longtemps ne tiendra Mets.* |

A major offensive ("great conflict") will be prepared around the city of "Nancy." "The Macedonian" of the Spanish campaign is found again here, as are the British. Upon including the metaphorical "wine" and "salt," one finds four separate subjects here that were also found in the southwestern front, helping link these two quatrains into the common theme of World War III. "Metz," less than thirty miles to the north of Nancy and possibly the corner of the northern and eastern fronts at the time, will be defended by "two" commanders named "Philip." They "will not" be able to hold it for "a long time."

There is one last quatrain about events along the eastern front and the final fate of the Islamic armies in this area:

(132) Century 8, Quatrain 10

| | |
|---|---|
| Putrid smell great will go out of Lausanne, | *Puanteur grande sortira de Lausanne,* |
| Which will not be known the origin of the fact, | *Qu'on ne saura l'origine du fait,* |
| The people will be put outside all the people far away, | *L'on mettra hors toute la gent lointaine,* |
| Fire seen to the sky, people foreign defeated. | *Feu vu au ciel, peuple étranger défait.* |

202

The "Putrid smell" will be from decaying corpses in a battlefield, near the Swiss city of "Lausanne," close to the French border. While they will smell the decaying corpses, the people of Lausanne will be ignorant of any nearby battles ("Which will not be known the origin of the fact"). Perhaps the "smell" will come from the seven million Muslim casualties in the Jura mountain campaign, only forty miles away. Afterwards the "foreign" (Muslim) "people" will be "defeated" and they "will be put outside" and driven "far away." Another nighttime artillery barrage ("Fire seen to the sky") is also forecast. The tone of the third line seems to indicate that this will be a permanent removal of the Islamic armies, and Switzerland, isolated from the rest of the Western forces for perhaps a few years, will be reunited with France and Great Britain again. It is possible that supplies may even begin to flow from France through Switzerland and into Milan again, as well.

This quatrain concludes the campaign along the eastern front. The farthest penetration here will be roughly the Rhone River, with major battles occurring in Avignon, Montelimar, Vienne, Lyon, Villefranche, Macon, Nancy, and Metz. At that point, the eastern front becomes continuous with the northern front. But before continuing with the northern front, Nostradamus has a quatrain detailing some of the economic effects of the war:

### (133) Century 7, Quatrain 25

| | |
|---|---|
| Through war long the entire army exhausted, | *Par guerre longue tout l'exercite épuiser,* |
| So that for soldiers there will be found no money, | *Qué pour soldats ne trouveront pécune,* |
| Instead of gold, instead of silver, leather they will coin, | *Lieu d'or, d'argent, cuir on viendra cuser,* |
| Gallic brass, seat, crescent of Moon. | *Gaulois airain, siège, croissant de Lune.* |

The length of World War III has been defined in other quatrains as lasting for twenty-seven years, so "war long" must be considered something of an understatement and "the entire army exhausted" is quite understandable. The lack of "gold" and "silver" is understandable as well, as all of the industrialized world abandoned the gold standard decades ago and now possesses only pennies of gold and silver for every dollar in circulation. Without gold and silver to back the currency, it is only the stability of the country itself that allows any country monetary stability at this time. The tremendous disruption of commerce caused by the meteor impact and the following war will change that situation greatly, not only resulting in hoarding of the precious metals, but a collapse of the current monetary system which is based on faith as well. Copper and nickel, the components of modern pocket change, will be too valuable as part of the war effort to waste in currency. The currency problem will be solved by creating a new type of money: a specially prepared leather with the seal of the government imprinted or burned into it. Actually, this will not be a new process. Folding money was invented by the Chinese thousands of years ago, and yes, they imprinted leather rather than paper.

The last line of this quatrain is somewhat unclear. Perhaps it will be Iran, the new Persia, who will "coin. . . leather" while the French will be coining "brass." Another option is that Nostradamus is describing the seals that will be burned into the leather. If he is describing the seals, then the French may imprint their money with an image of the Pope, the "seat" referring to the home of the Pope, and the currency of the enlarged Iran may contain the traditional Islamic symbol of the "crescent of Moon."

Discussion of the battle for the eastern front was left at Nancy, which appears to be the corner where the eastern front meets the northern front. Continuing 150 miles to the west-northwest from Nancy is the city of St. Quentin:

### (134) Century 4, Quatrain 8

| | |
|---|---|
| The great city by assault promptly unexpected | La grande cité d'assaut prompt repentin |
| Surprised at night, guards interrupted: | Surpris de nuit, gardes interrompus: |
| The guards and watches St. Quentin | Les excubies et veilles saint Quintin |
| Massacred, guards and the portals broken. | Trucidés, gardes et les portails rompus. |

This is a fairly clear and simple quatrain. "St. Quentin" is about seventy-five miles north-northeast of Paris, and less than fifty miles from the Belgian border. A surprise "night" attack will breach holes in the defensive works ("the portals") that will be erected around the city, and after the defensive forces ("the guards") are overcome, the inhabitants will be "massacred."

Continuing westward along the northern front is the following quatrain:

**(135) Century 9, Quatrain 88**

Calais, Arras, succor
  to Therouanne,
Peace and semblance simulated
  by the spy:
Mercenaries of Savoy will
  descend through Roanne,
Detoured people who would
  end the rout.

*Calais, Arras, secours á Theroanne,*
*Paix et semblant simulera l'escoute:*
*Soulde d'Alobrox descendre par Roane,*
*Détourné peuple qui défera la routte.*

"Arras" is thirty-five miles to the northwest of St. Quentin. "Calais," a port city on the English Channel, is sixty miles to the northwest of Arras, with the English city of Dover a mere twenty-five miles away across the Channel. Roughly halfway between Calais and Arras is the city of "Therouanne." If St. Quentin, from the prior quatrain, is included, then a nearly 100-mile-long perfectly straight line is formed. In this battle, the center of the front, located at Therouanne, will be in danger of collapse. It will be saved by reinforcements from the left and right flanks at Calais and Arras ("Calais, Arras, succor to Therouanne").

During this time a Muslim emissary will cross into French territory under the guise of discussing a "Peace" treaty, a treaty which the Mahdi will have no intention of honoring since it will be "simulated." The emissary's true purpose will be to "spy" on the French defensive positions.

In the third line the scene shifts back to the eastern front. "Roanne" is forty miles to the northwest of Lyon. What was then the country of "Savoy" in Nostradamus' time is today western Italy and southeastern France. "Mercenaries" from this area would likely be French and Italian citizens pressed into the Mahdi's service, or perhaps Nostradamus refers to mercenary troops from another part of the world piercing through the Rhone north of Lyon and penetrating as far as Roanne. The Allied troops capable of stopping this advance on the eastern front ("who would end the rout") will be "Detoured" elsewhere, probably to Therouanne.

This quatrain links simultaneous events on the eastern and northern fronts. During the time of the battle for Lyon, the northern front will still be in northern France on a line running from northwest to southeast. This line will not hold for the French, however. Perhaps it will be the collapse of St. Quentin that undermines it. As the front continues to the south the next major battle will be at Rouen:

**(136) Century 4, Quatrain 19**

Before Rouen by the Insubrians
   will be put the siege,
By land and sea shut off
   the passages:
Of Hainaut, and Flanders, of
   Ghent and those of Liege
By gifts cloaked
   ravaging the beaches.

*Devant Roüan d'Insubres mis le siège,*
*Par terre et mer enfermés les passages:*
*D'Haynault, et Flandres,*
   *de Gand et ceux de Liege*
*Par dons laenees raviront les rivages.*

"Rouen" is over 100 miles to the south of Calais. It will be surrounded and put under a "siege" by troops from north central Italy ("the Insubrians"). Perhaps these will be, once again, mercenary troops, or perhaps they will be Muslim units that will have previously participated in the battle for northern Italy. Rouen will be isolated ("shut off the passages") from the rest of France both "by land and sea."

The third line indicates the origin of the invaders. "Hainaut," "Flanders," "Ghent" and "Liege" are all from modern-day Belgium and the Netherlands. When taken together, the last three lines indicate that the Mahdi will launch invasions of the French beaches, something like the Normandy invasion of WW II. These invasions, unlike D-Day, will be from bases in Belgium and the Netherlands, not England. Also unlike D-Day, they may occur at any point along the coast, perhaps even as far as the Spanish border. Nostradamus does not indicate the extent of the invasions. It does appear, though, that a major thrust will penetrate to Rouen by both land and sea. These amphibious assaults will be successful enough to allow the Iranian navy to control the entire Atlantic offshore region for an unspecified period of time.

Additional support that the Calais—St. Quentin line will not hold is found in the following quatrain:

**(137) Century 9, Quatrain 86**

From Bourg-la-Reine they will
   come right to Chartres,
And will near to
   Pont d'Antony pause:
Seven for the peace
   crafty as Martens,
Will enter an army at Paris closed.

*Du bourg Lareyne parviendront*
   *droit à Chartres,*
*Et feront près du pont Anthoni pause:*
*Sept pour la paix cauteleux*
   *comme Martres,*
*Feront entrée d'armée à Paris close.*

"Bourg-la-Reine" and "Pont d'Anthony" are just a few miles south of "Paris," while "Chartres" is about forty-five miles to the southwest. The Allied troops south of Paris will leave the city and engage the enemy at Chartres. Afterwards, they will return to a point just south of Paris, at Pont d'Anthony, for a rest. They then will enter Paris and help to defend it. The verbatim translation of the last line does not help with the understanding of the passage. It is better understood as reading "The army will then enter Paris, which will be encircled." Capable of withdrawing from Paris, the French commander will elect to make a stand in the French capital. The meaning of the third line is completely obscure at this time.

How will this commander fare in Paris? The answer is found in the following:

(138) Century 6, Quatrain 43

Long time will be
    without inhabitants,
Where the Seine and Marne
    comes to water:
From La Tamise and
    warriors tested,
Deceived the guards in believing
    in the repulse.

*Longtemps sera sans être habitée,*
*Où Signe et Marne autour*
    *vient arroser:*
*De la Tamise et martiaux tentée,*
*Décus les gardes en cuidant repousser.*

The "Marne" River flows into the "Seine" just to the east of Paris, so there can be no doubt about which city Nostradamus intended here. The destruction of Paris will be so severe that for a "Long time" it "will be without inhabitants." What could cause such a calamity? Biological and chemical weapons are possible causes, but their use is unlikely at this point in the war by the forces of Islam, since they will be winning and unwilling to risk a counterattack from similar weapons. Besides, it is doubtful if even those weapons would leave the city unlivable, since after they dissipate, the physical structures would still be present and livable within a few years at most. Nuclear weapons are also unlikely, since the last line indicates that the defenders will believe themselves capable of repulsing the attack ("believing in the repulse") and no army is capable of repulsing nuclear weapons. Thus, the last line implies a conventional attack.

How will the Mahdi's troops make Paris unlivable? After taking the city, the simplest method would be to spread interconnected flammable materials throughout the streets, linking them so that a single match could ignite a firestorm, thus leaving nothing useful in the ashes and rubble. Afterwards, the Mahdi may use an old Roman tactic: salt. After several Punic wars with the Carthaginians in North Africa, the Romans sacked and burned Carthage and spread salt all over the grounds of the city and its surrounding fields. For over 2,000 years now, Carthage has remained uninhabited, its countryside a wasteland.

Another possible way of making a city unlivable was a tactic practiced by Saddam Hussein in his genocide of the Iraqi Khurds. After bombing entire villages to rubble, bulldozers were sent in to level the ruins. Land mines were then liberally distributed throughout the rubble piles, guaranteeing that the original inhabitants would not return, as the mines remain potentially explosive for generations. The second line of this quatrain indicates the direction from which the attack will come. La Tamise is a town near Antwerp, well to the north of Paris.

Since Nostradamus devotes so many quatrains to other battles, why are just a few devoted to the destruction of Paris? Several reasons are possible. First, the French may not make an all-out commitment to defend the city. Several times during the past few centuries they have had to defend Paris, most recently in World War II. What did they do then? The commanders realized that since Paris lies on a large plain, without the benefit of large hills or mountains, they could not possibly hold it and Paris was abandoned to the advancing Nazis. Something similar to that episode may happen again. Or, perhaps the quatrains that involve war and do not specify a location, and there are many of those, are meant for Paris. For whatever reason, there is only one other quatrain that specifically mentions Paris that is relevant to this setting:

**(139) Century 3, Quatrain 93**

| | |
|---|---|
| Into Avignon the chief of the entire empire | *Dans Avignon tout le chef de l'empire* |
| Will pause for Paris desolated: | *Fera arrêt pour Paris désolé:* |
| Troy will have the Hannibal's ire: | *Tricast tiendra l'Annibalique ire:* |
| Lyon by the change will be evilly consoled. | *Lyon par change sera mal consolé.* |

Here "the chief of the entire empire" appears to be the ruler of France. How can Nostradamus use the term "empire" when France does not even control half of its own territory, let alone the foreign lands required to make an empire? Either he intends an empire governing many nationalities (the refugees from all of Europe that will stream into France), or else Nostradamus looks forward to a time after the war, when France will once again be an empire. The man who "will pause" in "Avignon" will be the ruler of that coming French empire. Apparently the eastern front will hold at the Rhone while the northern front is collapsing as this "chief. . . Will pause" (to mourn?) while in "Avignon" for a "Paris desolated."

The commander that will destroy Paris is called "Hannibal" in this quatrain, perhaps a reference to his North African (Libyan?) origin, as Hannibal (247-163 B.C.) was the greatest of the Carthaginian generals. After this victory in Paris he will continue southward, making the city of "Troy" his next target. Troy is seventy-five miles to the east-southeast of Paris, and half way between Paris and Langres.

Why should Lyon "be evilly consoled" about these events? Probably because troops will be removed from the defense of Lyon and rushed to Troy to help shore-up the defenses on the northern front, leading to the fall of Lyon on the eastern front previously described in quatrain (126). Nostradamus does not say in this quatrain whether or not Troy will hold. After the fall of Paris, "Hannibal" will continue to advance southward, the next stop being Tours:

**(140) Century 4, Quatrain 46**

| | |
|---|---|
| Well defended the fact by excellence, | *Bien défendu le fait par excellence,* |
| Guard yourself Tours from your near ruin: | *Gardes-toi Tours de ta proche ruine:* |
| London and Nantes through Reims will make defense | *Londres et Nantes par Reims fera défense* |
| Not passing further at the time of the drizzle. | *Ne passe outre au temps de la bruine.* |

"Tours" is on the Loire River, 120 miles southwest of Paris. "Nantes" is also on the Loire, 100 miles to the west of Tours. In fact, the Loire River, lying on a line running from east to west for over 180 miles, then turning southeast for another 165 miles, will serve as the best natural defensive border in all of northern France. As the Loire originates only thirty miles to the west of Lyon, which will be the edge of the eastern front, the French could not ask for a better natural defense in the north. That is what Nostradamus means in the first line, which might be paraphrased as "well defended behind an excellent defense." If "Hannibal" can pierce through the Loire, then there is no terrain the French will be able to use to their advantage anywhere in the north, endangering the entire front. And should the northern front collapse at the Loire it is likely that all of France will fall as well.

In the southwest, the Garonne will be the final line of defense; on the eastern front it will be the Rhone, and on the northern front it will be the Loire. Behind these three rivers France will make its final stands. The strategic withdrawals all across Europe, trading land for time and inflicting large casualties on the Muslims, will stop here. Behind these three rivers the Allies will not retreat and will commit all of their reserves in do-or-die battles. Nostradamus seems to indicate that the Garonne and the Rhone (except at Lyon) will hold. Will the Loire hold? In the second line of this quatrain Nostradamus indicates that Tours will have a close call ("near ruin"). If Troy does not hold against the attack detailed in quatrain (139) it will be retaken, for here the French forces from Nantes, with British assistance, are found defending "Reims," sixty miles directly to the north of Troy.

Nostradamus has another quatrain detailing the defense of the Loire:

**(141) Century 1, Quatrain 20**

Tours, Orleans, Blois, Angers,
    Reims, and Nantes,
Cities vexed through
    sudden change:
Through languages foreign
    will be erected tents,
Rivers, darts at Rennes
    land and sea trembling.

*Tours, Orléans, Blois, Angiers,*
    *Reims, et Nantes,*
*Cités vexées par subit changement:*
*Par langues étranges seront*
    *tendues tentes,*
*Fleuves, dards Renes terre*
    *et mer tremblement.*

"Nantes," "Angers," "Tours," "Blois," and "Orleans" lie on the Loire River on a line from west to east that is over 160 miles long. As Reims, listed in the previous quatrain, is 120 miles to the northeast of Orleans, and "Rennes" is sixty miles to the north of Nantes and only thirty miles from the Atlantic ocean, this represents the entire northern front, a distance of 370 miles. This will be France's last stand on the northern front. The "languages foreign" expression was seen in the battle for the Balkans in Eastern Europe (quatrain 52), and referred to the Mahdi's armies. They will set up their camps ("erected tents") at "rivers" (possibly the Garonne, the Rhone, and/or the Loire?). Rennes will be subject to a missile attack of some sort ("darts"), and yet another aftershock earthquake of the great meteor strike will occur as the "land and sea" will be "trembling."

The Atlantic front has been hinted at in several quatrains. Here is one more quatrain discussing events on that front:

(142) **Century 3, Quatrain 9**

| | |
|---|---|
| Bordeaux, Rouen and the La Rochelle joined | *Bourdeaux, Roüan et la Rochelle joints* |
| Will hold around the great sea of the Ocean, | *Tiendront autour la grande mer Océan,* |
| English, Bretons and the Flemings conjoined | *Anglois, Bretons, et les Flamans conjoints* |
| The chase will be nearly to Roanne. | *Les chasseront jusqu'auprès de Roane.* |

"Bordeaux" was already mentioned as being the northwest corner of the Spanish front. Apparently it will be the southwest corner of the Atlantic front as well, as it is only a few miles from the ocean, quite close to the Gironde estuary of the Garonne River. "La Rochelle" is on the Atlantic Ocean, ninety miles to the north of Bordeaux. As "Rouen" is in northern France, and over thirty miles from the ocean, and will likely be under Muslim control at this time of the war, it is difficult to see how it fits unless troops originally from Rouen will participate in the defense of La Rochelle or Bordeaux.

In the third line, a combined "English," British (Scottish? Welsh? Irish? Perhaps even Canadian?) and Belgian ("Flemings") army will attack the Muslims on the eastern front, pushing them back to Roanne. While Nostradamus does not give the location from where "The chase" will start, the most likely site is a mountain range that extends for twenty miles from north to south, lying about ten miles to the west of Roanne. If this should be so, it implies that not only will the Allies lose Lyon to the Moslems, but that the Mahdi's troops will continue across the Rhone another forty-five miles to the west before they can be repulsed.

Another interpretation of this quatrain, however, is that after successfully repelling the Muslims on the Atlantic front, a combined Allied force will drive north along the coast, then turn east, flanking the Islamic Asian hordes. This flanking attack will continue eastward along the northern front, then loop southward along the eastern front, almost as far as Roanne.

Nostradamus has one final quatrain providing an overview of the Mahdi's entire campaign:

**(143) Century 5, Quatrain 68**

| | |
|---|---|
| Into the Danube and of the Rhine will come to drink | *Dans le Danube et du Rhin viendra boire* |
| The great Camel, not repenting it: | *Le grand Chameau, ne s'en repentira:* |
| Trembling by those of the Rhone, and more strongly those of the Loire, | *Trembler du Rosne, et plus fort ceux de Loire,* |
| And near the Alps the Cock will ruin him. | *Et près des Alpes Coq le ruinera.* |

"The great Camel" must be the Mahdi, as camels are to the peoples of the Middle East and North Africa what horses and cattle are to Western Civilization. His campaign is summarized here, his conquest of the "Danube" river in Eastern Europe, and the "Rhine" river in Germany and the Netherlands. Of these conquests, of the blood that he will shed, the Mahdi will have no regrets ("not repenting"). At the "Rhone" and "Loire" rivers the defenses will be severely tested ("tremble"), but hold. Note that Nostradamus indicates fiercer attacks against the Loire; apparently the bulk of the Mahdi's forces in France will be on the northern front. It is likely that those of the northern front will be veterans of the Eastern European and German campaigns; those on the eastern front will probably come from the Greek and Italian campaigns.

"The Cock," of course, has been a symbol for France for many centuries, and the French "will ruin him" (the Mahdi) "near the Alps." Implied is a counterattack on the eastern front, perhaps a continuation of the push to Roane, which will force the Muslims back to the Swiss and Italian borders. The Mahdi, unwilling to give ground after so many years of advances, with final victory so close, will dig in for a final defense and commit all his reserves to avoid being pushed out of France. This epic battle will result in the "ruin" of the Islamic forces and a complete victory for France and the Allies. Read the last line of the quatrain again. There is something about the tone of the words that indicates the "ruin" is something final, not just a temporary setback for the Mahdi.

Is it credible that the French, after years of defeats, will suddenly counterattack the Muslim forces, perhaps even completely destroying them? Yes, it is quite possible. Remember, after the disasters early in the war, in Eastern Europe, where Allied troops will stand and hold only to be overwhelmed by superior numbers, the Allied approach will be one of trading land for time. During World War II the Russians employed a similar tactic, retreating many hundreds of miles across the Russian steppes before finally turning defeat into victory. In World War III the Allies will pick out superior defensive positions, fortify them, and try to inflict ten or more casualties on the Muslims for every one they suffer. Then, when they are about to be finally overwhelmed, they will retreat to the next position. This will occur all across Europe, all the way to France. Along the way the defensive perimeter will continue to grow shorter, making it easier to defend, and the Muslim supply lines will grow longer. Even though the Mahdi will have hundreds of millions of troops at his disposal during the war, eventually these tactics by the Allies will leave even his massive forces weakened. The Allied commanders will not even risk a major offensive at any time during the war until they are sure the Muslims have been weakened enough to be driven from Europe permanently. When they are sure of complete victory they will strike, and strike hard, at the Mahdi and his armies.

# THE ALLIES
# COUNTERATTACK

T he last chapter closed with the thought that somehow, despite years of retreating across Europe, the Allies will succeed in driving the Islamic forces from France. Support for that idea is found in the following quatrain:

**(144) Century 2, Quatrain 60**

| | |
|---|---|
| The faith Punic in<br>   the East broken,<br>Ganges Jordan, and Rhone Loire,<br>   and Tagus will change:<br>When of the mule the hunger<br>   will be satisfied,<br>Fleet poured out, blood and<br>   bodies floating. | *La foi Punicque en Orient rompue,*<br>*Gang. Iud, et Rosne Loire,*<br>   *et Tag changeront:*<br>*Quand du mulet la faim sera repue,*<br>*Classe espargie, sang et corps nageront.* |

"The faith Punic" represents the religion of the peoples of northern Africa, in short, Islam. By also referring to countries "in the East," Nostradamus links this quatrain with those other quatrains which give the origin of the Blue and White Turbans, and hints at a unified Islamic nation. He then mentions five rivers that will be notable for the battles fought on them. The "Rhone" and the "Loire" rivers were discussed in some detail in the previous chapter during the battle for France. The "Ganges" is one of the major rivers of India; it starts in the far north and flows to the southeast before

215

entering Bangladesh on its way to the sea. It is worth noting that while India is primarily Hindu, Bangladesh is a country whose population is overwhelmingly Moslem. While Nostradamus makes little mention of battlefields during World War III outside of Europe, here he at least pays brief tribute to the fight between the Hindus of India and their Moslem neighbors. Since the Ganges is not especially far from China, perhaps even India and the Chinese will battle each other as well.

The Book of Revelation, discussed in the second chapter, indicates that the death toll in WW III will be in the billions, and that the surface area of the Earth that will see combat will be more than twice that of World War II. To come up with a death toll in the billions and a combat surface area of twenty-five percent of the planet, a very bloody war between China and India may not only be possible, it may be unavoidable. However, since Nostradamus saw himself first and foremost as a prophet for France, fighting in other parts of the world, thousands of miles away from France, was not of much concern to him.

The mention of the "Jordan" River is very interesting. Until this point, Nostradamus has not indicated that he had any vision of the restoration of the state of Israel. Yet, he must have been aware of the numerous prophecies from the Bible which speak of the reestablishment of a Jewish state. Perhaps, as with India, he felt no need to write of battles not directly involving France. Regardless, the location of the Jordan River, flowing from north to south and forming the border between Israel and Jordan, and the border between Israel and the Golan Heights farther to the north, indicates yet another major battle front. Implied is the conquest and captivity of Israel yet one more time, with at least one more restoration of the country before the Second Coming of Jesus and the final arrival of the "end-times." It is interesting that since Israel has been reestablished as an independent country that all scholars of biblical prophecy regard the end of the world as being imminent. There is no scriptural reason that Israel cannot be destroyed and resurrected as a country many more times before the end of the world!

The "Tagus" River flows from east to west in Spain and Portugal, nearly bisecting the Iberian peninsula in half. And only a few miles from the source of the Tagus is the source of the Jucaw River, which flows eastward, emptying into the Atlantic. Together they form a water barrier across the entire Iberian peninsula, a perfect natural defensive barrier, and the Allies can be expected to make the Muslim armies of Arab North Africa pay heavily in the crossing of these two rivers.

Nostradamus writes that these five rivers "will change," apparently when the Muslim forces will be defeated ("The faith Punic in the East broken"). The meaning of "when. . . the mule('s). . . hunger will be satisfied" is not clear at this time. Perhaps the "mule" will be one of the military commanders, and it will be his "hunger" for war that "will be satisfied." This thought is linked with disaster by sea; the last line indicating ships sunk ("fleet poured out") and sailors killed ("blood and bodies floating"). Since the rest of the quatrain deals with the defeat of Muslim forces, the implication is that the ships sunk in the last line will be from the Iranian navy as well. But how can the Allied forces, bottled up inside France, facing tremendous pressures on five fronts, mount any type of a sea campaign? The French navy will be small at best, their ports few and probably ill-equipped. Then from whence will come the fleet that will destroy Iran's navy? The answer is found in the following quatrain:

### (145) Century 4, Quatrain 50

| | |
|---|---|
| Libra will be seen to reign over the Hesperias, | *Libra verra regner les Hesperies,* |
| Of sky and earth keeping the monarchy: | *De ciel et terre tenir la monarchie:* |
| The Asian forces no one will see perished, | *D'Asie forces nul ne verra péries,* |
| Not until seven in a row of rank will hold the hierarchy. | *Que sept ne tiennent par rang la hiérarchie.* |

"Libra will be" in control ("seen to reign") "over the Hesperias," the land of the west. While in other quatrains "Hesperia" possibly refers to Spain, in this instance the Hesperias are the new lands of Nostradamus' time, the Americas. Allowing this, who can "Libra" be? While most Nostradamian scholars believe that this refers to a European state influenced by the constellation Libra, if Nostradamus could truly see into the future, then Libra can only be the United States. There are several reasons why this must be so. First, the constellation Libra is pictured in the heavens holding a scale, known as the scales of Justice. This same symbol is found in the form of the statue outside the Supreme Court building in Washington, D.C. Second, the Latin word for liberty is "Libertas." The Latin word "Libra" means balance, hence the scales for the constellation Libra. Nostradamus uses the word "Libra" here as an anagram of the Latin "Libertas." Third, many beautiful former coins of the larger denominations have images of "Lady Liberty" engraved on them, and the symbol "liberty" on U.S. coins signifies justice for all. Fourth, the Statue of Liberty, one of the most prominent of all of the U.S. landmarks, was a gift from the French people. Yes, if the French prophet Nostradamus really foresaw the future, the most likely symbol he would pick, from his French perspective, to represent the United States would be the symbol of "Libra."

In the second line of this quatrain Nostradamus indicates that at this point during the war the U.S. will have its internal problems under control, and will dominate the Americas by ground and air power ("Of sky and earth keeping the monarchy"), imposing peace on the other countries of North and South America. In the last two lines he indicates that "The Asian forces," representing the Mahdi and his Asian hordes, will not be defeated ("no one will see perished") until the seventh U.S. president to hold power during World War III takes office ("Not until seven in a row of rank will hold the hierarchy"). Since Nostradamus indicated in quatrain (32) that WW III will take twenty-seven years, this is an average of slightly less than four years per president, by no means unreasonable. For instance, the twenty-seven years between 1962 and 1989 saw seven Presidents: Kennedy, Johnson, Nixon, Ford, Carter, Reagan, and Bush. Also note that two of those seven, Nixon and Reagan, were elected to multiple terms. The fact that there will only be seven Presidents during the most tumultuous period in world history should argue for at least some domestic stability in the United States; unless of course they all hold power under martial law and finish their rule by being assassinated.

With its domestic problems somewhat under control, the U.S. will once again look overseas to Europe, and just as in World War I, will enter the war late in the contest. Yet, just as in WW I, the presence of the U.S. armed forces will be enough to assure victory. And now the question of who it was that sank the Iranian fleets in quatrain (144) can be answered. Since it can only be through its navy that the U.S. will be able to reach Europe, it will be the new United States' navy that will destroy the Muslim fleet and reestablish Allied control of the Mediterranean.

There is a specific quatrain linking United States and French forces together against the Muslims:

**(146) Century 8, Quatrain 46**

At Saint-Paul-de-Mausolee he
   will die three leagues
   from the Rhone,
Running away the two nearest
   Tarascon destroyed:
Because Mars will make the
   most horrible throne,
Of Cock and of Eagle of France
   brothers three.

*Pol mensolee mourra trois*
   *lieues du rosne,*
*Fuis les deux prochains tarasc destrois:*
*Car Mars fera le plus horrible trône,*
*De coq et d'Aigle de France frères trois.*

"St.-Paul-de-Mausolee" has been mentioned previously, during the campaign for the eastern front in France; in quatrain (127) was a prediction of the death of a French soldier who was to be buried there. In this quatrain another (or perhaps the same?) soldier will die and be buried there. Perhaps St.-Paul-de-Mausolee will become the national cemetery for the French war dead.

Tarascon is on the east bank of the Rhone River, just a few miles south of Avignon. Since it is on the east bank, and presumably under Muslim control, the "two nearest" ones "running away" are presumably Islamic armies, crumbling under an Allied onslaught. But who might the Allied attackers be? The last line indicates their nationality. Much has been written about the "brothers three" of the last line, and almost all commentators regard them as persons, but examine the context closely! The first three items of the last line are countries, so it is likely that the last item represents a country as well. The last line might be better understood as "Cock" (the symbol of France) is to "Eagle" (the symbol of the United States) as "France" (the country of France) is to "brothers three" (the country of the United States?)." Of course, the "brothers three" might also refer to the French, British and U.S. military forces, which will be "brothers" together for the third time during a world war. However, if the "brothers three" refers to America, who might the other two "brothers" be along with the U.S.? The most likely candidates are Mexico and Canada, who along with the United States, are the only three "brothers" of the North American continent. After the meteor-induced explosion and tsunami, the geopolitical state of the world will be permanently altered. Perhaps the North America Free Trade Agreement (NAFTA) will serve as a precursor for the eventual unification of the three into a commonwealth, or perhaps even a single country, a larger "united" states of all North America. Whatever may happen politically in North America, Nostradamus indicates that it will be the French, in combination with the United States (and possibly Mexican and Canadian forces under U.S. control), that will drive the armies of the Mahdi from the Rhone River in southern France. And it will be from the Rhone that the Allies will continue to drive eastward against the Muslims. Before continuing with that eastward march, however, there are just a few quatrains concerning events on other fronts that need to be addressed. Beginning with Spain:

**(147) Century 4, Quatrain 70**

| | |
|---|---|
| Fully contiguous from great mountains Pyrenees, | *Bien contiguë des grands monts Pyrenées,* |
| Against the Eagle a great army addressed: | *Un contre l'Aigle grande copie adresser:* |
| Opened veins, forces exterminated, | *Ouvertes veines, forces exterminées,* |
| That almost to Pau the chief will be pursued. | *Que jusqu'à Pau le chef viendra chasser.* |

The United States ("the Eagle" being the other great symbol of the United States besides "Justice," and the one with which most Americans would most identify themselves) will face a "great army" of Muslims. Presumably the U.S. will have made a landing on the beaches of Spain, pushing the armies of Islam eastward up against the "mountains Pyrenees." That the Muslims will suffer a crushing defeat ("forces exterminated") is seen in their retreat over the "Pyrenees," being chased all the way to "Pau." Obviously, the Islamic forces must hold southern France at this time as well as Spain. The Muslims will be trapped between the British on the north at the Garonne River, the French and the enigmatic "brothers three" at the Rhone River on the west, and by the approaching U.S. forces from the west. The final fate of the Islamic forces in Spain and southern France is found in the following quatrain:

**(148) Century 6, Quatrain 99**

The enemy doctor will find
    himself confused,
Great camp sick, and defeated
    by ambushes,
Mountains Pyrenees and Pennine
    Alps to him will in fact
    be refused,
Near of river discovering
    antique rocks.

*L'ennemi docte se trouvera confus,*
*Grand camp malade, et défait*
    *par embûches,*
*Monts Pyrenees et Poenus lui*
    *seront faits refus,*
*Proche du fleuve découvrant*
    *antiques roches.*

The "doctor" of the first line refers to the Islamic commander, who will be either a university professor with a Ph.D., or a medical doctor. He will be uncertain as to which way to turn, with a plague among his troops ("Great camp sick") and "ambushes" set against him with every attempted break-out. Upon being pushed out of Spain and unable to reach the armies of Islam in Italy ("Mountains Pyrenees and Penine Alps to him . . . refused"), he will be forced to surrender. The "antique rocks" of the last line is a mystery. The "river" is probably the Rhone, and it will be at the Rhone where the Islamic commander will surrender his forces. Implied in this quatrain is Allied control of the Mediterranean, doubtless by the U.S. Navy, since otherwise the Muslim commander could be resupplied from Italy or North Africa.

In the following quatrain Nostradamus writes about the Allied control of the seas:

**(149) Century 8, Quatrain 59**

By two times elevated by two
    times put lower,
The East also the West
    will weaken:
Its adversary after many combats,
By sea chased at the time
    of need failing.

*Par deux fois haut par deux*
    *fois mis à bas,*
*L'Orient aussi l'Occident faiblira:*
*Son adversaire après plusieurs combats,*
*Par mer chassé au besoin faillira.*

The first line is not entirely clear, possibly there will be two massive offensives by "The East" against the Allies sometime during the war. "The West" will repulse the attacks, but "will weaken" under the onslaught of hundreds of millions of Asian troops. "After many combats" the "East" will falter "by sea. . . at the time of need." With the collapse and surrender of all Islamic forces in Spain and southwestern France, this will definitely be a "time of need" for Islam; so perhaps this quatrain refers to the collapse of the Muslim forces in France. Nostradamus attributes their failure to loss of control of the "sea," probably the Mediterranean. If the U.S. Navy can take control of the Mediterranean from the Iranian navy, then not only will the Islamic armies in Spain be cut off from supply, but the Muslim occupation forces in Italy will be in danger of being isolated as well.

There is a quatrain which may or may not be appropriate at this juncture:

### (150) Century 8, Quatrain 49

| | |
|---|---|
| Saturn in Taurus, Jupiter in Aquarius, Mars in Sagittarius, | *Satur au boeuf iouë en l'eau,* |
| | *Mars en flèche,* |
| Sixth of February mortality handed over, | *Six de Février mortalité donnera,* |
| | *Ceux de Tardaigne à Bruge* |
| Those of Tardenois at Bruges so great breach, | *si grande brèche,* |
| | *Qu'à Ponteroso chef Barbarin mourra.* |
| That at Ponteroso chief of Barbarians will die. | |

While the first line presents a fairly uncommon conjunction, dating it may be useless due to the previously noted difficulties with Nostradamus' ability to accurately predict a configuration given the inaccurate data regarding planetary motions during the 16th century. This book assumes that his predicted configurations do not necessarily correlate with the years he had in mind! The configuration in the first line does not occur between the years of 2000 and 2030, so if Nostradamus foresaw the sky correctly, then this quatrain does not belong to World War III. Assuming that it does belong to WW III, the events of this quatrain are fairly simple. "Tardenois" was the area just to the northwest of Paris. The French from this area will successfully attack the Muslim "Barbarians" near the city of "Bruges" in Belgium, and the attack will result in the death of a famed Muslim general at "Ponteroso." This name presents something of a difficulty and is probably best translated as "red bridge." Perhaps it will be red from all of the blood spilled in trying to capture it.

Returning now to the eastern front, the front from which the Allies will launch their effort to reclaim Europe from the Mahdi, is another quatrain involving the united armies of the French and the United States:

**(151) Century 8, Quatrain 9**

| | |
|---|---|
| During which time the Eagle and the Cock at Savona | *Pendant que l'Aigle et le Coq à Sauone* |
| Will be united, Sea, Levant and Hungary: | *Seront unis, Mer, Levant et Ongrie:* |
| The army to Naples, Palermo, March of Ancona, | *L'armée à Naples, Palerne, Marque d'Ancone,* |
| Rome, Venice by the Barbarians horrible cry. | *Rome, Venise par Barbe horrible cri.* |

"Savona" is a coastal Italian city, twenty-five miles west of Genoa. A joint attack ("Will be united") against Savona by the U.S. ("the Eagle") and the French ("the Cock") will result in the liberation of that city from the forces of Islam. This attack will come by "Sea," probably with support from land-based forces coming from the north. Nostradamus then provides an overview of the campaign to reclaim Europe from the Mahdi. The drive will come from southern France and proceed to "Hungary" and Turkey ("Levant") in the east and Italy in the south.

In Italy Nostradamus makes special mention of Allied victories at "Naples, Palermo," "Ancona, Rome" and "Venice." The "Barbarians" will make a "horrible cry" because of their defeats throughout Italy. If the U.S. navy successfully neutralizes the Iranian fleet, then the Allies will trap millions of Muslim soldiers in Italy, and prevent their resupply and reinforcement as the Allies drive southward through the Italian peninsula

There are other quatrains fleshing out the theme of the Allies returning to Italy. Here is the first:

**(152) Century 7, Quatrain 4**

| | |
|---|---|
| The Duke of Langres besieged within Dole, | *Le Duc de Langres asségé dedans Dole,* |
| Accompanied by Autun and those of Lyon: | *Accompagné d'Autun et Lyonnois:* |
| Geneva, Augsburg, joined those of Mirandola, | *Genève, Ausbourg, joint ceux de Mirandole,* |
| To pass the mountains against the Anconians. | *Passer les monts contre les Anconnois.* |

223

"Langres" lies on the Marne River, roughly sixty miles southwest of Nancy and sixty-five miles north of Chalon. The French commander from there will find himself trapped inside of "Dole," surrounded by the Muslims. Dole, thirty-five miles to the northeast of Chalon, will be well behind the farthest westward advance of the Mahdi. Apparently this commander will survive inside an Allied pocket besieged within Dole and be relieved at a later date, for here he commands a multi-national force comprised of soldiers from "Lyon," "Autun" (fifty miles to the west of Dole), "Geneva" (Switzerland), "Augsburg" (Germany), and "Mirandola" (Italy). These soldiers, remnants from their original much larger units, will be blended into a single elite veteran force that will cross the Alps ("pass the mountains") into Italy. What will their goal be? The last line of this quatrain indicates that it will be the Adriatic port city of Ancona.

And here is the second quatrain describing the return of the Allies to Italy:

**(153) Century 7, Quatrain 31**

| | |
|---|---|
| From Languedoc, and Guienne more than ten | *De Languedoc, et Guienne plus de dix* |
| Thousand will want the Alps to pass again: | *Mille voudront les Alpes repasser:* |
| Great Savoyards will march against Brindisi, | *Grands Allobroges marcher contre Brundis,* |
| Aquino and Bresse will come to chase them again. | *Aquin et Bresse les viendront rechasser.* |

"Languedoc" and "Guienne" were ancient provinces of southwestern France. The entry of the U.S. into the war and the surrender of the Islamic forces on the Spanish front will free Allied troops from that area to move to the eastern front. "Ten thousand" survivors of the retreat from Italy years before "will want the Alps to pass again." They will be accompanied by troops from southeastern France ("Great Savoyards") and the area around Lyon ("Bresse"), as well as Italian refugees from "Aquino" (located in southern Italy). Their attack will carry them to "Brindisi," an Adriatic port city located in the heel of the so-called Italian boot. As in southern France, the return of the naval power of the United States will serve to isolate the Islamic forces in Italy and prevent their reinforcement or escape.

The last two quatrains provide an overview of the campaign to retake Italy from the Islamic armies. Returning to a slightly earlier time, Nostradamus has a quatrain about Genoa:

(154) Century 7, Quatrain 39

| | |
|---|---|
| The conductor of the army French, | *Le conducteur de l'armée Francoise,* |
| Thinking to lose the | *Cuidant perdre le principal phalange:* |
|    principal phalanx: | *Par sus pavé de l'avoine et d'ardoise,* |
| Upon the street of oats | *Soi parfondra par Gennes gent étrange.* |
|    and of slate, | |
| Undermining themselves through | |
|    Genoa the people foreign. | |

The Muslim commander will over-commit his troops to the defense of "Genoa," trying to stop the Allied advance, but by doing this he will risk the entire Italian front. The loss of Genoa will result in the Muslims "Undermining themselves" throughout all of Italy. The French commander ("conductor of the army French") will be prepared to lose his "principal phalanx" of troops, knowing reinforcements from the west will be available. Nostradamus predicts that the fighting will be especially fierce at a location he denotes as "the street of oats and of slate."

After the liberation of Genoa will come the relief of Milan. The next quatrain was discussed during the fall of Italy and is presented here once again:

(85) Century 7, Quatrain 15

| | |
|---|---|
| In front of the city of | *Devant cité de l'Insubre contrée,* |
|    the Insubrian country, | *Sept ans sera le siège devant mis:* |
| Seven years will the siege | *Le très grand Roi y fera son entrée,* |
|    be before: | *Cité puis libre hors des ennemis.* |
| The very great King | |
|    there will himself enter, | |
| City then liberated | |
|    put out from enemies. | |

Milan, "the city of the Insubrian country," will hold out against the "siege" of the Islamic hordes for "Seven years." Thus, during the twenty-seven years of World War III, war within France itself probably cannot last for more than a seven-year period, and possibly quite less. The city of Milan will then be liberated and "The very great King" of the

225

French "will himself enter" into it. This theme of the French being ruled by a king once again will be expounded upon in the next chapter.

There is one final quatrain about fighting in Italy:

**(155) Century 2, Quatrain 33**

| | |
|---|---|
| Through the torrent which descends from Verona | *Par le torrent qui descend de Verone* |
| Through which to the Po guided his entry, | *Par lors qu'au Pau guidera son entrée,* |
| A great shipwreck, and no less in Garonne, | *Un grand naufrage, et non moins en Garonne,* |
| When those of Genoa will march against their country. | *Quand ceux de Gennes marcheront leur contrée.* |

This quatrain describes the Allied attack upon northeastern Italy. "Verona," slightly over fifty miles to the east of Venice, lies on the Adige River. This river and the Po are only about ten miles apart, and they both flow into the Adriatic Sea. "A great shipwreck" on a river can only come from an attempted crossing in which the riverboats are blown out of the water by artillery and small arms fire. Nostradamus likens this battle to the one that will be fought in southwestern France (obviously prior to this time) in which the Muslims will try to cross the "Garonne." Since the attackers at this time will be Italian natives of "Genoa" who will "march against their country" in an attempt to liberate it, while the Muslims are the ones apparently defending, it must be the Allies who will suffer the greater losses here.

On the northern aspect of the eastern front, the Allies march back into Germany as shown in the following quatrain:

**(156) Century 10, Quatrain 31**

| | |
|---|---|
| The Holy Empire will come into Germany, | *Le saint Empire viendra en Germanie,* |
| Ishmaelites will find places open: | *Ismaëlites trouveront lieux ouverts:* |
| Asses will demand also the Carmania, | *Ânes voudront aussi la Carmanie,* |
| The supporters by earth all covered. | *Les soutenants de terre tous couverts.* |

As the European states are liberated in a piecemeal fashion by the Allies they will be governed by France, the only Western European country that will have any type of functioning government at that time. Thus, as France expands into Italy and "Germany," Nostradamus now refers to it as an "Empire." The Christian character of France, home of the Papacy, and the religious nature of WW III will make it a "Holy Empire." With Allied victories in hand, a debate will arise about how far to push back the "Ishmaelites." A group that Nostradamus describes as "Asses" will want to continue the fighting all the way to "Carmania," probably to take the Middle East oil fields at the mouth of the Persian Gulf. Why does he call them "Asses"? Probably because it will not be possible to push the Allied attack this far east without incurring massive casualties, and the Allies will be exhausted at this point after decades of continuous war. While still taking Germany, the "Ishmaelites" (who are Arabs descended from Abraham's son Ishmael) will be counterattacking, finding openings in the Allied lines. In the last line "The supporters" will be buried ("by earth all covered"), but Nostradamus does not say to which side "The supporters" belong.

Continuing eastward through Europe the Allies return to Hungary in the following quatrain:

**(157) Century 5, Quatrain 89**

| | |
|---|---|
| Within Hungary through Bohemia, Navarre, | *Dedans Hongrie par Boheme, Navarre,* |
| And through banner holy seditions: | *Et par bannière saintes séditions:* |
| By the fleurs-de-lis region carrying the bar, | *Par fleurs-de-lis pays portant la barre,* |
| Against Orleans will cause emotions. | *Contre Orleans fera émotions.* |

The fleur-de-lis ("fleurs" is the plural form) was a heraldic device having the shape of an iris (which is French for the flower-of-lily). With a diagonal line in the corner, the fleur-de-lis comprises the coat of arms of one of the junior branches of the House of Bourbon, making this yet another quatrain implying that France will abandon democracy and return to a government ruled by a king.

If the chronologic placement of this quatrain is correct, then the House of Bourbon will again see a king on the throne in only a few decades. "Navarre," in far southwestern France, may provide a clue as to which branch it will be, as the Vendome branch of the Bourbons originate from Navarre. This king-to-be will lead his army into the former Czechoslovakia and then Hungary, encouraging revolutions ("holy seditions") against the Mahdi along the way.

The road to kingship will not be simple; in the last line, the House of "Orleans" will apparently have their own candidate for king. Despite the period of time since the French have had a king, the two major royal lines, the Bourbons and the Orleans, still maintain their own internal order of succession. Each is prepared to put a king on the throne at a moment's notice. With the ineffectiveness of democracy in the aftermath of the meteor, the masses of most countries will eventually turn again to an authoritarian form of government, and since France has a long history of rule by kings, another king will be coronated. While Nostradamus indicates that the king will be from the Bourbons, unfortunately he does not indicate exactly when he will take power as the supreme authority in France. A hint when that will be, however, is found in the next quatrain:

**(158) Century 5, Quatrain 50**

| | |
|---|---|
| The year that the brothers of lily will come of age, | *L'an que les frères du lis seront en âge,* |
| The one of them will hold the great Romania: | *L'un d'eux tiendra la grande Romanie:* |
| Trembling the mountains, opened Latin passage, | *Trembler les monts, ouvert Latin passage,* |
| Treaty to march against fort of Armenia. | *Pache marcher contre fort d'Armenie.* |

The "lily" is once again the fleur-de-lis, the "brothers" represent different branches of the House of Bourbon rather than individual leaders. Bourbon "will come of age" when it again becomes the ruling house in France, implying the time of the coronation of the new king. This will occur at the time when the Allies will be liberating Italy ("opened Latin passage") and when Eastern Europe will already have been taken (assuming that "Romania" means the country of Romania rather than the area around Rome). An agreement ("treaty") will be signed by the Allied forces, the World War III equivalent of the Yalta agreement, dictating that the Allies continue the fight eastward until Armenia is reached. This "fort of Armenia" was described in quatrain (56) as the staging area that the Mahdi used as his theater headquarters for his invasion of Turkey and Eastern Europe. The direction of the campaign indicates that this will be an attempt by the Allies to make a broad sweep through Europe and the republics of the former Soviet Union, descending upon Turkey from the north. While Nostradamus indicates that the Allies will make the attempt to take Armenia, he does not say here whether or not they will be successful.

The next quatrain discusses the return of the Allies to Greece:

**(159) Century 6, Quatrain 21**

| | |
|---|---|
| When those of the pole arctic will be united together, | *Quand ceux du pôle arctique unis ensemble,* |
| In Orient great terror and fear: | *En Orient grand effrayeur et crainte:* |
| Elected new, supported the great trembling, | *Élu nouveau, soutenu le grand tremble,* |
| Rhodes, Byzantium from blood Barbarian tainted. | *Rodes, Bisance de sang Barbare teinte.* |

While the only significant powers of the arctic circle ("pole arctic") in the twentieth century have been the United States and the Soviet Union, it is doubtful if Russia can be the power referred to here. Even without the destruction wrought by the comet and meteor, Russia will probably have collapsed into anarchy by the year 2020, its cities a vast wasteland of toxic and nuclear waste, its peoples splintering into ever smaller ethnic groups. Of course, should Russia revive as a country and join the Allies' side in World War III, that would explain the "great terror and fear" amongst the Mahdi's troops at this time.

Another possibility for "those of the pole arctic" is a combined U.S. and Canadian force, or perhaps even the emergence of a united Scandinavian army. A leader "elected new," possibly a pope since "the great trembling" appears as a reference to the Church in other quatrains, will support the Church. This will occur during a time of Islamic ("Barbarian") defeats on the island of Rhodes and in Turkey.

While this quatrain may also apply to the period occurring many years prior, when the Mahdi will overrun Turkey and Greece, this seems unlikely because the implication of this quatrain is that "Orient" will be the ones receiving the "terror and fear," not inflicting it.

In the next quatrains the Allies continue their eastward advance, even reaching into Turkey:

**(160) Century 6, Quatrain 85**

| | |
|---|---|
| The great city of Tarsus<br>    by those of Gaul<br>Will be destroyed, captives<br>    the whole of the Turban:<br>Succor by sea from the great one<br>    of Portugal,<br>First of summer the day<br>    of the holy Urban. | *La grande cité de Tharse par Gaulois*<br>*Sera détruite, captifs tous a Turban:*<br>*Secours par mer du grand Portugalois,*<br>*Premier d'été le jour du sacre Vrban.* |

"Tarsus" was an ancient city in southeastern Turkey, just a few miles from the Mediterranean. With the Allies in control of the seas, an invasion into Tarsus will occur, well behind the front lines. It is this quatrain that assures that France will eventually be victorious over the Mahdi, since the French troops ("those of Gaul") from this invasion will destroy "Tarsus" and make "captives" of "the whole of the (Blue) Turban."

In the third line is one of the few references to the Portuguese in World War III. Even though their country was destroyed, enough of them will survive to man a fleet late in the war, or perhaps just the commander of the fleet will be Portuguese. This fleet will either land the French in Tarsus or reinforce them. There are many St. Urbans, but none of them have their feast day on the first day of summer. Perhaps the name of a new pope is intended, or another individual named Urban will be declared a saint. Anyway, the time of the attack on Tarsus will be in early summer.

Another quatrain describes the Allied attack upon Turkey:

**(161) Century 5, Quatrain 80**

| | |
|---|---|
| Ogmios the great Byzantium<br>    will approach,<br>He will pursue the<br>    Barbaric League:<br>Of two laws the one heathen<br>    will give out,<br>Barbarian and Frank<br>    in perpetual fighting. | *L'Ogmion grande Bisance approchera,*<br>*Chassée sera la Barbarique Ligue:*<br>*Des deux lois l'une l'estinique lâchera,*<br>*Barbare et franche*<br>    *en perpétuille brigue.* |

"Ogmios" was an old god of pagan French mythology before the coming of Christianity to France, very similar in nature to Hercules.

Why Nostradamus should use this name for a Frenchman is not clear. Perhaps his deeds of valor during the war will be near-Herculean in nature, or perhaps his name will be an anagram of "Ogmios" or even of Hercules. Regardless, this "Ogmios" "will pursue the Barbaric (i.e. Barbarian) League" all the way to "the great Byzantium," in other words, Istanbul. The "two laws" are Christianity and Islam. The "one heathen will give out," which must be Islam to the thinking of Nostradamus, who was of the Christian faith. In the fourth line Nostradamus notes the "perpetual" nature of the "fighting." While the word "perpetual" means without end or forever, twenty-seven years of constant fighting is close enough to justify Nostradamus' use of the word.

The Allied attacks into Turkey will not only be on Tarsus and Istanbul, however, as shown in the following quatrain:

**(162) Century 1, Quatrain 74**

| | |
|---|---|
| After staying they will wander into Epirus: | *Après séjourné vagueront en Epire:* |
| The great succor will come towards Antioch, | *Le grand secours viendra vers Antioche,* |
| The black bristle beard will strain strongly at the Empire: | *Le noir poil crêpe tendra fort à l'Empire:* |
| Beard of bronze will roast him on a spit. | *Barbe d'airain le rôtira en broche.* |

After some rest, an Allied force "will wander into Epirus," which is in northwestern Greece. Shortly afterwards another (or perhaps the same?) Allied force ("the great succor") will take the ancient city of "Antioch," located in far southern Turkey, near the border with Lebanon and Syria. "Black bristle beard," was seen previously in quatrain (66), where he set up a "trophy" during the Islamic conquest of Italy. In this quatrain he "will strain strongly at the" French "Empire."

"Beard of bronze" is probably the same person as "Redbeard," who was mentioned previously also, in quatrain (110), where he came to the rescue on the Allied Spanish front after the "English chief" stayed too long at Nimes. In quatrain (162), the one currently under study, they meet face to face. What will the result be? "Redbeard" will impale "black bristle beard" upon a spear ("roast through a spit"), apparently in battle.

231

There is yet another quatrain about an Allied attack on Istanbul:

**(163) Century 5, Quatrain 70**

| | |
|---|---|
| From the regions subject to the Balance, | *Des régions sujettes à la Balance,* |
| They will trouble the mountains through great war, | *Feront troubler les monts par grande guerre,* |
| Captives of both sexes due and all of Byzantium, | *Captifs tout sexe dû et tout Bisance,* |
| Which people will cry at dawn from land to land. | *Qu'on criera à l'aube terre à terre.* |

The "Balance" stands for Libra and represents, of course, the United States, as has been previously shown. The "regions subject to the Balance" probably are the Mexican and Canadian allies of the United States. The "mountains" troubled "through great war" could refer to the Pyrenees, the Alps, or even the Apennines, but given the context a mountain range within Turkey itself is indicated. Perhaps the U.S. will be descending from the north, after taking the previously noted "fort of Armenia." If so, then a three-pronged attack upon Istanbul will occur, with the U.S. coming from the east after liberating Armenia (or possibly coming from the north across the Black Sea), an unspecified Allied group coming eastward from Greece, and the French from Tarsus to the southeast. The Mahdi's forces in Turkey will then find themselves isolated from Iran and the rest of Asia, and completely surrounded. They will surrender, male and females ("captives of both sexes"), throughout "all of Byzantium," and the news of this surrender will be cried from door to door "at dawn" throughout Western Europe.

With the loss of Turkey, the armies of Islam will finally realize that they will be unable to win the war. The Allies, exhausted after twenty-seven years of horrible war, and having driven the Muslims from the European continent, will be unwilling to continue onward into Iran and the jungles of southern Asia. What will happen then? A negotiated peace settlement is the only option. Nostradamus has a quatrain about that, too:

**(164) Century 7, Quatrain 36**

| | |
|---|---|
| God, the sky all of the divine words in the waves, | *Dieu, le ciel tout le divin verbe à l'onde,* |
| Carried by red seven shaven heads to Byzantium: | *Porté par rouges sept rases à Bizance:* |
| Against the anointed three hundred from Trebizond | *Contre les oints trois cents de Trebisconde* |
| Two laws will be set, and horror, then credence. | *Deux lois mettront, et horreur, puis crédence.* |

The "red shaven heads" will be Cardinals of the Catholic Church, as their "red" hats are the symbol of their office. Why their heads will be shaven is unclear—perhaps they will do it as mourning for all of those killed during World War III, perhaps it will be something as simple as a treatment for a head lice infestation. These Cardinals will be the Allied peace negotiators. Trebizond, known today as Trabzon, was mentioned previously in quatrain (34), in which someone, presumably the White Turban, came from Persia to occupy it. If it does become the White Turban's residence, then it will likely become the seat of the Islamic government of the Mahdi's kingdom, and the "three hundred" will be the Islamic representatives from that government. The two sides will negotiate two treaties ("Two laws will be set"), the first met with "horror," presumably an outbreak of hostilities again, and the second met with "credence." Thus will end the hostilities of World War III, the worst of times that mankind will have ever seen.

After the war is over, the Pan-Muslim state created by the Mahdi will eventually crumble. The following quatrain describes part of that (apparently) peaceful crumbling:

**(165) Century 3, Quatrain 97**

| | |
|---|---|
| New law the new land will occupy | *Nouvelle loi terre neuve occuper* |
| Towards Syria, Judea and Palestine: | *Vers la Syrie, Iudée et Palestine:* |
| The great empire barbarian will decay, | *Le grand empire barbare corruer,* |
| Before the Moon its century is finished. | *Avant que Phebés son siècle determine.* |

The "New law" and "the new land" imply the formation of a new country, comprised of "Syria," "Judea" (Israel) and "Palestine." Will Israel be re-established yet one more time? If so, will it be given even more land than it currently possesses? Can the newest version of the state of Israel include not only the Israel of the 1990s but part of Jordan and Syria as well? It would appear that these lands will be wrested from their current owners and given to a new Israel, perhaps as part of the reparations at the end of the war.

"The great barbarian empire" can only be the Mahdi's empire. At its greatest extent during World War III it will cover the entire Middle East and North Africa, reaching into India in the south, Indonesia (perhaps even to Australia) in the east, Russia in the north, Spain and France in the west. After the war this "empire" "will decay," rather than be conquered. The "century" of "the Moon," and when it will be finished, is as unclear as all of Nostradamus' other astrologically-dated predictions.

How can Nostradamus devote so many quatrains to the Islamic advances into Europe and so few to the Allies pushing them back out? Because of the twenty-seven years of World War III, most of them will be spent with the Allies retreating, suffering defeat after defeat, but making the Mahdi pay dearly for the land he will take. The entry of the United States into the war may not occur until twenty-five years or so into the war, but that entry, combined with the immense prior losses of men that the Muslims will suffer, will allow the Allies to defeat the Mahdi in only a short period of time. There is also the consideration of morale. As long as the Mahdi is conquering new lands, moving across the European continent, he will be fulfilling what has been predicted for him, and regardless of the casualties his troops will love him. But, once he begins to suffer defeats, and once it appears that he will not be able to conquer the "infidel" Christians, the question of his Mahdi-ship will arise. Unable to fulfill the prophecies set for him, talk about the man who will come to be known as "The Blue Turban" not being the true Mahdi sent by Allah will circulate amongst his armies. As defeat follows defeat, he will be regarded as a fraud, and his multi-national coalition, held together by religious beliefs, will collapse. And what will be the fate of the Mahdi himself? Nostradamus has a quatrain about that, too:

**(166) Century 2, Quatrain 2**

The head blue will bring
  to the head white
As much evil as France
  has brought good to them:
Dead at the antenna the great
  one hung with the branch,
Since when caught the King
  will tell how many.

*La tête bleue fera la tête blanche*
  *Autant de mal que France*
    *a fait leur bien:*
*Mort à l'antenne grand pendu*
  *sus la branche,*
*Quand pris des siens*
  *le Roi dira combien.*

"The head blue," also known as the Blue Turban and the Mahdi, will be the military leader of the unified Muslim state; "the head white," also known as the White Turban, will be the religious leader of the civilian government. Based on information discussed in prior quatrains, the capital of the new Persia appears to be located in the Turkish city of Trebizond. In the end, the Mahdi will have brought "as much" destruction and "evil" to the Middle East "as France has brought good to them." What good has France brought to this part of the world? Even a cursory look at the amount of trade today between France and the Arab states of the Middle East shows that business with France has indeed been very good to them. The third and fourth lines are difficult to understand, but the last line indicates that the man who will be known as the "King" of Islam, the Blue Turban, the Mahdi, will be "caught." Apparently, the third line also refers to him as well. He will eventually be executed by hanging, perhaps by a military tribunal after the war, but more likely by a revolt among his own troops. By that time, however, he will be responsible for the deaths of hundreds of millions of people, and much of Europe and Asia will have been turned into a wasteland for many generations to come.

# AFTER
# THE WAR

With the Third World War concluded, Nostradamus still has a group of quatrains relevant to events after the war. Here is the first one:

### (167) Century 6, Quatrain 24

| | |
|---|---|
| Mars and the sceptre with each other found conjoined, | *Mars et le sceptre se trouvera conjoint,* |
| Under Cancer calamitous war: | *Dessous Cancer calamiteuse guerre:* |
| A little after will be a new King anointed, | *Un peu après sera nouveau Roi oint,* |
| Who for a long time will pacify the earth. | *Qui par longtemps pacifiera la terre.* |

The first two lines provide a conjunction: "Mars" and Jupiter ("the sceptre" denoting kingship and Jupiter was the king of the gods) "with each other found conjoined" in "Cancer." Dr. Christian Wollner published a commentary in German on Nostradamus' works in 1926 titled Das Mysterium des Nostradamus, apparently becoming the first commentator on Nostradamus' works to calculate the astrological configurations present in many of Nostradamus' quatrains. Dr. Wollner's dating of these configurations has been carried by most commentators since that time, but apparently no author quoting Wollner has ever rechecked the accuracy of his dates for Nostradamus' configurations! As previously described, attempting to date the quatrains may be useless as Nostradamus (and apparently Dr. Wollner as well) possessed incomplete knowledge of planetary motions. Small errors in predicted movements become multiplied over the years, leaving a planet many constellations away from its predicted astronomical position for a given month and year.

Of course, if in seeing the future Nostradamus could also actually see the configurations in the skies, then the configurations will be accurate. While this book assumes that Nostradamus calculated his configurations rather than actually viewing them in the future sky, and that trying to date most of Nostradamus' conjunctions is pointless, the configuration in this quatrain will be assessed.

Dr. Wollner predicted that the only time this conjunction (Mars and Jupiter in Cancer) would occur will be on June 21, 2002. In fact, for a period of time a few weeks on either side of July 1, 2002, both planets will be in Cancer. If Nostradamus was correct with this conjunction, then World War III will begin in late June or July of 2002, not quite three years after the destruction to be wrought by the meteor contained within the comet's tail.

"A little after" the end of World War III "a new King will be anointed" (crowned). This "King" will probably be French since no other country is specified. In the exhausted aftermath of World War III no one will be interested in fighting again for quite a while ("long time") afterwards, and this "King. . . will pacify the earth." That the king will indeed be French is shown in the following quatrain:

**(168) Century 8, Quatrain 61**

| | |
|---|---|
| Never by the discovery of day, | *Jamais par le descouvrement du jour,* |
| Will he attain to the sign | *Ne parviendra au signe sceptrifere:* |
|   of the scepter-bearer: | *Que tous ses sièges ne soient en séjour,* |
| Not until all his sieges | *Portant au coq don du TAG armifere.* |
|   and cares are at rest, | |
| Bearing to the cock the gift | |
|   of the legion armed. | |

The first line of this quatrain is just a long way of saying "never." In English it might also be paraphrased as "never by the light of day." In the second line the individual who will become ("attain") king will not be crowned as king ("the scepter-bearer") until after the war is over ("Not until all his sieges and cares are at rest"). That he will be French is shown in the last line, since he will bring to France ("the cock") the "gift of the legion armed." The last line might be better translated as "bringing to France the gift of the army at his command." Implied here is that the new king will be the Commander-in-Chief of the armed forces of France during World War III. There is nothing unusual about this. From Julius Caesar to Charles de Gaulle to Dwight Eisenhower, great wartime generals have subsequently become peacetime political leaders of their countries.

That he will be a descended from French royal lineage is shown next:

**(169) Century 5, Quatrain 74**

| | |
|---|---|
| Of blood Trojan born a heart Germanic | *De sang Troyen naîtra coeur Germanique* |
| Which will grow into so much of an elevated: | *Qui deviendra en si haute puissance:* |
| Chasing out people foreign Arabic, | *Hors chassera gent étrange Arabique,* |
| Returning the Church to pristine preeminence. | *Tournant l'Eglise en pristine prééminence.* |

The country of France is named after Francus, son of Priam, a king of the ancient state of Troy, and French kings for many centuries have claimed to trace their ancestry back to him ("Of blood Trojan"). The "Germanic" peoples have been noted for their warlike tendencies for centuries, and the world wars of this century have done nothing to dispel that image. Combining the two metaphors gives the picture of a Frenchman of royal lineage skilled in matters of war. That this is indeed the new king is shown by him growing "into so much of an elevated" place, i.e. becoming the leader of the government.

"Chasing out people foreign Arabic" places this quatrain squarely into the future; there has been no Arab nation at war with France on French soil since Nostradamus' time. Raids from the Arabic Barbary Pirates of North Africa occurred during Nostradamus' life and for several centuries afterwards, but they were quick coastal raids and not invasions which required "chasing out" of the invaders from French soil. Many commentators regard the "new King" of Nostradamus as being failed predictions for Henry II, who ruled France at the time of the writing of the quatrains, but the linkage of this new king with the theme of an "Arabic" invasion of France indicates that this quatrain must pertain to the future.

In the last line the religious nature of World War III is again mentioned. After winning the war, this man "Of blood Trojan" will help the Catholic Church to undergo a period of purification and renewal ("Returning the Church to pristine preeminence"). It is also possible that "the Church" will return to the position of preeminent power and influence in political affairs that it once had in Europe in the days prior to the Protestant Reformation.

That this new king will rule more than France is shown in the following quatrain:

(170) **Century 10, Quatrain 95**

| | |
|---|---|
| Into Spain will come King very powerful, | *Dans les Espaignes viendra Roi très-puissant,* |
| By sea and land subjugating the South: | *Par mer et terre subjuguant le Midi:* |
| This evil will cause, re-lowering the crescent, | *Ce mal fera, rebaissant le croissant,* |
| Lowering the flanks of those of Friday. | *Baisser les ailes à ceux du Vendredi.* |

Since the "King" "Into Spain will come" he cannot be a Spanish king, and since no other country is specified, the "King" is French. He will be the supreme commander of the Allied forces that will liberate Spain. By both "sea" (from America?) "and land" (from France) he will retake Spain, which is to "the South" of France. "Subjugating the South," however, may also imply that the Allies will take control of the former French colonies of Arab North Africa as well. The "crescent" refers to the crescent moon, a symbol of Islam, and "relowering the crescent" implies their defeat. "Those of Friday" also refers to Islam, since Friday is their day of worship, so there can be no doubt that a final Islamic defeat is predicted.

So Nostradamus' "King" will control Spain as well as France. But that is not all, as the following quatrain attests:

(171) **Century 6, Quatrain 27**

| | |
|---|---|
| Within the Isles of five rivers to one, | *Dedans les Isles de cinq fleuves à un,* |
| Through the increase of the great Chyren Selin: | *Par le croissant du grand Chyren Selin:* |
| Through the drizzles of the air fury of the one, | *Par les bruines de l'air fureur de l'un,* |
| Six escaped, cached burdens of flax. | *Six échappés, cachés fardeaux de lin.* |

The "Isles of five rivers to one" is generally regarded by Nostradamian scholars as being the British Isles, since at the height of its power England controlled the Thames, Nile, Ganges, Indus, and St. Lawrence Rivers. As Egypt, India, and Canada have now gained their independence, Great Britain now controls only the Thames. Of course, Great Britain controlled many more great rivers than these, and the list of exactly which five Nostradamus had in mind is debatable, but there is no other island country ("Within the isles of") that has had total control of five great rivers in the past and now only of one ("five rivers to one").

In the second line Nostradamus finally indicates the name of the new king: "Chyren Selin." "Chyren" is regarded by all Nostradamian scholars as being an anagram of "Henry," fueling speculation that Nostradamus was referring to his own king, Henry II. As has been shown, however, this is not possible. The new Henry will be Henry V, and will take as his symbol the moon, since "Selin" is generally regarded to be an anagram of "Selene," meaning "crescent." Perhaps he will put the symbol in his coat of arms because he will defeat the Islamic armies, who historically have used the crescent moon as their symbol. While the last two lines are completely murky, the tone of the first two lines indicates that Henry V will control what is left of the tsunami-destroyed British Isles as well. The total extent of his conquests is hinted at in the following:

(172) **Century 6, Quatrain 70**

The chief of the world
    the great "Chyren" will be,
After "Plus Ultra" loved,
    feared, dreaded:
His din and praise the skies
    will surpass,
And with the sole title Victor
    strongly contented.

*Au chef du monde le*
    *grand CHIREN sera,*
*PLVS OVTRE après aimé,*
    *craint, redouté:*
*Son bruit et los les cieux surpassera,*
*Et du seul titre Victeur fort contenté.*

Nostradamus predicts that "Chyren," the future Henry V, will be "chief of the world." While this must be an exaggeration, Henry will control much of Europe, which was all the world that Nostradamus cared about. Further proof that Nostradamus believed this to be so is found in the expression "Plus Ultra," which was the motto of Holy Roman Emperor Charles V. Charles, a contemporary of Nostradamus, was Holy Roman Emperor from 1519 to 1546. The Holy Roman Empire of that time included all of the lands of the modern countries of the Netherlands, Belgium, Luxembourg, Germany, southeastern France (Savoy), Switzerland, the Czech Republic, Slovakia, and Austria. Charles V also ruled Milan (which controlled northern Italy), the kingdom of Naples (which controlled southern Italy), and Spain, too! Also, through his Spanish overseas possessions Charles V ruled much of South and Central America.

After World War III is over, Henry V will likely control the same European countries that Charles V controlled, along with all of France and possibly England and North Africa as well. Incidentally, the Europeans have been struggling for years with the establishment of a common European Economic Community. Nostradamus predicts that this will finally come about in the next century, but not in the manner most expect!

In the aftermath of World War III, with France the only intact European government, the people of Western and Central Europe will gladly accept inclusion into a new French Empire as the price to pay for peace and stability; for the establishment of law and order; for the final creation of a new European Common Market. Nostradamus also predicts that the new Henry will be "loved, feared," and "dreaded" like no ruler since Charles V, and the "din" of his "praise" and his fame will be renowned ("the skies (it) will surpass"). As another comparison, it is also fascinating that Charles fought his own battles with Islam, clashing with the Turks and even invading North Africa. In the last line Nostradamus claims that Henry will be "contented" to claim "the sole title" of "Victor" against the Asian Islamic hordes in World War III. As the only intact Allied country to survive the war, and probably the only one to fight for all of the twenty-seven years of the war, this title will be justly deserved.

Henry will not be perfect, however. The next quatrain details what appears to be a major flaw in his character:

**(173) Century 4, Quatrain 86**

| | |
|---|---|
| The year that Saturn in Aquarius will be conjoined | *L'an que Saturne en eau sera conjoint* |
| With the Sun, the King strong and powerful | *Avec Sol, le Roi fort et puissant* |
| At Reims and Aix will be received and anointed, | *À Reims et Aix sera reçu et oint,* |
| After conquests murdering the innocent. | *Après conquêtes meurtrira innocent.* |

242

Once again the problem with astrological dating is present. Several different astronomy computer programs place Saturn in Aquarius from February 2023 to April 2025. Since other quatrains indicate World War III will last for twenty-seven years, and others that the war will not start until the early years of the next century, perhaps Henry will be crowned king before the war is over, rather than waiting for its conclusion. It is also possible that this quatrain does not belong here, or perhaps Nostradamus was wrong in his astrological calculations, or perhaps the author of this book is entirely wrong in writing this book!

Of course it is also possible that World War III will begin as an inter-Muslim conflict (like the Iran-Iraq war) or a Western-Arab conflict (like the Gulf War) sometime before 1998, escalating into the next world war only after the destruction brought by the comet. After all, in 1939 no one declared the fighting between Germany and Poland to be World War II. "The King strong and powerful" is of course Henry V, future ruler of Europe. He will be crowned king ("received and annointed") "At Reims," the traditional coronation site of the French kings, as well as at "Aix," which was the coronation site for the Emperors of the Holy Roman Empire from 813 to 1531. Implied here is that Henry will rule not only France but also the territory that was previously part of the Holy Roman Empire. The last person to accomplish this was Charlemagne, almost 1,200 years ago. The last line of the quatrain is most fascinating. "After conquests" can only mean after the end of World War III. But what can "murdering the innocent" mean? And why will Henry do it? While the answer is not certain, the following quatrain provides a likely answer:

(174) **Century 2, Quatrain 7**

| | |
|---|---|
| Amongst many to the isles deported, | *Entre plusieurs aux isles déportés,* |
| The one to be born with two teeth in the mouth | *L'un être né à deux dents en la gorge* |
| They will die of famine the trees stripped of leaves, | *Mourront de faim les arbres esbrotés,* |
| For them new King, new edict for them forged. | *Pour eux neuf Roi, nouvel édit leur forge.* |

After the war, "many" will be "to the isles deported." The "isles" probably refer to the islands along the southern coast of France, used as prison colonies by the French for many years in the past. One of those deported will be the one "born with two teeth in the mouth," apparently the same individual mentioned in quatrain (16), born while the Earth passes through the tail of the comet. Nostradamus records his birth and his death; one can only wonder what will happen during this man's interim years. Will he be one of the "innocent" ones murdered by Henry? And why will all of this happen? The answer is found in the quatrains, also quoted in the first chapter, linking the Mahdi with Genghis Khan.

The Mahdi will follow the Great Khan's example of giving his opponents the opportunity of surrendering and enrolling in the front ranks of his army, rather than being executed after defeat. Many will choose this course rather than certain death. After the war, after the liberation of Europe, Henry will face the question of what to do with these former European collaborators of the Mahdi. Having fought for the entire duration of the war, having watched many, including his own son (as will be shown later) die during the war, Henry will have little sympathy for the collaborators. Times will be hard after World War III, and compassion will be in short supply. The collaborators will be shipped to Mediterranean island-based prisoner colonies, and the term "many" by Nostradamus implies overcrowding. The prisoners will overtax the ability of the islands to produce food, and the prisoners will strip the trees of leaves before starving to death.

Yet, as when any form of justice is handed out simultaneously to large numbers, there will be mistakes, and many innocent of their charges will die of starvation in the island camps. That Henry V will be to blame is indicated in the last line, where Nostradamus attributes their deaths to a "new King" (Henry), whose "new edict" (apparently the banishment to the prison islands for the crime of collaboration) will be the cause of the overcrowding and starvation. As happens occasionally in criminal justice, some innocent will be included with the punishment of the guilty.

And what will be the end of Henry V?

**(175) Century 4, Quatrain 77**

| | |
|---|---|
| Selin monarch Italy peaceful, | *Selin monarque l'Italie pacifique,* |
| Reigns united by the King Christian of the world: | *Regnes unis par Roi Chrétien du monde:* |
| Dying will want to lie in the earth of Blois, | *Mourant voudra coucher en terre blesique,* |
| After the pirates will have been chased from the waves. | *Après pirates avoir chassé de l'onde.* |

In quatrain (171) Henry V was also described as "Selin." Further proof of his identity is given by: "Reigns united by the King Christian of the world." Already described in many quatrains as the unifier of most of Europe, and in previous chapters as supporting the Catholic Church and giving it sanctuary in France, this can only be Henry V. After his death he will want to be buried near Blois, the traditional home of the Valois dynasty. Whereas other quatrains show the fleur-de-lis, the traditional emblem of the Bourbons, being carried into Eastern Europe, this quatrain indicates that Henry will be of the Valois. Perhaps he will be descended from both bloodlines. This quatrain shows Henry's death as occurring sometime after the end of World War III, since "the pirates" refers to the Barbary Pirates, who were Muslims from North Africa. After the end of World War III, but before Henry's death, there will be some kind of disturbance (riots? a revolt?) in Italy, which will be resolved ("Italy peaceful").

And what of the sons of Henry V? The next quatrain shows the fate of one of them:

**(176) Century 10, Quatrain 63**

| | |
|---|---|
| Cydonia, Ragusa, | *Cydron, Raguse, la cité* |
|     the city of St. Jerome, |     *au saint Hieron,* |
| Will revive the healing help: | *Reverdira le medicant secours:* |
| Dead son of King through death | *Mort fils de Roi par mort* |
|     of two heroes, |     *de deux heron,* |
| The Arabs, Hungary will take | *L'Arabe, Hongrie feront* |
|     the same course. |     *un même cours.* |

Ancient "Cydonia" is the modern city of Canea, located on the island of Crete, while the ancient city of "Ragusa" is today known as Dubrovnik, now in Croatia. "St. Jerome" was born in Stridon, today known as Tesanj, part of Bosnia (of course, the geography in this part of the world changes frequently!), and lived his later years at Aquileia, near Venice, so "the city of" St. Jerome could be either Stridon or Aquileia. What any of these cities might have in common, and how they "will revive the healing help" is obscure at this time. However, the setting of these three cities, in Eastern Europe, along with the events of the last line ("Hungary" capitulating to, and then allying with, "the Arabs") tends to place these events early in the war. Since quatrains (48) and (49), which Nostradamus numbered as Century 10,

245

Quatrains 61 and 62, have already been placed during the struggle of Eastern Europe, perhaps this quatrain, Century 10, Quatrain 63, belongs to that time frame as well. Should that be the case, this represents three quatrains in a row left in their original order.

An interesting aside in this quatrain is Nostradamus' apparent difficulty in finding a rhyme for the word "Hieron" at the end of the first line. Most commentators believe that the word "heron" at the end of the third line should really be "heroes," instead. In that case, because of the "death of two heroes" a "son of King (Henry)" will die. Perhaps the "two heroes" will be decorated soldiers who will die while fighting a delaying action in the Balkans, and the son of the future Henry V will die with them.

With the death of his son, who will reign after the death of Henry V? The next quatrain provides that answer:

**(177) Century 6, Quatrain 42**

| | |
|---|---|
| To Ogmios will be given the realm, | *À l'ogmyon sera laissé le regne,* |
| Of the great Selin, who more will in fact do: | *Du grand Selin, qui plus fera de fait:* |
| Through Italy will he extend his teachings, | *Par les Itales étendra son enseigne,* |
| Administered will he be by a prudent deformed one. | *Regi sera par prudent contrefait.* |

"Ogmios," mentioned in quatrain (161) as being the French commander who will lead the Allied attack on Istanbul near the end of the war, "will be given the realm of the great Selin" (Henry). In quatrain (175) Nostradamus stated that Italy will be peaceful at the time of Henry's death. There is no point in mentioning a peace in Italy if there will not be some disturbances prior to that. After Henry's death, "Ogmios" will consolidate his rule "Through Italy" as well. His closest adviser is described as being "a prudent deformed one" by Nostradamus, probably suffering from an orthopedic disorder of some kind.

What will be the relationship between Henry and "Ogmios"? Just because Henry will have one son die in the battle of Eastern Europe does not mean that he cannot have another; besides, choosing a king from an open field of candidates would likely result in open civil war in Europe, which is something all parties will want to avoid so soon after World War III. Thus, Ogmios will be the clear successor of Henry, probably another son.

Nostradamus even has a quatrain about the third of the new kings of France:

(178) **Century 8, Quatrain 44**

| The offspring natural of Ogmios, | *Le procrée naturel dogmion,* |
| From seven to nine on account of the road will turn aside: | *De sept à neuf du chemin détourner:* |
| To the King of long and friend to the half-man. | *À Roi de longue et ami au mi-homme.* |
| Destruction of the Navarre fort from Pau protests. | *Doit à Navarre fort de Pau prosterner.* |

"The offspring natural of Ogmios" can only be his son. What the meaning of the second line can be is a total mystery, as is the rest of this quatrain. If Henry is crowned king around 2030 and reigns for ten years (a conservative estimate), and then Ogmios reigns for another twenty or thirty years after that (quite possible since he may not even be born until the late 1990s), it is possible that this quatrain may not be fulfilled until late in the next century. The "fort" of "Navarre" could be fortifications built against the invading Muslims during the next World War, but why the city of "Pau" might object to its "Destruction" almost 100 years from now cannot even begin to be guessed at.

Enough has been said about the French kings. Nostradamus has a few other topics that may be relevant to the postwar world:

(179) **Century 6, Quatrain 4**

| The Celtic river will change from its banks, | *Le Celtique fleuve changera de rivage,* |
| No more your city of Agrippina: | *Plus ne tiendra la cité d'Agripine:* |
| All transmuted but the old language, | *Tout transmué hormis le vieil langage,* |
| Saturn, Leo, Mars, Cancer in plunder. | *Saturne, Leo, Mars, Cancer en rapine.* |

"The Celtic river" is the Rhine, and the "city of Agrippina" is Cologne. That the river should change its course is not surprising; rivers naturally wander back and forth across their valleys, depositing silt until the river bottom has been elevated above the lowest spot of the surrounding countryside, at which time the river takes up a new course. It is only in recent times that mankind has confined rivers to their current banks. Nostradamus sees a time coming when the Germans will either be unwilling or unable to keep the Rhine flowing in its current course. This will occur at a time when everything in Germany will be changed except for the spoken German language itself. Perhaps this will occur at the time of the Mahdi's conquests, and if not at that time, then certainly after the war, when France will govern Germany. Of course, in the post-comet, postwar Germany it is doubtful if much of anything will look like it did in the early 1990s.

The last line provides yet another astrological conjunction. The interpretation might be better translated as "There will be plundering when Saturn is in Leo and Mars is in Cancer." Disregarding all of the noted potential problems with astrological datings, if this conjunction is accurate, it occurs during the spring of 2008, and again in the late spring and summer of 2038. While plundering will be occurring in Eastern Europe in 2008, it seems doubtful that the war will have reached Germany by that time. By 2038, the war should be over for at least a few years, making the source of the plundering questionable.

As noted several times previously, calculating when Nostradamus' conjunctions will occur with accuracy may be a nearly impossible task. Wollner, the most often quoted Nostradamian astrologer, wrote in his 1926 book about the conjunction appearing in the following quatrain:

**(180) Century 10, Quatrain 67**

| | |
|---|---|
| The trembling very strong in the month of May, | *Le tremblement si fort au mois de Mai,* |
| Saturn, Capricorn, Jupiter, | *Saturne, Caper, Jupiter,* |
| Mercury in the bull: | *Mercure au boeuf:* |
| Venus also, Cancer, Mars in Virgo, | *Venus aussi, Cancer, Mars en Nonnay,* |
| Will fall hail then more large than an egg. | *Tombera grêle lors plus grosse qu'un oeuf.* |

Wollner interpreted the conjunction as: "Saturn" in "Capricorn," "Jupiter" and "Mercury" "in the bull" (Taurus), "Venus also" in "Cancer," and "Mars in Virgo." Wollner calculated that between the years of the writing of the prophecy and the year 3797 this conjunction could occur only in April 1929, and May 3755. However, consulting another of those super-accurate computer astronomy programs shows that in May 3755, Saturn will be in Sagittarius instead of Capricorn, Jupiter in Pisces, and Mercury in Aquarius, rather than either one being in Taurus, Venus will be in Aquarius with Mercury instead of in Cancer, and Mars in Taurus instead of Virgo. Every single calculation is wrong!

Even Wollner's calculation for the predicted configuration for April 1929, only three years after the writing of his book, is inaccurate. At that time Saturn was in Sagittarius, Jupiter in Aries and Mercury near the border of Aquarius and Pisces (two constellations away from where it was supposed to be), Venus in Aries (three constellations off) and Mars in Gemini (also three constellations off from its predicted location). To be that far off in his calculations for a prediction only three years after the publication of his book, Wollner must either have been using old, outdated charts, or else he was incompetent in astronomical theory and planetary computations. Apparently he never stood outside and looked at the night sky to check his work either, and obviously none of the other commentators who quote Wollner's dates, even to this time, have ever bothered to check his accuracy! And if these are the results that Wollner achieved in 1926, for a 1929 conjunction, who knows *what* kind of configurations Nostradamus came up with in the 1500s for specific configurations in future years. His predicted astrological configurations are probably so far off from the dates he intended that all of his conjunctions are useless. The only hope that his predicted conjunctions will match the actual events is if in seeing the future Nostradamus also turned his gaze to the stars to record their actual positions.

There is one final quatrain about the events that will occur after the war:

(181) **Century 3, Quatrain 92**

| | |
|---|---|
| The world near of the period last, | *Le monde proche du dernier période,* |
| Saturn again will be tardy of return: | *Saturne encore tard sera de retour:* |
| Transferring the empire towards nation Dusky, | *Translat empire devers nation Brodde,* |
| The eye removed at Narbonne by Goshawk. | *L'oeil arraché à Narbon par Autour.* |

The first line provides the time frame: "near" the end of "The world." Perhaps Nostradamus looked into the sky on this one, and instead of concluding that his astrological calculations were in error decided that Saturn would "be tardy" "again" in appearing where,

249

based on his calculations, he thought that it should be. The French "empire" will be transferred towards a new place. The "nation Dusky" could also be translated as the "black" nation (will France become a colonial power in Africa again?), or the "decadent" nation (something that all great civilizations go through after reaching their peak). The meaning of the last line is unclear, and a good way to finish any commentary on the quatrains of this strange 16th-century prophet.

# APPENDIX A:
# NOSTRADAMUS' OTHER SPECIFICALLY DATED QUATRAINS

This book began with Nostradamus' final specifically dated quatrain, one involving events of the year 1999. The placement of the quatrains that follow that one are based, to some extent, on whether that quatrain will occur as predicted. However, as noted in the first chapter, Nostradamus was not infallible in his predictions. Presented here in chronological order are his other quatrains that mention specific dates. Since they are not relevant to the group of quatrains presented in this book, the author has not included them in his numbering system. By examining how closely these other quatrains came to fulfillment, a rough idea can be obtained of the chances of the Earth being struck by a cometary fragment during 1999. Beginning with the period shortly after Nostradamus' death is the following:

**Century 6, Quatrain 2**

In the year five hundred
   eighty more or less,
One will await the century
   very strange:
In the year seven hundred and
   three the heavens as witness,
That several kingdoms one to
   five will make a change.

*En l'an cinq cent octante*
   *plus et moins,*
*On attendra le siècle bien étrange:*
*En l'an sept cent et trois*
   *cieux en témoins,*
*Que plusieurs regnes un à*
   *cinq feront change.*

As with Nostradamus' other quatrains, the assumption will be made that since no other country is mentioned, this quatrain refers to France. "In the year five hundred eighty" (1580), France was torn by a civil war that ended later that year, and it appeared that France might not survive as a country. Yet, by 1680, only one century later, France had become the strongest power in all of Europe, displacing Spain from that position. The change from one of the weakest to the strongest European state in a "century" is certainly "very strange."

"In the year seven hundred and three" (1703), France was fighting The War of the Spanish Succession in an attempt to put the grandchild of Louis XIV on the throne in Spain. After successfully concluding the war in 1714, this grandson became known as Philip V (the "five" of the last line). The "several kingdoms" of the last line refers not only to Philip's rule of Spain (the "one"), but also his control of The Kingdom of the Two Sicilies, parts of the Netherlands, and many areas in North and South America.

Nostradamus did very well with this quatrain, and it is considered by scholars of his work to be a perfectly fulfilled prediction. In the next quatrain he did not fare as well:

**Century 8, Quatrain 71**

| | |
|---|---|
| Increase the number so very greatly of astrologers | *Croîta le nombre si grand des astronomes* |
| Chased, banished and books censured: | *Chassés, bannis et livres censurés:* |
| The year thousand six hundred seven by sacred assemblies, | *L'an mil six cent et sept par sacrés glomes,* |
| That not any from the sacred ones will be secure. | *Que nul aux sacres ne seront assurés.* |

This quatrain is generally interpreted as meaning that in "The year thousand six hundred seven" (1607) there was to be a persecution of "astrologers." They were to be "banished" from France, their "books" banned and burned. The cause of this was to be the "sacred assemblies," probably the French Inquisition. In the last line Nostradamus predicted that no astrologer would be safe from the "sacred ones," i.e. the priests and bishops of the Inquisition. These events simply did not take place. There was no assembly in 1607, and there was no persecution of astrologers. While it is not likely, there is a slim possibility that instead of connecting the "sacred assemblies" of the third line with the "book" burnings in the second line and the "sacred ones" of the last line, Nostradamus meant that only the events of the third line were related. In that case, the quatrain occurs one thousand six hundred and seven years after an important assembly of the Church, perhaps something similar to Vatican II, called by Pope John XXIII a few decades ago. In his letter to his son, Nostradamus wrote that his predictions extended to as far as the year 3797, so perhaps this council has not even been called yet! Again, this is not the standard interpretation of the quatrain, but possible. Nonetheless, it will be counted as a failure, making Nostradamus 1-for-2 at this point.

Strangely, with all the years to choose from, Nostradamus had another for the year 1607:

**Century 6, Quatrain 54**

| | |
|---|---|
| At the point of day at the second crowing of the cock, | *Au point du jour au second chant du coq,* |
| Those of Tunis, of Fez, and of Bougie, | *Ceux de Tunes, de Fez, et de Bugie,* |
| By the Arabs captured the King of Morocco, | *Par les Arabes captif le Roi Maroq,* |
| The year thousand six hundred and seven, of the Liturgy. | *L'an mil six cent et sept, de Liturgie.* |

Nostradamus predicted that at daybreak an "Arab" force would conquer "Morocco," capturing their "King." Also to be conquered was "Tunis," "Bougie" (400 miles to the west of Tunis), and the inland Kingdom of "Fez." These events never happened. But once again, note the "of the Liturgy" quote after the year, just as in the third line of the prior quatrain. Is it possible that Nostradamus intended that one thousand six hundred and seven years were to be added to the time when a Church convention regarding the "Liturgy" of the Mass was to be called? An interesting possibility, but a cynical approach will be taken and this quatrain will also be regarded as a failure, making Nostradamus now 1-for-3. His next dated quatrain refers to the election of a pope:

### Century 10, Quatrain 91

| | |
|---|---|
| Clergy Roman the year thousand six hundred and nine, | *Clergé Romain l'an mil six cents et neuf,* |
| At the beginning of the year will be an election: | *Au chef de l'an feras élection:* |
| Of one gray and black of the Campania issued, | *D'un gris et noir de la Compagne issu,* |
| Which never was there one so malicious. | *Qui onc ne fut si malin.* |

This prophecy is fairly clear. In "the year thousand six hundred and nine" (1609), "At the beginning of the year," the Cardinals were to have elected a new pope. This pope was to have been a native of "Campania," situated on the western coast of Italy. Since there was no priestly order of both "black" and "gray" colors the origin of the supposed new Pope was uncertain. Possibilities included the Benedictines (known for their "black" garb) and the Franciscans (known for their "gray" color of dress ). However, Pope Paul V reigned continuously from 1605 to 1621, making the quatrain a failure. For those who believe that in the two previous quatrains the year 1607 has to be added to the date of a major Church Council, then it is (remotely) possible that since this quatrain also involves the Church that the same number of years must be added to this prophecy. They will also point out that since a "gray and black" order did not exist at the time Nostradamus wrote this quatrain, the quatrain must apply to a future time when an order with both of those colors will exist. Perhaps, but this does not seem likely. Nostradamus is now 1-for-4. His next quatrain was for the year 1660:

### Century 10, Quatrain 100
*(a duplicate number)*

| | |
|---|---|
| When the fork will be supported by two stakes, | *Quand le fourchu sera soutenu de deux paux,* |
| With six half bodies and six scissors open: | *Avec six demi-corps et six ciseaux ouverts:* |
| The very powerful Lord, heir of the toads, | *Le trés-puissant Seigneur, héritier des crapauds,* |
| Then will subjugate, under him the entire universe. | *Alors subjuguera, sous soi tout l'univers.* |

This quatrain is designated as a duplicate number since Nostradamus had two different quatrains which he labeled as Century 10, Quatrain 100. "The fork supported by two stakes" is an M, the Roman numeral symbol for 1000. The "six half bodies" are letter Cs, C being the Roman numeral for one hundred. Six of them total 600. The "six scissors open" are Xs, X being the Roman numeral for 10, thus 60. Adding all of these together gives the year: 1660; and "toads" refers to an ancient symbol for France, indicating that France is the country under consideration.

The quatrain predicted that in the year 1660 the French ruler ("The very powerful Lord, heir of the toads") would become the pre-eminent power in Europe ("Then will subjugate"), with some colonies oversea as well (about as far as the "universe," or known world, extended at that time). In fact, in March 1661, Louis the XIV, the greatest of the French Kings, assumed power. An infant king since 1643, Cardinal Mazarin was the real power behind the throne. After the Cardinal's death, just a few months after this quatrain expired, France entered a period where it became the most prominent of all the European powers. Was this quatrain a success? While he was only a few months off, the year is still wrong. Perhaps Nostradamus felt constrained in naming the exact year by verse length and rhyme in the quatrain. Also, while France did enter a period of political stability, economic growth, and imperial expansion, it did not quite "subjugate" "under him (Louis) the entire universe." This quatrain, while not a complete success, was not a failure either. For counting purposes it will be counted as half-right. Nostradamus is now one-and-a-half for five.

The next dated quatrain of Nostradamus was for the year 1700:

**Century 1, Quatrain 49**

| | |
|---|---|
| Much, much before such leadings | *Beaucoup, beaucoup avant telles menées* |
| Those of the East by | *Ceux d'Orient par la vertu lunaire:* |
|     virtue of the moon: | *L'an mil sept cent feront* |
| The year thousand seven |     *grands emmenées,* |
|     hundred will cause great | *Subjugant presque le coin Aquilonaire.* |
|     to be taken away, | |
| Subjugating nearly the corner | |
|     of the North. | |

"Those of the East" were the Turks, led by their Islamic symbol of the crescent "moon." Nostradamus predicted that in "The year thousand seven hundred" (1700) the Turks would win a large campaign, taking many prisoners and extending their rule as far north as Scandinavia. It did not happen. Beginning in 1682, the Turks began advancing farther westward into Europe. This war continued until 1699, at which time Turkey signed a treaty that ceded almost all of its territory north of the Balkans. Additionally, in 1700 the Turks lost territory to the Russians as well. This quatrain was a complete failure. Nostradamus is now one-and-a-half for six. There is one more dated quatrain:

### Century 3, Quatrain 77

| | |
|---|---|
| The third climate under Aries comprised | *Le tiers climat sous Aries compris* |
| The year thousand seven hundred twenty and seven in October, | *L'an mil sept cent vingt et sept en Octobre,* |
| The King of Persia by those of Egypt prisoner: | *Le Roi de Perse par ceux d'Egypte pris:* |
| Conflict, death, ruin: to the cross great approbation. | *Conflit, mort, perte: à la croix grand approbre.* |

The first line is not entirely clear, apparently indicating the "third" country under the astrological sign of "Aries." Which one Nostradamus intended is unknown. While the Turks and the Persians did sign a peace treaty in 1727, "The King of Persia" was not taken as a "prisoner. . . by those of Egypt," nor was there any discredit ("approbation") to Christianity ("the cross") in the process, so this quatrain is another failure.

Nostradamus' final accuracy rate for his dated quatrains is one-and-a-half for seven, slightly over 21%. For those of the opinion that the two quatrains of 1607 and the following one of 1609 have not yet occurred as the years of "the Liturgy" or "the sacred assembly" must be added to them, Nostradamus' accuracy rate then improves to one-and-a-half for four, almost 38%. However, Century 2, Quatrain 6, the quatrain that was a perfectly accurate prediction, would also seem to be the most important of the dated quatrains from France's perspective. Predicting France to change from one of the weakest of the European powers to the strongest in only one century would seem to be much more important than a generalized persecution of astrologers, an intra-Arab war in North Africa, or the election of a pope. Perhaps Nostradamus could see more clearly, and thus be more accurate, when the events were closer to France and of greater importance. In that case, if the significance that this author has attached to the final dated prediction of 1999 is accurate, then it seems likely that the possibility of this prediction coming true is greater than only 20–30%.

There is one other factor that may affect Nostradamus' accuracy rate as well: human free will. It is always possible that human free-will can change some of the prophecies; the path of life is not predetermined, the future is not set in stone. Why, the Bible even records instances of God changing his mind about things he had planned to do. This free-will factor may contribute somewhat to the failure of some of the dated quatrains. An appearance of a comet in the sky and a meteor impact on the Earth; however, is not under human control. Perhaps, to some extent, human free will can change Nostradamus' predictions on Earth, but free will cannot change the orbit of a comet on a collision course with the Earth.

For whatever reason, Nostradamus was not infallible, being wrong more often than he was right. Still, he was right at least part of the time. If past successes and failures are predictive of future results, then the chances of a comet becoming visible during the great European eclipse of 1999 stand between 21% and 38%, at the minimum. Thus, it probably will not occur, but what if it does? In today's world it is considered foolish not to buy insurance for one's life, house, health, auto, business, etc., yet the chances of dying in a given year are less than 21%, and the chances of one's house burning down are much, much less than that. Yet the potential scale of devastation described in this book is far worse than the loss of a single life, home, or business. All individuals, yes, and countries as well, should prepare for the possibility that Nostradamus correctly foresaw a meteor impact in 1999. There is simply too much to lose to assume he was wrong. Besides, even if Nostradamus was wrong, the coming disasters from the trends outlined in Chapter 3 seem likely to occur anyway. Additionally, for those Christians who believe in the infallibility of the New Testament, the the events of Revelation, outlined in Chapter 2 of this book, will eventually occur as well. In the world of the 1990s, very few are ready. Be prepared!

# APPENDIX B: MISCELLANEOUS QUATRAINS

There are still a few quatrains that may be relevant to events of the next generation or so. They are placed here either because they seemed too general to allow for placement in a specific chapter earlier in the book, or because they might not even belong to the time frame in which the events predicted in this book are to occur. Since they cannot be placed with any certainty, they are numbered only as Nostradamus numbered them.

### Century 1, Quatrain 17

For forty years the rainbow
   will not appear,
For forty years in all of the days
   will it be seen:
The earth will wax more dry,
And great floods
   when it will appear.

*Par quarante ans l'iris n'apparaîtra,*
*Par quarante ans tous les*
   *jours sera vu:*
*La terre aride en siccité croîtra,*
*Et grands déluges quand sera aperçu.*

There is no history anywhere in the world of a drought lasting "For forty years" that was followed by "forty years" of continuous rain, and it seems rather remarkable that Nostradamus would predict such a thing. However, since no date is specified here, there is really very little risk in making such a prediction; it could always occur at some date in the unspecified future, couldn't it? "When it will appear," in the last line, refers to something, but what is "it"? Perhaps this is a reference to the appearance of the comet, since tsunami-driven "great floods" will accompany the explosion from the meteor impact. In that case, the drought-stricken area most likely to change would be the Sahara Desert, parts of which have averaged less than one inch of rain per year for longer than forty years, and a few areas of which have received no rain for forty years.

Should this quatrain apply to the time after the meteor impact, "The forty years" of rain indicate a permanent, not just temporary, change in climate, with North Africa receiving far more rain than it now does. This is not as preposterous as it sounds. During the last Ice Age, less than 10,000 years ago, there were several huge lakes in what is now the middle of the Sahara Desert. A massive energy release in the Atlantic from the explosion of the meteor might permanently change the weather of this part of the world once again. But remember, even without the comet, global warming threatens massive climate change in the next century!

**Century 10, Quatrain 49**

| | |
|---|---|
| Garden of the world near the city new, | *Jardin du monde auprès de cité neuve,* |
| Inside the road of mountain caves: | *Dans le chemin des montagnes cavées:* |
| It will be seized and plunged into the Tub, | *Sera saisi et plongé dans la Cuve,* |
| To drink by force waters sulfur poisoned. | *Buvant par force eaux soufre envenimées.* |

The key to this quatrain is interpreting "the city new." There are several possibilities, the most likely of which is the city of Naples, since in Greek "new city" is "nea polis," and Naples in Italian is "Napoli," literally meaning "new city." In this case the "Garden of the world" would refer to the soil of the Campanian plain, located between Naples and Mt. Vesuvius, which has been frequently enriched by the ash fallout from prior Vesuvian eruptions. Other possible cities include New York, the "new" city of North America, or perhaps even the "new" capital of France after the fall of Paris.

The second line places this quatrain in modern times since "Inside the" city will be "roads" of "mountains" with "caves" in them, in other words, skyscrapers. Something will be "seized and plunged," indicating deliberate action rather than accident, "into the Tub." The most likely candidate for this "Tub" would be the modern reservoir systems that serve large cities. This impression is expanded upon in the last line, which indicates "sulfur(ous)" poisoning of the water system. While the "sulfur" poisoning could occur in Naples as a result of sulfuric acid fall-out from an eruption of Mt. Vesuvius, it seems more likely that some-one, somewhere, sometime, will deliberately poison the water treatment system of a city known only as "the city new." Of course, if it does refer to Vesuvius, this quatrain might also belong to the time period just after the meteor strike since the initial earthquake, along with a sec-ondary tremblor along the African-European Plate boundary, might well allow deep-seated magma pockets to rise near the surface.

**Century 1, Quatrain 87**

| | |
|---|---|
| Volcanic fire from center of earth | *Ennosigeé feu du centre de terre* |
| Will cause trembling | *Fera trembler autour de cité neuve:* |
| around the city new: | *Deux grands rochers longtemps* |
| Two great rocks long time | *feront la guerre,* |
| will make the war, | *Puis Arethuse rougira nouveau fleuve.* |
| Then Arethusa will redden | |
| a new river. | |

Here is another quatrain indicating an eruption near "the city new." It seems likely that Naples is the intended city here, so perhaps the prior quatrain refers to Naples, after all. The "two great rocks" who will for a "long time make the war" could be the Muslims and the Allies in World War III, in which case Vesuvius will be erupting either just before or during the Italian campaign. "Arethusa" was a nymph transformed by the goddess Diana into a fountain on the island of Sicily. How she might "redden a new river" is uncertain. Perhaps there will be a great deal of blood spilled in a battle in Sicily at the time of the eruption of Vesuvius.

**Century 2, Quatrain 22**

| | |
|---|---|
| The camp imprudent of Europe | *Le camp Ascop d'Europe partira,* |
| will set out, | *S'adjoignant proche de* |
| Adjoining itself near | *l'isle submergée:* |
| the isle submerged: | *D'Araon classe phalange pliera,* |
| On account of the weak fleet | *Nombril du monde plus* |
| the phalanx will fold up, | *grande voix subrogée.* |
| Navel of the world | |
| greater voice substituted. | |

At some point during World War III the Allies will launch a fleet against the Mahdi's forces. This fleet will gather "near the isle submerged." Great Britain is the most likely candidate for the title of "the isle submerged," since quatrain (12) indicates that it will be half-drowned by the tsunami. Nostradamus describes this fleet as "imprudent," indicating that the risk in their plans will be far greater than the potential rewards. This fleet will not prove equal to its task, and because of its failure the Allies will have an entire army surrender somewhere ("the phalanx will fold up"). Where the "Navel of the world" might be is not agreed upon by any commentators; some feel it might be the Middle East, others specifically mention Egypt, still others say it will be Italy. The failure of the fleet and loss of "the phalanx" will result in a "greater voice" displacing the existing authority. Either the Allies will change commanders or the Islamic forces will conquer a large amount of Allied territory and form a new government to rule the residual civilian population

**Century 10, Quatrain 86**

| | |
|---|---|
| Like a griffin will come the King of Europe, | *Comme un griffon viendra le Roi d'Europe,* |
| Accompanied by those of Aquilon: | *Accompagné de ceux d'Aquilon.* |
| Of reds and whites will he conduct a great troop, | *De rouges et blancs conduira grande troupe,* |
| and fight against the King of Babylon. | *Et iront contre le Roi de Babylon.* |

Some commentators see this quatrain as being fulfilled in Napoleon's Egyptian campaign, but it seems unlikely that Nostradamus would refer to Napoleon here as a "King," since he does not use that title in any of the other quatrains applied to Napoleon or the period of the French Revolution. It seems more likely that this quatrain applies to Henry V, the new Henry. He will "fight against the King of Babylon," which will either be the forces of the Blue or the White Turban. Exactly who the "reds and whites" might be is unclear. In Nostradamus' time the Spanish wore red battle colors and the French wore white, so perhaps Henry will lead a force into the Middle East composed primarily of French and Spanish soldiers, "Accompanied by those of Aquilon."

"Aquilon" is mentioned at least nineteen times in Nostradamus' writings, but no commentator has been able to offer an explanation about to whom it might refer. "Aquilon" is described elsewhere in Nostradamus' writings as a great "country of the north." Since these quatrains seem to have little in common with the events of World War III they have not been integrated into the main body of this book. However, if this quatrain applies to the new Henry, then sometime before the end of the next World War, the "northern" European countries, including perhaps Norway, Sweden, Finland, Denmark, Lithuania, Estonia, Latvia, and part of Russia, may find themselves united as a single country, much as Henry will rule over the rest of Europe. Since Nostradamus seems to make little mention of German troops helping to defend France during World War III, perhaps Germany will withdraw its troops to the north during its retreat from the Mahdi, rather than into a France already overcrowded with refugees from Spain, Italy, and Eastern Europe.

If the northern European country of "Aquilon" is to be formed during World War III why does Nostradamus have so little to say about it during the war? Remember that Nostradamus' desire as a prophet was to help France in her time of greatest need. There will be many, many other events occurring in the world at that time that Nostradamus ignored, since they will be irrelevant to France and its direct interests at the time. However, since "Aquilon" may persist as a country after the war, the vast majority of the quatrains related to it may not take place for hundreds of years.

**Century 6, Quatrain 44**

| | |
|---|---|
| During the night by Nantes the rainbow will appear, | *De nuit par Nantes l'iris apparaîtra,* |
| Through arts marine resuscitating the rain: | *Des arts marins susciteront la pluie:* |
| Arabic gulf great fleet will sink to the bottom, | *Arabiq gouffre grande classe parfondra,* |
| A monster in Saxony born from bear and sow. | *Un monstre en Saxe naîtra d'ours et truie.* |

How is it possible to have a "rainbow. . . During the night"? The only way this is possible is if it occurs shortly after sunset, while sunlight still is reaching the upper portions of the sky in the west. Perhaps it will be seen after the meteor impact when there will be tremendous amounts of dust in the far-upper portion of the atmosphere. In the western sky at that time, even several hours after sunset, the dust will reflect large amounts of light back to the Earth, perhaps even making something similar to a "rainbow. . . appear." "Resuscitating. . . the rain" implies a drought, a theme found in the book of Revelation, occurring a year or two after the impact. It appears that the French will begin bringing "rain" to their fields by artificially seeding the clouds ("through marine arts"), something tried in the past with only limited success.

At the time of these events in France a "great fleet will sink to the bottom" in an "Arabic gulf," probably the Persian Gulf. Unfortunately, Nostradamus does not indicate to whom the fleet belongs. Perhaps this represents part of the inter-Muslim fighting (Iran against Saudi Arabia and Kuwait?) that will occur early in World War III. The "monster" that will be "born from bear and sow" is uncertain, although it seems likely that countries, rather than individuals, are intended here. In that case the "bear" might be Russia, but who the "sow" will be is a mystery. Saxony is an ancient German province near the city of Leipzig. Can it represent some sort of Russian-German alliance that will be formed early in the war, an alliance that will collapse shortly afterwards?

### Century 6, Quatrain 97

Five and forty degrees
    the sky will burn,
Fire to approach the great
    city new:
Instant great flame
    scattered will leap,
When one will demand of the
    Normans to make proof.

*Cinq et quarante degrés ciel brûlera,*
*Feu approcher de la grande cité neuve:*
*Instant grande flamme éparse sautera,*
*Quand on voudra des Normans*
    *faire preuve.*

Another quatrain of the "city new" theme, but this time Nostradamus describes the city as being near the 45th degree of latitude ("Forty and five degrees"). This rules out Naples, which is near the 40th degree of parallel, not the 45th. Other possible candidate cities include Bordeaux, Lyons, Turin, Milan, Genoa, Venice, and Avignon. Since it has already been predicted that the Papacy will move to Avignon, perhaps Nostradamus intends it to be the "city new" of the Pope. The "Instant great flame" that "will leap" up into the sky calls to mind anti-aircraft fire or Patriot-type missiles. What "proof. . . will" be "demand(ed)" "of the Normans" (those from Normandy) and who "will demand" it makes this quatrain unclear and frustrating to decipher.

### Century 3, Quatrain 23

If France passes beyond
    sea Ligurian,
You yourself in islands
    and seas enclosed:
Mahomet contrary,
    more sea Adriatic:
Horses and of asses you
    gnaw the bones.

*Si France passe outre mer lygustique,*
*Tu te verras en îles et mers enclos:*
*Mahommet contraire,*
    *plus mer Hadriatique:*
*Chevaux et d'ânes tu rongeras les os.*

The "sea Ligurian" is the Gulf of Genoa. Nostradamus seems to be warning the French to not pass beyond Genoa into Italy. If they do they will "gnaw the bones" of "Horses and of asses," obviously near starvation, somewhere "in islands." The "Mahomet" theme places this in World War III; the problem is when and where will this occur? As described in the conquest of Italy, the Allies will be surrounded and pocketed around Rome, cut off from assistance. This location is a possibility, except that Rome is hardly an "island" and why does Nostradamus mention the Adriatic Sea, which is on the east coast of Italy? Perhaps Nostradamus warns against moving into the Greek islands, or even into Crete. What is also frustrating in this quatrain is that there is no way to tell if it occurs during the early years of the war, while the Allies are retreating, or while they retake those areas near the end of the war.

### Century 9, Quatrain 43

Near to the descension
    the army of the Cross,
Will be ambushed
    by the Ishmaelites,
From all sides struck by
    ship Impetuosity,
Promptly assailed from
    ten galleys elite.

*Proche à descendre l'armée Crucigere,*
*Sera guettée par les Ismaëlites,*
*De tous côtés battus par nef Rauiere,*
*Prompt assaillis de dix galères élites.*

"The army of the Cross" refers, of course, to the Christian armies of Henry V and the mention "of the Cross" with "Ishmaelites" places the theme squarely in World War III. While "descending" from some location, either a mountain or moving southwards and thus "descending" towards the equator, the French "Will be ambushed."

Part of the ambush will include ten elite ships of the Iranian navy ("ten galleys elite") led by a "ship" to which Nostradamus gives the specific name of "Impetuosity." Unfortunately, there is no way to pinpoint this quatrain to a specific time or place during the war.

### Century 4, Quatrain 38

| | |
|---|---|
| While Duke, King, Queen will be occupied, | *Pendant que Duc, Roi, Reine occupera,* |
| Chief of Byzantium captive in Samothrace: | *Chef Bizant du captif en Samothrace:* |
| Before the assault the one the other will eat: | *Avant l'assaut l'un l'autre mangera:* |
| Edge of metal will follow of blood the trace. | *Rebours ferré suivra du sang la trace.* |

The "King" would appear to be Henry V, "occupied" with his wife ("Queen") and son ("Duke," could it possibly be Ogmios?) while the "Chief of Byzantium" will be held "captive in Samothrace," which is the northernmost of the Greek islands, just a few miles west of the Dardanelles. Who will the "Chief of Byzantium" be? In quatrain (33) a man described as being the White Turban was banished to Byzantium, so perhaps the White Turban will be captured as the war is winding down, while the final "assault" is being prepared. The last two lines, however, are completely obscure. Will the White Turban actually be eaten by Henry V? That seems preposterous, yet there seems to be no clearer meaning, either, and Nostradamus' intention in the final line is even more obscure.

# AUTHOR'S NOTE

As the author of this book, do I really believe the events that it contains will happen as I have recorded them? Do I actually think that a cometary fragment will impact the Earth in 1999, causing such unspeakable devastation and resultant war that over four billion people will lose their lives as a result? I am not sure, but it is my fervent hope that I am wrong. After all, who could possibly want to be right about something that will bring such pain and suffering to so many people?

On the one hand, it is eerie how Nostradamus' quatrains can be linked in a series so that a cohesive theme emerges, and when that theme can be correlated with prophetic passages from the Bible, Muslim eschatology, and current food production trends, the result is positively scary. With trends from different areas converging, it seems possible that I may be right. On the other hand, Nostradamus was wrong more often than he was right, and even if he is right about the seventh month of 1999, that does not mean that my interpretation is correct, nor does it mean that the quatrains that follow are necessarily right, either.

I hope I am wrong about 1999, that nothing appears during the solar eclipse in Europe that August. However, even if I am wrong, planet Earth is still in danger. Growing food shortages, increasingly violent societies, the growing arms race in the Third World, the spread of nuclear weapons, the Greenhouse Effect, continued deterioration of the environment, population growth, moral decay, and deficit spending by national governments are but a few of the items that could destroy Western Civilization. Have you prepared for disaster? How *can* you prepare for it? Such simple things as keeping extra food, water and candles at home and learning how to garden may save your life someday. Organizing a local civil-defense survival plan with neighbors would be even better. Don't count on the government for help—they may be the first casualty in a large disaster. Self-sufficiency and self-reliancy were the foundations of the United States; now no one practices them. How sad. How stupid. How dangerous!

Whether I am right or wrong, we are all going to die anyway, within a few short decades at most. Suppose I am right and all these things happen. Suppose further that you have prepared yourself and are one of the few that manage to come through World War III unscathed. Would that be a great success? Not if you lost your immortal soul in the process! Jesus said it far better than I can:

> Be careful not to let yourselves become occupied with too much feasting and drinking and with the worries of this life, or that Day may suddenly catch you like a trap. For it will come upon all people everywhere on earth. Be on watch and pray always that you will have the strength to go safely through all those things that will happen and to stand before the Son of Man.

I wish you peace.

*Stefan Paulus*
*Pentecost Day, 1996*

# REFERENCES

"Acid-Flecked Candy-Colored Sunscreen." *Discover* XIII(1):44-46, January 1992.

Arjomand, Said Amir. *The Turban for the Crown.* Oxford University Press, 1988.

Barraclaugh, Jeffrey, Editor. *The Times Atlas of World History.* Hammond, Inc., Third Edition edited by Norman Stone, 1989.

Brandon, S. G. F., General Editor. *A Dictionary of Comparative Religion.* Charles Scribner's Sons, 1970. Subentry: Mahdi.

Brewe, Bryan. *Eclipse.* Earth View, 1978.

Brown, Lester R., et al. *State of the World 1988.* W.W. Norton & Company, 1988.

———. *State of the World 1989.* W.W. Norton & Comapny, 1989.

———. *State of the World 1990.* W. W. Norton & Company, 1990.

———. *State of the World 1991.* W. W. Norton & Comapny, 1991.

———. *State of the World 1992.* W. W. Norton & Company, 1992.

———. *State of the World 1993.* W. W. Norton & Company, 1993.

Budiansky, Stephen, et al. "The Nuclear Epidemic." *U. S. News & World Report* CXII(36): 40-44, 16 March 1992.

Bullfinch, Thomas. *Bullfinch's Mythology.* Avenel Book Edition, 1979.

Caldwell, Mark. "Resurrection of a Killer." *Discover* XIII(12):58-64, December 1992.

Carson, Rachel L. *The Sea Around Us*. The New American Library, 1950.

Cavendish, Richard, Editor-in-Chief. *Man, Myth & Magic, The Illustrated Encyclopedia of Mythology, Religion and the Unknown*. Marshall Cavendish, 1983. Subentry: Mahdi.

Cheetham, Erika. *The Final Prophecies of Nostradamus*. Perigree Books, 1989.

"Climate and the Rise of Man." *U.S. News and World Report* CXII (48): 60-67, 8 June 1992.

"Climate Watch." *Discover* XIII (10):18, October 1992.

Cohen, Joel."How Many People Can the Earth Hold?" *Discover* XIII (11):114-119, November 1992.

Crabb, Charlene. "Soiling the Planet." *Discover* XIV(1):74-75, January 1993.

Crim, Keith, General Editor. *Abingdon Dictionary of Living Religions*. Abingdon, 1981. Subentry: Mahdi.

*The Europa World Book 1992, Volume 1*. Europa Publications Ltd., 1992.

*FAO Production Yearbook*. Food and Agriculture Organization of the United Nations, 1990.

Byron Farwell. *Prisoners of the Mahdi*. Harper & Row, 1967.

Folger, Tim. "All About Asteroids." *Discover* XIV(1):34, January 1993.

de Fontbrune, Jean-Charles. *Nostradamus: Countdown to Apocalypse*. Translated from the French by Alexis Lykiard. Holt, Rhinehart and Winston, 1983.

"Fully Loaded." *Time* CXLI(9):14, 1 March 1993.

Gibb, H. A. R. and J. H. Kramers, Editors. *Shorter Encyclopaedia of Islam*. Cornell University Press, 1965. Subentry: Mahdi.

Glasse, Cyril, Editor. *The Concise Encyclopedia of Islam*. Harper, 1989. Subentries: ad-Dajjal, Eschatology.

Gleadow, Rupert. *The Origin of the Zodiac*. Castle Books, 1968.

de Hartog, Leo. *Genghis Khan: Conqueror of the World.* St. Martin's Press, 1982.

Hastings, James, Editor. *Encyclopaedia of Religion and Ethics, Volume 8.* Charles Scribner's Sons, No year of publication given. Subentry: Mahdi.

Hayes, R. Dennis. "Ravaged Republics." *Discover* XIV(3):66-75, March 1993.

Hinnells, John R., Editor. *The Facts on File Dictionary of Religions.* Facts on File, 1984. Subentry: Mahdi.

von Hippel, Frank. "Bombs Away." *Discover* XII(4):32-35, April 1992.

Jackson, James O. "Nuclear Time Bombs." *Time* CXL(49):44-45, 7 December 1992.

Jackson, Samuel Macauley, Editor-in-Chief. *The New Schaff-Herzog Encyclopedia of Religious Knowledge.* Baker Book House, 1950. Subentries: Islam, Mahdi.

"Jove the Unforgiving." *Discover* XIV(8):15, August 1993.

Keegan, John, Editor. *The Times Atlas of the Second World War.* Harper & Row, 1989.

Knight, Robin. "Northern Exposure." *U.S. News & World Report* CXII(38):43, 30 March 1992.

Knight, Robin, et al."Easier Said Than Done." *U.S. News & World Report* CXIII(17):53-54, 2 Novermber 1992.

Kunzig, Robert. "Twilight of the Cod." *Discover* XVI(4):44-58, April 1995.

Leoni, Edgar. *Nostradamus and His Prophecies.* Bell Publishing Company, 1982.

Lief, Louise. "Fire, Fury and Nationalism." *U.S. News & World Report* CXII(52):44-47, 6 July 1992.

Lief, Louise. "Iran's Familiar Face." *U.S. News & World Report* CXIII(20):51-53, 23 November 1992.

Lief, Louise, with Richard Z. Chesnoff. "Freeing Hostages, Hiring Hit Squads." *U.S. News & World Report* CXII(13):52, 7 October 1991.

Lief, Louise, with Gabriella Gamini and Bruce B. Auster. "Iran's New Offensive." *U.S. News & World Report* CXII(38):40-42, 30 March 1992.

Littmann, Mark, and Ken Wilcox. *Totality: Eclipses of the Sun.* University of Hawaii Press, 1991.

Marks, John. "Derailing Troubled Turkey." *U.S. News & World Report* CXIII(18):73-75, 9 November 1992.

Marsden, Brian G. "Comet Swift-Tuttle: Does it Threaten Earth?" *Sky & Telescope* CXXXV(1):16-19, January 1993.

Matthews, Robert. "Death in June." *Discover* XIII(6):16, June 1992.

Meagher, Paul Kevin, Thomas C. O'Brien, and Consuelo Maria Aherne, Editors. *Encyclopedic Dictionary of Religion, Volume F-N.* Corpus Publications, Washington, 1979. Subentry: Mahdi.

Naeye, Robert. "The Hole in Nebraska." *Discover* XIV(4):18, April 1993.

Nelan, Bruce W. "An Army Out of Work." *Time* CXL(49):48-49, 7 December 1992.

Oliwenstein, Lori. "Lava and Ice." *Discover* XIII(10):18, October 1992.

Pasternak, Douglas. "Moscow's Dirty Nuclear Secrets." *U.S. News & World Report* CXII(31):46-47, 10 February 1992.

"Perseid Burst." *Sky and Telescope* LXXXIV(5):493, November 1992.

Pope, Victoria. "The Wreck of Russia." *U.S. News & World Report* CXIII(22):40-51, 7 December 1992.

Pope, Victoria. "Poisoning Russia's Rivers of Plenty." *U.S. News & World Report* CXII(40):49-51, 13 April 1992.

Randi, James. *The Mask of Nostradamus.* Charles Scribner's Sons, 1990.

Robbins, Carla Anne, et al. "The X Factor in the Proliferation Game." *U.S. News & World Report* CXII(36):44-51, 16 March 1992.

Rukeyser, Louis. "Threats to Computer Systems Spur Hot New Industry." *Individual Investor* XI(125):50, May 1992.

Sagan, Carl, and Ann Druyan. *Comet.* Random House, 1985.

Saunders, J. J. *The History of the Mongol Conquests.* Barnes and Noble, 1971.

"Sabotage." *U.S. News & World Report* CXIII(20):25, 23 November 1992.

Schone, D. Justin. *Chronology of Eclipses and Comets.* The Boydell Press, 1984.

Sergeant, David R. *Vagabonds of Space.* Doubleday, 1982.

Sivard, Ruth Leger. *World Military and Social Expenditures 1987-88, 12th Edition.* World Priorities, Washington, 1987.

Stanglin, Douglas. "Breathing Sulfur and Eating Lead." *U.S. News & World Report* CXII(40):46-48, 13 April 1992.

Stanglin, Douglas, and Robin Knight, et al. "Sailing into the Sunset." *U.S. News & World Report* CXII(32):31-33, 17 February 1992.

Stanglin, Douglas, et al. "Toxic Wasteland." *U.S. News & World Report* CXII(40):40-46, 13 April 1992.

Suitil, Kathy. "Holey War." *Discover* XIV(1):75-76, January 1993.

"Sweeping Up Space Junk." *Discover* XIII(1):11, January 1992.

Svitil, Kathy A. "Hurricane from Hell." *Discover* XVI(4):26, April 1995.

Vacca, Roberto. *The Coming Dark Age.* Translated from the Italian by J. S. Whale. Doubleday & Co., 1973.

*Van Nostrand's Scientific Encyclopedia, Sixth Edition.* P.E. Van Nostrand Reinhold Company, 1983. Subentry: Earthquakes, Seismology and Plate Tectonics.

Watson, Russell, et al. "The Devil's Work." *U.S. News & World Report* CXII(32):30-31, 17 February 1992.

Whipple, Fred L. *The Mystery of Comets.* Smithsonian Institution Press, 1985.

Wilson, Edward O. *The Diversity of Life.* Harvard University Press, 1992.

*The World Almanac and Book of Facts 1991.* Pharos Books, 1990.

*The World Fact Book 1992.* Central Intelligence Agency, 1992.

Yeomans, Donald K. *Comets: A Chronological History of Observation, Science, Myth, and Folklore.* John Wiley & Sons, 1991.

Zimmerman, Tim. "Tragic Inaction." *U.S. News & World Report* CXIII(18):66-69, 9 November 1992.

REFERENCES

# INDEX

NOSTRADAMUS

NOSTRADAMUS

INDEX

279

# STAY IN TOUCH. . .

## Llewellyn publishes hundreds of books on your favorite subjects

On the following pages you will find listed some books now available on related subjects. Your local bookstore stocks most of these and will stock new Llewellyn titles as they become available. We urge your patronage.

## Order by Phone

Call toll-free within the U.S. and Canada, 1–800–THE MOON.
In Minnesota call (612) 291–1970.
We accept Visa, MasterCard, and American Express.

## Order by Mail

Send the full price of your order (MN residents add 7% sales tax) in U.S. funds to:
Llewellyn Worldwide
P.O. Box 64383, Dept. K515–0
St. Paul, MN 55164–0383, U.S.A.

## Postage and Handling

- $4.00 for orders $15.00 and under
- $5.00 for orders over $15.00
- No charge for orders over $100.00

We ship UPS in the continental United States. We cannot ship to P.O. boxes. Orders shipped to Alaska, Hawaii, Canada, Mexico, and Puerto Rico will be sent first-class mail. International orders: Airmail—add freight equal to price of each book to the total price of order, plus $5.00 for each non-book item (audiotapes, etc.). Surface mail— Add $1.00 per item. Allow 4–6 weeks delivery on all orders. Postage and handling rates subject to change.

## Group Discounts

We offer a 20% quantity discount to group leaders or agents. You must order a minimum of 5 copies of the same book to get our special quantity price.

## FREE CATALOG

Get a free copy of our color catalog, *New Worlds of Mind and Spirit*. Subscribe for just $10.00 in the United States and Canada ($20.00 overseas, first-class mail). Many bookstores carry *New Worlds*—ask for it!

# PREDICTIONS FOR
# A NEW MILLENNIUM

Noel Tyl

He predicted the exact dates of the Gulf War and the fall of the Soviet Union. Now Noel Tyl foresees key events, with 58 predictions about the dramatic political, economic, and social changes that will occur between now and the year 2012. *Predictions for a New Millennium* prepares us to see beyond the crisis of the moment to understand world changes strategically. Here are just a few of the momentous events that we will witness as we enter the 21st century: assassination of another U.S. president... China abandons communism... Saddam Hussein toppled from power... Hitler revival in Germany. The new millennium is a pivotal time in our history. How will these events affect the economy, the world powers... how will they affect you? The answers are here.

1-56718-737-4, 304 pp., 6 x 9, maps, graphs, index, softcover    $14.95

**To order call 1-800-THE MOON**

# HOROSCOPE FOR THE NEW MILLENNIUM

E. Alan Meece

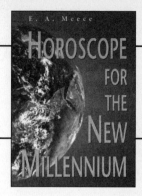

For anyone interested in the meaning of the great events of our time, and for those who want to know how these events might affect their lives, *Horoscope for the New Millennium* offers the first revealing mirror of humanity in this age. Understand the great moments of history—and of the upcoming critical and progressive opportunities—through astrology presented as a fascinating, gripping story of our evolution from social enslavement to individual freedom ... and acceptance of personal responsibility within the planetary environment.

Scan the vast landscape of human destiny for the larger astrological rhythms and prophetic insights. Then focus in on our own times with the engaging narrative that traces the path of our transition from one Age to another. When the book becomes a crystal ball to divine where we're headed, discover what it means for you, with intriguing prophecies of specific events. Find out how we will soon find ourselves entering a "new Golden Age"—if we make the right choices.

1-56718-461-8, 432 pp., 7 x 10, softcover                                      $19.95

# JUDE'S HERBAL HOME REMEDIES

## Natural Health, Beauty & Home-Care Secrets

Jude C. Williams, M.H.

There's a pharmacy—in your spice cabinet! In the course of daily life we all encounter problems that can be easily remedied through the use of common herbs—headaches, dandruff, insomnia, colds, muscle aches, burns—and a host of other afflictions known to humankind. *Jude's Herbal Home Remedies* is a simple guide to self-care that will benefit beginning or experienced herbalists with its wealth of practical advice. Most of the herbs listed are easy to obtain.

Discover how cayenne pepper promotes hair growth, why cranberry juice is a good treatment for asthma attacks, how to make a potent juice to flush out fat, how to make your own deodorants and perfumes, what herbs will get fleas off your pet, how to keep cut flowers fresh longer... the remedies and hints go on and on!

This book gives you instructions for teas, salves, tinctures, tonics, poultices, along with addresses for obtaining the herbs. Dangerous and controversial herbs are also discussed.

Grab this book and a cup of herbal tea, and discover from a Master Herbalist more than 800 ways to a simpler, more natural way of life.

0-87542-869-X, 240 pgs., 6 x 9, illus., softcover                    $12.95